Entertainment Directory

ROME

TRAVEL GUIDE

SHOPS, RESTAURANTS, ATTRACTIONS & NIGHTLIFE

The Most Positively
Reviewed and Recommended
by Locals and Travelers

EGP
Editorial

ROME
TRAVEL GUIDE

SHOPS, RESTAURANTS, ATTRACTIONS & NIGHTLIFE

ROME TRAVEL GUIDE 2022
Shops, Restaurants, Attractions & Nightlife

© Herman W. Stewart
© E.G.P. Editorial

Printed in USA.

ISBN-13: 9798748771481

INDEX

ROME TRAVEL GUIDE

Shops, Restaurants, Attractions & Nightlife

*This directory is dedicated to Rome Business Owners and Managers
who provide the experience that the locals and tourists enjoy.
Thanks you very much for all that you do and thank for being the "People Choice".*

*Thanks to everyone that posts their reviews online and
the amazing reviews sites that make our life easier.*

*The places listed in this book are the most positively reviewed
and recommended by locals and travelers from around the world.*

*You will find in this book 2,000 places to visit organized in five groups
to make your life easier when you decide to go out.*

*500 Shops, 500 Restaurants, 100 Landmarks & Historical Buildings,
400 Arts & Entertainment Attractions and 500 Nightlife Spots.*

*Thank you for your time and enjoy the directory that is
designed with locals and tourist in mind!*

TOP 500 SHOPS

Most Recommended by Locals & Trevelers
Ranking (from #1 to #500)

#1
Palazzo Delle Esposizioni
Category: Museum, Art Gallery
Average Price: Modest
Area: Centro Storico
Address: Via Nazionale 194
00184 Rome Italy
Phone: +39 06 39967200

#2
Fahrenheit 451
Category: Bookstore
Average Price: Modest
Area: Centro Storico
Address: Piazza Campo De' Fiori 44
00186 Rome Italy
Phone: +39 06 6875930

#3
Galleria Alberto Sordi
Category: Shopping Center
Average Price: Expensive
Area: Centro Storico
Address: Piazza Colonna 53
00187 Rome Italy
Phone: +39 06 69190769

#4
Il Mercatino Del Pigneto
Category: Arts, Crafts, Antiques, Food
Average Price: Expensive
Area: Pigneto
Address: Via Del Pigneto
00176 Rome Italy
Phone: +39 06 2155194

#5
Discoteca Laziale
Category: Vinyl Records
Average Price: Modest
Area: Termini
Address: Via Mamiani 62A
00185 Rome Italy
Phone: +39 06 447141

#6
Elvis Lives
Category: Fashion, Watches, Gift Shop
Average Price: Inexpensive
Area: Termini, San Giovanni
Address: Via Dei Volsci 48
00185 Rome Italy
Phone: +39 06 89534823

#7
Galleria Porta Di Rome
Category: Department Store
Average Price: Modest
Area: Bufalotta
Address: Via Alberto Lionello 201
00139 Rome Italy
Phone: +39 06 87074216

#8
Ikea
Category: Furniture Store
Average Price: Inexpensive
Area: Bufalotta
Address: Via Casale Redicicoli 501
00139 Rome Italy
Phone: +39 199 114646

#9
Aseq
Category: Bookstore
Average Price: Modest
Area: Centro Storico
Address: Via Sediari 10
00186 Rome Italy
Phone: +39 06 6868400

#10
Citt' Del Sole
Category: Toy Store
Average Price: Expensive
Address: Viale Somalia 61
00199 Rome Italy
Phone: +39 06 86218879

#11
Zara
Category: Accessories, Shoe Store,
Women's Clothing
Average Price: Expensive
Area: Centro Storico
Address: Via Del Corso 189
00186 Rome Italy
Phone: +39 06 69791711

#12
Transmission
Category: Vinyl Records
Area: Termini
Address: Via Dei Salentini 27
00185 Rome Italy
Phone: +39 06 44704370

#13
Too Much
Category: Home Decor
Average Price: Expensive
Area: Centro Storico
Address: Via Santa Maria Dell'anima 29
00186 Rome Italy
Phone: +39 06 68301187

#14
TAD
Category: Cosmetics, Beauty Supply,
Women's Clothing, Florist
Average Price: Expensive
Area: Flaminio
Address: Via Del Babuino, 155
00187 Rome Italy
Phone: +39 06 96842085

#15
Polvere Di Tempo
Category: Arts, Crafts
Average Price:
Area: Trastevere
Address: Via Del Moro 59
00153 Rome Italy
Phone: +39 06 5880704

#16
Sephora
Category: Cosmetics, Beauty Supply
Average Price: Modest
Area: Centro Storico
Address: Via Del Corso 480
00186 Rome Italy
Phone: +39 06 3215704

#17
Tech It Easy
Category: Home Decor
Average Price:
Area: Centro Storico
Address: Via Del Gambero 1
00187 Rome Italy
Phone: +39 06 69380924

#18
Cherubini
Category: Musical Instruments
Average Price: Modest
Area: San Lorenzo
Address: Via Tiburtina 366
00159 Rome Italy
Phone: +39 06 432191

#19
Caff' Letterario
Category: Bar, Books, Mags, Music
Average Price: Expensive
Area: Testaccio, Ostiense
Address: Via Ostiense 95
00154 Rome Italy
Phone: +39 06 57302842

#20
Strategic Business Unit
Category: Men's Clothing,
Women's Clothing
Average Price: Modest
Address: Via Di San Pantaleo 68
00186 Rome Italy
Phone: +39 06 68802547

#21
Di Cori Gloves
Category: Leather Goods
Average Price: Modest
Area: Centro Storico
Address: Piazza Di Spagna 53
00187 Rome Italy
Phone: +39 06 6784439

#22
Scuderie Del Quirinale
Category: Art Gallery,
Landmark/Historic, Museum
Average Price: Modest
Area: Centro Storico
Address: Via XXIV Maggio 16
00184 Rome Italy
Phone: +39 06 39967500

#23
Mondo Bizzarro Gallery
Category: Art Gallery, Street Art
Average Price: Modest
Area: Termini
Address: Via Sicilia 251
00187 Rome Italy
Phone: +39 06 44247451

#24
Hollywood Video
Category: Videos, Video Game Rental,
Bookstore, Music & Dvds
Average Price:
Area: Centro Storico
Address: Via Di Monserrato 107
00186 Rome Italy
Phone: +39 06 6869197

#25
Bartolucci
Category: Toy Store
Average Price: Modest
Area: Centro Storico
Address: Via Dei Pastini 98
00186 Rome Italy
Phone: +39 06 69190894

#26
Louis Vuitton
Category: Shoe Store, Leather Goods
Average Price: Exclusive
Area: Centro Storico
Address: Piazza San Lorenzo In
Lucinia 36, 00186 Rome Italy
Phone: +39 06 68809520

#27
Lush Italia
Category: Cosmetics, Beauty Supply
Average Price: Expensive
Area: Centro Storico
Address: Via Del Gambero 25
00187 Rome Italy
Phone: +39 06 69924344

#28
Pink Moon
Category: Books, Mags, Music &Video
Average Price: Modest
Area: Ostiense
Address: Via Antonio Pacinotti 3C
00146 Rome Italy
Phone: +39 06 5573868

#29
Fotoforniture Guido Sabatini
Category: Photography Store
Average Price: Exclusive
Area: Prati
Address: Via Germanico 168
00192 Rome Italy
Phone: +39 06 36003966

#30
Video Elite
Category: Videos, Video Game Rental
Average Price: Exclusive
Area: Nomentano
Address: Via Nomentana 166A
00162 Rome Italy
Phone: +39 06 86209826

#31
T -Nobile
Category: Leather Goods
Average Price: Modest
Area: Centro Storico
Address: Via Dei Pettinari, 47
00186 Rome Italy
Phone: +39 06 68392205

#32
Officine Fotografiche Rome
Category: Art Gallery
Average Price:
Area: Ostiense
Address: Via Giuseppe Libetta 1
00154 Rome Italy
Phone: +39 06 97274721

#33
Musicarte
Category: Musical Instruments
Average Price: Exclusive
Area: Prati
Address: Via Germanico 170B
00192 Rome Italy
Phone: +39 06 3225302

#34
Hydra II Leather &More
Category: Fashion
Average Price: Modest
Area: Monti
Address: Via Urbana 139
00184 Rome Italy
Phone: +39 06 48907773

#35
Borghetto Flaminio
Category: Vintage
Average Price: Modest
Area: Flaminio
Address: Piazza Della Marina 32
00196 Rome Italy
Phone: +39 06 5880517

#36
Mercatino Conca d'Oro
Category: Shopping, Festival
Average Price: Modest
Area: Nomentano
Address: Via Conca d'Oro 113
00141 Rome Italy
Phone: +39 06 88644327

#37
Libreria Spagnola
Category: Bookstore, Library
Average Price: Modest
Area: Centro Storico
Address: Piazza Navona 90
00186 Rome Italy
Phone: +39 06 68806950

#38
Libreria Il Mare
Category: Bookstore
Average Price: Expensive
Area: Flaminio
Address: Via Di Ripetta 239
00186 Rome Italy
Phone: +39 06 3612155

#39
Forbidden Planet
Category: Bookstore
Average Price: Expensive
Area: San Giovanni
Address: Via Pinerolo 11
00182 Rome Italy
Phone: +39 06 70305702

#40
L'Orbita
Category: Active Life, Hobby Shop
Average Price: Modest
Area: Termini, San Giovanni
Address: Via Dei Volsci, 81
00185 Rome Italy
Phone: +39 06 44709062

#41
Hellnation Store
Category: Vinyl Records, Fashion
Average Price: Expensive
Area: Nomentano
Address: Via Nomentana 113
00198 Rome Italy
Phone: +39 06 44252628

#42
Gallerie Auchan
Category: Shopping Center, Grocery
Average Price: Modest
Area: San Lorenzo
Address: Via Alberto Pollio 59
00159 Rome Italy
Phone: +39 06 432071

#43
Farmacia Igea
Category: Drugstore
Average Price: Modest
Area: Balduina/Montemario
Address: Largo Cervinia 23
00135 Rome Italy
Phone: +39 06 35343691

#44
Arte5
Category: Art Gallery, Jazz &Blues
Average Price: Expensive
Area: Centro Storico
Address: Corso Vittorio Emanuele II 5
00186 Rome Italy
Phone: +39 06 69921298

#45
La Feltrinelli Libri E Musica
Category: Bookstore
Average Price: Modest
Area: San Giovanni
Address: Via Appia Nuova 427A
00178 Rome Italy
Phone: +39 06 7804545

#46
Libreria Scuola E Cultura
Category: Bookstore
Average Price: Modest
Area: Montesacro/Talenti
Address: Via Ugo Ojetti 173
00137 Rome Italy
Phone: +39 06 8274166

#47
Rome Store Profumi
Category: Cosmetics, Beauty Supply
Average Price: Expensive
Area: Trastevere
Address: Via Della Lungaretta 63
00153 Rome Italy
Phone: +39 06 5818789

#48
Vecchia America
Category: Vintage
Average Price: Inexpensive
Area: Esquilino, Aventino
Address: Via Ostilia 4
00184 Rome Italy
Phone: +39 335 8201488

#49
Fellini
Category: Leather Goods
Average Price: Modest
Area: Centro Storico
Address: Via Del Corso 340
00186 Rome Italy
Phone: +39 06 6785800

#50
Anteprima
Category: Women's Clothing
Average Price: Expensive
Area: Centro Storico
Address: Via Delle Quattro Fontane 38
00184 Rome Italy
Phone: +39 06 4828445

#51
Invito Alla Lettura
Category: Vinyl Records, Bookstore
Average Price:
Area: Centro Storico
Address: C. Vittorio Emanuele II, 283
00186 Rome Italy
Phone: +39 06 6861396

#52
Aspesi
Category: Fashion
Average Price: Exclusive
Area: Centro Storico
Address: Via Del Babuino 144
00187 Rome Italy
Phone: +39 06 32628760

#53
La Casa Delle Bambole
Category: Toy Store
Average Price: Inexpensive
Address: Via Flaminia 58A
00196 Rome Italy
Phone: +39 06 6790058

#54
Dear Camera
Category: Photography Store
Average Price: Modest
Area: San Giovanni
Address: Via Giuseppe Manno, 3
00179 Rome Italy
Phone: +39 06 77073770

#55
Blue Marlin
Category: Men's Clothing,
Women's Clothing
Average Price:
Area: Pinciano, Salario
Address: Via Salaria 224
00198 Rome Italy
Phone: +39 06 8553551

#56
Bonini
Category: Jewelry
Average Price: Expensive
Area: Appia Antica
Address: Via Lorenzo Bonincontri 18
00147 Rome Italy
Phone: +39 06 5139629

#57
Blitz
Category: Accessories
Average Price:
Area: Appia Antica
Address: Via Attilio Ambrosini 186
00147 Rome Italy
Phone: +39 06 5402568

#58
Studio 13
Category: Cosmetics, Beauty Supply
Average Price: Modest
Area: Prati
Address: Piazza Cavour 13
00193 Rome Italy
Phone: +39 06 68803977

#59
House &Kitchen
Category: Appliances, Home Decor
Average Price: Expensive
Area: Centro Storico
Address: Via Del Plebiscito 103
00186 Rome Italy
Phone: +39 06 6794208

#60
La Cornucopia
Category: Home Decor,
Interior Design
Average Price:
Area: Centro Storico
Address: Piazza Rondanini 32
00186 Rome Italy
Phone: +39 06 97275476

#61
Citt' Del Sole
Category: Toy Store
Average Price: Expensive
Area: Centro Storico
Address: Via Della Scrofa 65
00186 Rome Italy
Phone: +39 06 68803805

#62
Delfini
Category: Accessories, Luggage
Average Price: Exclusive
Area: Centro Storico
Address: Piazza Barberini 14
00187 Rome Italy
Phone: +39 06 42011016

#63
Ciuff Ciuff
Category: Toy Store
Average Price: Expensive
Area: San Giovanni
Address: Via Etruria 4
00183 Rome Italy
Phone: +39 06 70496454

#64
La Bancarella Di Andy Capp
Category: Comic Books, Local Flavor
Average Price: Inexpensive
Area: Nomentano
Address: Piazza Alessandria 2
00198 Rome Italy
Phone: +39 06 8530371

#65
Libreria Il Minotauro
Category: Bookstore
Average Price: Expensive
Area: Monteverde, Ostiense
Address: Via Di Monteverde, 11/A
00152 Rome Italy
Phone: +39 06 5374060

#66
Centro Carta Vertecchi
Category: Cards, Stationery
Average Price: Expensive
Area: Centro Storico
Address: Via Della Croce 70
00187 Rome Italy
Phone: +39 06 69190071

#67
Cinecitt' Due
Category: Shopping Center
Average Price: Modest
Area: Tuscolano
Address: Via Palmiro Togliatti 2
00173 Rome Italy
Phone: +39 06 7220910

#68
Tra Le Righe
Category: Bookstore
Average Price: Modest
Area: Nomentano
Address: Viale Gorizia 29
00198 Rome Italy
Phone: +39 06 85354165

#69
Centro Commerciale Primavera
Category: Shopping Center, Grocery
Average Price: Modest
Area: Casilino
Address: Viale Della Primavera, 194
00172 Rome Italy
Phone: +39 06 24406805

#70
Rome Est
Category: Shopping Center
Average Price: Expensive
Area: Casilino
Address: Via Collatina 800
00155 Rome Italy
Phone: +39 06 22511059

#71
Galleria Doria Pamphilj,
Category: Art Gallery
Average Price:
Area: Centro Storico
Address: Via Della Reginella 26
00186 Rome Italy
Phone: +39 06 87452131

#72
Empresa
Category: Men's Clothing
Average Price: Expensive
Area: Centro Storico
Address: Via Dei Giubbonari 25
00186 Rome Italy
Phone: +39 06 6832428

#73
Joseph De Bach
Category: Shoe Store
Average Price: Exclusive
Area: Trastevere
Address: Vicolo Del Cinque 19
00153 Rome Italy
Phone: +39 06 5562756

#74
Officina Della Carta
Category: Shopping
Average Price:
Area: Trastevere
Address: Via Benedetta 26/B
00153 Rome Italy
Phone: +39 06 58955578

#75
GAP
Category: Women's Clothing,
Men's Clothing
Average Price: Modest
Area: Centro Storico
Address: Via Del Corso 472
00186 Rome Italy
Phone: +39 06 68408800

#76
Peroni
Category: Kitchen &Bath
Average Price:
Area: Prati
Address: Piazza Unit'29
00192 Rome Italy
Phone: +39 06 3210852

#77
Marchese Di Sassinoro
Category: Leather Goods,
Accessories, Shoe Store
Average Price: Modest
Area: Pinciano
Address: Via Salaria 150
00198 Rome Italy
Phone: +39 06 93572908

#78
Mino - Tessuti E Biancheria
Category: Furniture Store
Average Price:
Area: San Lorenzo
Address: Viale Ippocrate 48
00161 Rome Italy
Phone: +39 06 44236003

#79
Flanella Grigia
Category: Men's Clothing
Average Price:
Area: Parioli
Address: Piazza Pitagora, 8
00197 Rome Italy
Phone: +39 06 6873793

#80
Dark Star
Category: Vinyl Records
Average Price:
Area: Appia Antica
Address: Viale Delle Accademie 53
00147 Rome Italy
Phone: +39 06 5407836

#81
Eco Store
Category: Office Equipment, Computers
Average Price: Modest
Area: Appia Antica
Address: Viale Caravaggio 119
00147 Rome Italy
Phone: +39 06 45439160

#82
Eco Store
Category: Office Equipment
Average Price: Modest
Area: Tuscolano
Address: Piazza Dell'alberone 30
00181 Rome Italy
Phone: +39 06 45420494

#83
Colosseum Computer
Category: Computers
Average Price: Expensive
Area: Nomentano
Address: Via Di Santa Costanza 20
00198 Rome Italy
Phone: +39 06 85357540

#84
Adidas Originals
Category: Sports Wear
Average Price: Modest
Area: Corso Francia
Address: Piazza Filippo Carli 5
00191 Rome Italy
Phone: +39 06 96031216

#85
L'Occhialaio
Category: Eyewear, Opticians
Area: Tuscolano
Address: Via Lucio Papirio 9
00174 Rome Italy
Phone: +39 06 71546946

#86
Cinzia
Category: Vintage
Average Price: Expensive
Area: Centro Storico
Address: Via Del Governo Vecchio 45
00186 Rome Italy
Phone: +39 06 6832945

#87
Livia Risi
Category: Accessories,
Women's Clothing
Average Price: Modest
Area: Trastevere
Address: Via Dei Vascellari, 37
00153 Rome Italy
Phone: +39 06 58301667

#88
Kokoro
Category: Women's Clothing, Accessories
Average Price: Modest
Area: Monti
Address: Via Del Boschetto 75
00184 Rome Italy
Phone: +39 06 4870657

#89
Formiche Verdi
Category: Florist
Average Price: Modest
Area: Centro Storico
Address: Via Arenula 22
00186 Rome Italy
Phone: +39 06 68193266

#90
Farmacia Giannangeli
Category: Drugstore
Average Price:
Area: Centro Storico
Address: Piazza Benedetto Cairoli, 5
00186 Rome Italy
Phone: +39 06 68307058

#91
Almost Corner Bookshop
Category: Bookstore
Average Price: Modest
Area: Trastevere
Address: Via Del Moro 45
00153 Rome Italy
Phone: +39 06 5836942

#92
Arion Minerva
Category: Bookstore
Average Price: Inexpensive
Area: Pinciano
Address: Piazza Fiume 57
00198 Rome Italy
Phone: +39 06 8553043

#93
Mandarina Duck
Category: Accessories, Luggage
Average Price: Inexpensive
Area: Centro Storico
Address: Via Due Macelli 59F
00187 Rome Italy
Phone: +39 06 6786414

#94
Twice Vintage Shop
Category: Vintage
Average Price: Inexpensive
Area: Trastevere
Address: Via Di San Francesco A Ripa
105A, 00153 Rome Italy
Phone: +39 06 31050610

#95
Casa Del Materasso
Category: Mattresses
Average Price: Inexpensive
Area: Tuscolano, Appia Antica
Address: Via Appia Nuova 545 A
00179 Rome Italy
Phone: +39 06 786706

#96
1000 Articoli A 1000
Category: Discount Store
Average Price: Inexpensive
Area: Tuscolano
Address: Via Di Tor Pignattara 52A
00177 Rome Italy
Phone: +39 347 8302242

#97
Libreria Esoterica Aradia
Category: Bookstore
Average Price: Inexpensive
Area: Nomentano
Address: Via Mantova 42
00198 Rome Italy
Phone: +39 06 85358638

#98
Borrini Shoes
Category: Shoe Store
Average Price: Inexpensive
Area: Nomentano
Address: Piazzale Delle Provincie, 18
00162 Rome Italy
Phone: +39 06 44232123

#99
Le Vesti Di Messalina
Category: Vintage
Average Price: Inexpensive
Area: Monti
Address: Via Leonina 24
00184 Rome Italy
Phone: +39 06 4881114

#100
Ibs.It Bookshop
Category: Used Bookstore, Books, Mags
Average Price: Inexpensive
Area: Centro Storico
Address: Via Nazionale 254
00184 Rome Italy
Phone: +39 06 4885405

#101
Spazio Margherita
Category: Shopping
Average Price: Inexpensive
Area: Nomentano
Address: Viale Regina Margherita 181B
00198 Rome Italy
Phone: +39 06 5570157

#102
Casa Del Fumetto
Category: Comic Books
Average Price: Inexpensive
Area: Balduina/Montemario, Prati
Address: Via Gino Nais 19
00136 Rome Italy
Phone: +39 06 39749003

#103
Pepe E Co
Category: Fashion
Average Price: Inexpensive
Area: Centro Storico
Address: Via Del Monte Della Farina 13
00186 Rome Italy
Phone: +39 06 6864740

#104
Vintage Clothing
Category: Vintage
Average Price: Inexpensive
Area: Centro Storico
Address: Via Dei Coronari, 115A
00186 Rome Italy
Phone: +39 06 68802121

#105
Eco Store
Category: Office Equipment
Average Price: Inexpensive
Area: Nomentano
Address: Viale XXI Aprile 13D
00198 Rome Italy
Phone: +39 06 45615878

#106
Essemme Servizi
Category: Wholesale Store,
Eyewear, Opticians
Average Price: Inexpensive
Area: Pigneto
Address: Via Muzio Attendolo 79A
00176 Rome Italy
Phone: +39 06 27800748

#107
Bierre Centro Copie
Category: Furniture Store,
Printing Services
Average Price: Inexpensive
Area: Nomentano
Address: Via Spalato, 6-8-10
00198 Rome Italy
Phone: +39 06 45491714

#108
Il Sesto Senso
Category: Flowers, Gifts, Jewelry,
Baby Gear &Furniture
Average Price: Inexpensive
Area: Nomentano
Address: Via Tripoli, 1
00199 Rome Italy
Phone: +39 06 86390136

#109
Fratelli Tocci
Category: Shoe Repair, Leather Goods
Average Price: Inexpensive
Area: Casilino
Address: Via Dei Frassini 156
00172 Rome Italy
Phone: +39 06 2312450

#110
Oviesse
Category: Women's Clothing
Average Price: Inexpensive
Area: Corso Francia
Address: Corso Di Francia, 124
00191 Rome Italy
Phone: +39 06 33213063

#111
Wunderkammern
Category: Art Gallery, Cultural Center
Average Price: Inexpensive
Area: Tuscolano
Address: Via Gabrio Serbelloni 124
00176 Rome Italy
Phone: +39 06 86903806

#112
Millerecords
Category: Music & Dvds, Vinyl Records
Average Price: Modest
Area: Esquilino
Address: Via Merulana 91
00185 Rome Italy
Phone: +39 06 70490109

#113
Cappelleria Dell'urbe
Category: Fashion
Average Price: Modest
Area: Monti, Termini
Address: Via Merulana 12
00185 Rome Italy
Phone: +39 06 4465820

#114
L'Artigianino
Category: Arts, Crafts
Average Price: Modest
Area: Trastevere
Address: Vicolo Del Cinque, 49
00153 Rome Italy
Phone: +39 392 6132710

#115
Ars-Imago
Category: Photography Store
Average Price: Modest
Area: Prati
Address: Via Degli Scipioni 24
00192 Rome Italy
Phone: +39 06 45492886

#116
Trast
Category: Fashion
Average Price: Modest
Area: Ostiense
Address: Piazza Di Santa Apollonia 13A
00153 Rome Italy
Phone: +39 06 88978393

#117
Pulp
Category: Vintage, Women's Clothing,
Men's Clothing
Average Price: Modest
Area: Monti
Address: Via Del Boschetto 140
00184 Rome Italy
Phone: +39 06 485511

#118
RGB46
Category: Bookstore
Average Price: Modest
Area: Testaccio, Ostiense
Address: Piazza Di Santa Maria Liberatrice
46 00153 Rome Italy
Phone: +39 06 45421608

#119
Hobo Art Club
Category: Bookstore, Winery
Average Price: Modest
Area: San Giovanni
Address: Via Ascoli Piceno 3
00176 Rome Italy
Phone: +39 06 648019

#120
Giunti Al Punto
Category: Bookstore
Average Price: Modest
Area: Centro Storico
Address: Piazza Santissimi Apostoli 59
00100 Rome Italy
Phone: +39 06 6784356

#121
Le Nuvole Parlanti
Category: Hobby Shop, Comic Books
Average Price: Modest
Area: San Lorenzo
Address: Viale Ippocrate 13
00161 Rome Italy
Phone: +39 06 4402688

#122
Accessorize Jacaranda
Category: Leather Goods, Jewelry
Average Price: Modest
Area: Centro Storico
Address: Via Del Corso, 405
00186 Rome Italy
Phone: +39 06 68136764

#123
Pifebo
Category: Vintage, Women's Clothing,
Men's Clothing
Average Price: Modest
Area: San Lorenzo, San Giovanni
Address: Via Dei Volsci 101
00185 Rome Italy
Phone: +39 338 3896371

#124
Libreria La Rinascita
Category: Bookstore
Average Price: Modest
Area: Pinciano
Address: Via Savoia 30
00198 Rome Italy
Phone: +39 389 4251173

#125
Federica Malori
Category: Shoe Store
Average Price: Modest
Area: Corso Francia
Address: Via Flaminia 628
00191 Rome Italy
Phone: +39 06 3338653

#126
Farmacia Rizzo
Category: Drugstore
Average Price: Modest
Area: Corso Francia
Address: Corso Francia 174
00191 Rome Italy
Phone: +39 06 36388584

#127
Paris
Category: Men's Clothing, Women's
Clothing, Shoe Store
Average Price: Modest
Area: Salario
Address: Via Di Priscilla 97
00199 Rome Italy
Phone: +39 06 86214671

#128
H&M
Category: Women's Clothing, Men's
Clothing, Children's Clothing
Average Price: Modest
Area: Tuscolano
Address: Via Tuscolana 785
00174 Rome Italy
Phone: +39 06 76964067

#129
EuRome2
Category: Shopping Center,
Department Store
Average Price: Modest
Area: Eur
Address: Via Cristoforo Colombo
00144 Rome Italy
Phone: +39 06 5262161

#130
Zou Zou
Category: Adult
Average Price: Modest
Area: Centro Storico
Address: Vicolo Cancelleria 9A
00186 Rome Italy
Phone: +39 06 6892176

#131
Peak-A-Book
Category: Bookstore, Italian
Average Price: Modest
Area: Centro Storico
Address: Via Arco Dei Banchi 3A
00186 Rome Italy
Phone: +39 06 64760087

#132
Arion Eritrea 2000
Category: Bookstore
Average Price: Modest
Area: Nomentano
Address: Viale Eritrea 72 F/G
00199 Rome Italy
Phone: +39 06 86212752

#133
Ricami Veronica
Category: Children's Clothing,
Swimwear, Arts, Crafts
Average Price: Modest
Area: Centro Storico
Address: Via Della Croce 77A
00187 Rome Italy
Phone: +39 06 6789184

#134
Fabriano Botique
Category: Arts, Crafts
Average Price: Modest
Area: Flaminio
Address: Via Del Babuino 173
00187 Rome Italy
Phone: +39 06 32600361

#135
L'image
Category: Art Gallery
Average Price: Modest
Area: Centro Storico
Address: Via Della Scrofa, 67
00186 Rome Italy
Phone: +39 06 6864050

#136
Medina Oriental Design
Category: Arts, Crafts
Average Price: Modest
Area: Nomentano
Address: Via Alessandria 121
00198 Rome Italy
Phone: +39 06 8558831

#137
Arion Veneto
Category: Books, Mags, Music &Video
Average Price: Modest
Area: Centro Storico
Address: Via Veneto 42
00187 Rome Italy
Phone: +39 06 4825308

#138
Cinius
Category: Furniture Store
Average Price: Modest
Area: San Giovanni
Address: Via Appia Nuova 215
00182 Rome Italy
Phone: +39 06 7014539

#139
La Stanza Della Musica
Category: Musical Instruments, Bookstore
Average Price: Modest
Area: Flaminio, Centro Storico
Address: Via Savoia 58
00198 Rome Italy
Phone: +39 06 85355065

#140
Star Shop
Category: Comic Books
Average Price: Modest
Area: Flaminio
Address: Via Laurina 4
00187 Rome Italy
Phone: +39 06 3223502

#141
Il Mercatino Dell'usato
Category: Vintage
Average Price: Modest
Area: Monteverde, Aurelia
Address: Via Ludovico Micara 32
00165 Rome Italy
Phone: +39 06 39388832

#142
Baby's Store Giocattoli
Category: Toy Store
Average Price: Modest
Area: Nomentano
Address: Viale XXI Aprile, 56/64
00162 Rome Italy
Phone: +39 06 44238806

#143
Farmacia Dott. Maurizio Spinelli
Category: Drugstore
Average Price: Modest
Area: Ostiense
Address: Piazza Andrea Ampere, 2
00149 Rome Italy
Phone: +39 06 55363007

#144
Capuani Sergio
Category: Tobacco Shop
Average Price: Modest
Area: Nomentano, Salario
Address: Piazza Istria, 1
00198 Rome Italy
Phone: +39 06 8606395

#145
Farmacia Spadazzi
Category: Drugstore
Average Price: Modest
Area: Corso Francia
Address: Piazzale Ponte Milvio 15
00191 Rome Italy
Phone: +39 06 3333753

#146
Libreria Nuova Europa I Granai
Category: Bookstore
Average Price: Modest
Area: Eur
Address: Via Mario Rigamonti, 100
00142 Rome Italy
Phone: +39 06 51955770

#147
Branciforte
Category: Fashion, Fabric Store,
Knitting Supplies
Average Price: Modest
Area: Centro Storico
Address: Piazza Paganica 12
00186 Rome Italy
Phone: +39 06 6865271

#148
Libreria Internazionale Croce
Category: Bookstore
Average Price: Modest
Area: Termini
Address: Via Solferino 7A
00185 Rome Italy
Phone: +39 06 4453222

#149
La Feltrinelli Libri E Musica
Category: Bookstore
Average Price: Modest
Area: Ostiense
Address: Viale Guglielmo Marconi,
188, 00146 Rome Italy
Phone: +39 06 5534171

#150
Le Gallinelle
Category: Fashion
Average Price: Modest
Area: Monti
Address: Via Panisperna 61
00184 Rome Italy
Phone: +39 06 4881017

#151
Video Video
Category: Videos, Video Game Rental
Average Price: Modest
Area: Ostiense
Address: Circonv. Ostiense, 155
00154 Rome Italy
Phone: +39 06 57300671

#152
Catenella Rome
Category: Women's Clothing
Average Price: Modest
Area: Prati
Address: Viale Eritrea 2
00199 Rome Italy
Phone: +39 06 86217309

#153
Kestrano
Category: Leather Goods, Accessories
Average Price: Modest
Area: Tuscolano
Address: Via Santa Maria
Ausiliatrice 43, 00181 Rome Italy
Phone: +39 06 78393974

#154
Ready Books
Category: Bookstore
Average Price: Modest
Area: Monti
Address: Via Cavour 255
00184 Rome Italy
Phone: +39 06 4882821

#155
**Libreria Galleria Il Museo
Del Louvre**
Category: Art Gallery, Bookstore
Average Price: Modest
Area: Centro Storico
Address: Via Della Reginella 26-28
00186 Rome Italy
Phone: +39 06 68807725

#156
Calzature Alberto
Category: Shoe Store
Average Price: Modest
Area: Centro Storico
Address: Piazza Benedetto Cairoli, 13/15,
00186 Rome Italy
Phone: +39 06 6861188

#157
Fratelli Bassetti Tessuti
Category: Department Store
Average Price: Modest
Area: Centro Storico
Address: Corso Vittorio Emanuele II
00186 Rome Italy
Phone: +39 06 6892326

#158
Taba
Category: Fashion
Average Price: Modest
Area: Centro Storico
Address: Piazza Campo DE' Fiori, 13
00186 Rome Italy
Phone: +39 06 68806478

#159
Il Papiro
Category: Cards, Stationery
Average Price: Modest
Area: Centro Storico
Address: Via Pantheon, 50
00186 Rome Italy
Phone: +39 06 6795597

#160
Berte
Category: Toy Store
Average Price: Modest
Area: Centro Storico
Address: Piazza Navona 108
00186 Rome Italy
Phone: +39 06 6875011

#161
Sandro Ferrone
Category: Women's Clothing
Average Price: Modest
Area: Centro Storico
Address: Via Del Tritone 120
00187 Rome Italy
Phone: +39 06 42020522

#162
WP Windsurf Paradise
Category: Outlet Store
Average Price: Modest
Area: Centro Storico
Address: Corso Vittorio
Emanuele II 206, 00186 Rome Italy
Phone: +39 06 68806564

#163
Trast
Category: Fashion
Average Price: Modest
Area: Centro Storico
Address: Vicolo Delle Vacche 18
00186 Rome Italy
Phone: +39 06 88978393

#164
Hassan Calzature
Category: Shoe Store
Average Price: Modest
Area: San Giovanni
Address: Via Faleria 18
00183 Rome Italy
Phone: +39 06 51435341

#165
Gallerie Josephine
Category: Flowers, Gifts,
Knitting Supplies
Average Price: Modest
Area: Ostiense
Address: Viale Guglielmo Marconi 168
00146 Rome Italy
Phone: +39 06 5570993

#166
Danielle
Category: Shoe Store
Average Price: Modest
Area: Prati
Address: Piazza Risorgimento 39
00192 Rome Italy
Phone: +39 06 39744675

#167
Marango Sport
Category: Sporting Goods
Average Price: Modest
Area: San Lorenzo
Address: Viale Delle Provincie, 168
00162 Rome Italy
Phone: +39 06 44232039

#168
PIM - Punto Ideal Market
Category: Home &Garden
Average Price: Modest
Area: Tuscolano, Appia Antica
Address: Via Satrico, 27
00183 Rome Italy
Phone: +39 06 770182

#169
Talassa
Category: Sporting Goods
Average Price: Modest
Area: San Lorenzo, Montesacro/Talenti
Address: Via Vincenzo Morello 21
00157 Rome Italy
Phone: +39 06 4396631

#170
La Placa
Category: Photography Store
Average Price: Modest
Area: Nomentano
Address: Via Val Trompia 12
00141 Rome Italy
Phone: +39 06 8173765

#171
Zucca Stregata
Category: Children's Clothing
Average Price: Modest
Area: Corso Francia
Address: Via Di Vigna Stelluti 179
00191 Rome Italy
Phone: +39 06 36306073

#172
Ultrasuoni Records
Category: Vinyl Records
Average Price: Modest
Area: Monti
Address: Via Degli Zingari 61A
00184 Rome Italy
Phone: +39 06 4745485

#173
Voland
Category: Art Gallery
Average Price: Modest
Area: Monti
Address: Via Del Boschetto, 129
00184 Rome Italy
Phone: +39 06 47823674

#174
King Size Vintage Shop
Category: Vintage
Average Price: Modest
Area: Monti
Address: Via Dei Volsci 101D
00185 Rome Italy
Phone: +39 06 491092

#175
Il Punto Editoriale
Category: Bookstore
Average Price: Modest
Area: Centro Storico
Address: Via Cordonata, 4
00187 Rome Italy
Phone: +39 06 6795805

#176
Archivia
Category: Home Decor
Average Price: Modest
Area: Monti
Address: Via Del Boschetto 23
00184 Rome Italy
Phone: +39 06 4741503

#177
Freestyler Rider's Shop
Category: Fashion
Average Price: Modest
Area: Monti
Address: Via Leonina 87
00184 Rome Italy
Phone: +39 06 473811

#178
Danza Bazar
Category: Fashion
Average Price: Modest
Address: Via Cavour 93
00184 Rome Italy
Phone: +39 06 4874598

#179
Libreria Croce
Category: Bookstore
Average Price: Modest
Area: Centro Storico
Address: Corso Vittorio
Emanuele II 156, 00186 Rome Italy
Phone: +39 06 68802269

#180
Centro Cucito Creativo
Category: Knitting Supplies,
Fabric Store
Average Price: Modest
Area: Esquilino
Address: Via Dello Statuto 70
00185 Rome Italy
Phone: +39 06 4872814

#181
Rendi
Category: Shoe Store
Average Price: Modest
Area: Centro Storico
Address: Via Nazionale 35
00184 Rome Italy
Phone: +39 06 4743326

#182
Tricolore
Category: Shopping
Average Price: Modest
Area: Centro Storico
Address: Via Nazionale 249
00184 Rome Italy
Phone: +39 06 4882885

#183
Giu.Pa.R.
Category: Electronics
Average Price: Modest
Area: Testaccio, Ostiense
Address: Via Dei Conciatori, 34/40
00154 Rome Italy
Phone: +39 06 57300045

#184
Pisapia Calzature
Category: Shoe Store
Average Price: Modest
Area: Termini
Address: Via Volturno 54
00185 Rome Italy
Phone: +39 06 4440647

#185
Pianeta Magia
Category: Hobby Shop
Average Price: Modest
Area: San Giovanni
Address: Via Pontremoli, 34
00182 Rome Italy
Phone: +39 06 70450154

#186
Sakurashu
Category: Shopping
Average Price: Modest
Area: San Giovanni
Address: Via Ceneda 13
00183 Rome Italy
Phone: +39 06 64821651

#187
Magic Sound
Category: Music & Dvds
Average Price: Modest
Area: San Giovanni
Address: Piazza Dei Re Di Rome18
00183 Rome Italy
Phone: +39 06 77208984

#188
Libreria Mondadori Di Voltapagina
Category: Bookstore
Average Price: Modest
Area: Termini
Address: Via Piave, 18
00187 Rome Italy
Phone: +39 06 42014726

#189
Bonsai Lucaferri
Category: Tree Services, Florist
Average Price: Modest
Area: Prati
Address: Via Lucrezio Caro 59
00193 Rome Italy
Phone: +39 06 3216148

#190
Libreria Anomalia
Category: Bookstore
Average Price: Modest
Area: San Giovanni
Address: Via Dei Campani 73
00185 Rome Italy
Phone: +39 06 491335

#191
Bertozzini
Category: Cosmetics, Beauty Supply,
Tanning, Perfume
Average Price: Modest
Area: Prati
Address: Via Cola Di Rienzo 192
00192 Rome Italy
Phone: +39 06 6874662

#192
Maremoto
Category: Toy Store
Average Price: Modest
Area: Prati
Address: Via Duilio 5
00192 Rome Italy
Phone: +39 06 3210682

#193
Vetreria Majorana
Category: Home Decor,
Windows Installation
Average Price: Modest
Area: Ostiense
Address: Via Quirino Majorana 141
00152 Rome Italy
Phone: +39 06 5583691

#194
Libreria Il Corsaro
Category: Bookstore
Average Price: Modest
Area: San Giovanni
Address: Via Macerata, 46
00176 Rome Italy
Phone: +39 06 97603761

#195
La Valigeria
Category: Luggage
Average Price: Modest
Area: San Giovanni
Address: Via Cesare Baronio 18
00179 Rome Italy
Phone: +39 06 7886754

#196
Il Seme
Category: Bookstore
Average Price: Modest
Area: Prati
Address: Via Monte Zebio, 3
00195 Rome Italy
Phone: +39 06 3728377

#197
Euronics Nova
Category: Mobile Phones,
Electronics, Computers
Average Price: Modest
Area: San Lorenzo
Address: Viale Ippocrate 23
00161 Rome Italy
Phone: +39 06 22769227

#198
**Alecci E Di Paola
Artefici D'Interni**
Category: Shopping
Average Price: Modest
Area: Monti
Address: Via Cardello, 14
00184 Rome Italy
Phone: +39 06 4824850

#199
Celli / UGO
Category: Shoe Store
Average Price: Modest
Area: Centro Storico
Address: Via Arenula, 86
00186 Rome Italy
Phone: +39 06 68803555

#200
Vertigo Vintage Boutique
Category: Women's Clothing,
Vintage, Accessories
Average Price: Modest
Area: Centro Storico
Address: Via Del Ges'71
00186 Rome Italy
Phone: +39 06 95216720

#201
Natura E Spirito
Category: Cosmetics, Beauty Supply
Average Price: Modest
Area: Nomentano, Salario
Address: Via Bisagno 23
00199 Rome Italy
Phone: +39 06 86324284

#202
Becker &Music'
Category: Tobacco Shop
Average Price: Modest
Area: Centro Storico
Address: Via San Vincenzo 29
00187 Rome Italy
Phone: +39 06 6785435

#203
Puntacco
Category: Shoe Store
Average Price: Modest
Area: Ostiense
Address: Viale Dei Colli Portuensi 382
00151 Rome Italy
Phone: +39 06 65740762

#204
Il Giardino Della Talpa
Category: Toy Store,
Baby Gear &Furniture
Average Price: Modest
Area: Testaccio, Ostiense
Address: Via Aldo Manuzio 61
00153 Rome Italy
Phone: +39 06 57302232

#205
Libreria Godel
Category: Bookstore
Average Price: Modest
Area: Centro Storico
Address: Via Poli, 46
00187 Rome Italy
Phone: +39 06 6790331

#206
Farmacia Piram
Category: Drugstore
Average Price: Modest
Area: Centro Storico
Address: Via Nazionale, 228
00184 Rome Italy
Phone: +39 06 48986001

#207
Aleeza
Category: Women's Clothing
Average Price: Modest
Area: San Giovanni
Address: Via Gallia 41A
00183 Rome Italy
Phone: +39 06 77201161

#208
Libri Angelo Curati
Category: Thrift Store, Bookstore,
Hobby Shop
Average Price: Modest
Area: Termini, Centro Storico
Address: Via Delle Terme Di Diocleziano
00185 Rome Italy
Phone: +39 339 2170406

#209
La Pallina
Category: Jewelry
Average Price: Modest
Area: Centro Storico
Address: Via Margutta, 61/C
00187 Rome Italy
Phone: +39 06 32110232

#210
La Gallina Bah
Category: Shopping
Average Price: Modest
Area: Salario
Address: Via Nemorense, 51/D
00199 Rome Italy
Phone: +39 06 8845949

#211
The Lion Bookshop
Category: Books, Mags, Music &Video
Average Price: Modest
Area: Flaminio, Centro Storico
Address: Via Dei Greci 33/36
00187 Rome Italy
Phone: +39 06 32650437

#212
Libreria Suspense
Category: Bookstore
Average Price: Modest
Area: Salario
Address: Via Ceresio 87
00199 Rome Italy
Phone: +39 06 85358291

#213
Chiaridea
Category: Women's Clothing, Accessories
Average Price: Modest
Area: Termini
Address: Via Quintino Sella 16
00187 Rome Italy
Phone: +39 00 39064814188

#214
Cartoplastica Colombo
Category: Cards, Stationery,
Party Supplies
Average Price: Modest
Area: Appia Antica
Address: Via Badia Di Cava 40
00142 Rome Italy
Phone: +39 06 5412413

#215
Mini Garden
Category: Florist
Average Price: Modest
Area: Ostiense
Address: Via Giuseppe Candeo, 20/22
00154 Rome Italy
Phone: +39 06 57300004

#216
Il Calzolaio
Category: Arts, Crafts
Average Price: Modest
Area: Tuscolano
Address: Via Di Tor Pignattara 35
00177 Rome Italy
Phone: +39 06 2413614

#217
Il Tesoro
Category: Arts, Crafts
Average Price: Modest
Area: Monti
Address: Via Dei Serpenti, 135-136
00184 Rome Italy
Phone: +39 06 4871927

#218
Cult 123
Category: Women's Clothing
Average Price: Modest
Area: Salario
Address: Viale Libia 123/125
00199 Rome Italy
Phone: +39 06 45437312

#219
Altromercato
Category: Women's Clothing,
Flowers, Gifts, Health Markets
Average Price: Modest
Area: Flaminio
Address: Via Di Ripetta 262
00186 Rome Italy
Phone: +39 06 3223023

#220
Dipalo Giornali
Category: Newspapers &Magazines
Average Price: Modest
Area: Appia Antica
Address: Via Meropia 105B
00147 Rome Italy
Phone: +39 06 5120253

#221
Tabacchi Monteleone
Category: Tobacco Shop
Average Price: Modest
Area: Appia Antica
Address: Via Giulio Aristide Sartorio, 31
00147 Rome Italy
Phone: +39 06 5132503

#222
Tiger
Category: Office Equipment,
Hobby Shop
Average Price: Modest
Area: Tuscolano
Address: Via Tuscolana, 1252
00174 Rome Italy
Phone: +39 06 7480917

#223
Maga
Category: Fashion
Average Price: Modest
Area: Nomentano
Address: Viale Eritrea 100
00199 Rome Italy
Phone: +39 06 86217547

#224
Tech It Easy
Category: Home Decor
Average Price: Modest
Area: Parioli
Address: Via Chelini 19
00197 Rome Italy
Phone: +39 06 8078904

#225
Trony
Category: Electronics, Computers,
Appliances
Average Price: Modest
Area: Casilino
Address: Viale Agosta 46
00171 Rome Italy
Phone: +39 06 2589700

#226
Rinascita
Category: Bookstore
Average Price: Modest
Area: Casilino
Address: Largo Agosta, 36
00171 Rome Italy
Phone: +39 06 25204819

#227
Ferramenta
Category: Hardware Store
Average Price: Modest
Area: Casilino
Address: Viale Delle Gardenie 49
00172 Rome Italy
Phone: +39 06 2410140

#228
Intimissimi
Category: Lingerie
Average Price: Modest
Area: Eur
Address: Viale Europa 11
00144 Rome Italy
Phone: +39 06 54282619

#229
Gamers Videogiochi
Category: Shopping
Average Price: Modest
Area: Nomentano
Address: Viale Tirreno, 88
00141 Rome Italy
Phone: +39 06 87179410

#230
Farmacia Gravina
Category: Cosmetics &Beauty Supply
Average Price: Modest
Area: Nomentano
Address: Via Nomentana 566
00141 Rome Italy
Phone: +39 06 86895602

#231
Blu Rosso Giallo
Category: Vinyl Records
Average Price: Modest
Area: Montesacro/Talenti
Address: Via Ugo Ojetti 144
00137 Rome Italy
Phone: +39 06 8273107

#232
By Simon
Category: Jewelry
Average Price: Modest
Area: Tuscolano
Address: Via Tuscolana 1434
00174 Rome Italy
Phone: +39 06 64781057

#233
Stazi
Category: Jewelry
Average Price: Modest
Area: Salario
Address: Via Monte Cervialto, 171
00139 Rome Italy
Phone: +39 06 8124408

#234
New Optical
Category: Eyewear, Opticians
Average Price: Modest
Area: Eur
Address: Piazza Hazon 10
00144 Rome Italy
Phone: +39 06 5292871

#235
Todis
Category: Discount Store
Average Price: Modest
Area: Eur
Address: Via Del Fiume Giallo 50
00144 Rome Italy
Phone: +39 06 52277107

#236
Casamaria
Category: Cosmetics, Beauty Supply
Average Price: Modest
Area: Ostiense
Address: Via Oderisi Da Gubbio 55
00146 Rome Italy
Phone: +39 06 5562258

#237
Tiffany
Category: Home Decor,
Watches, Jewelry
Average Price: Expensive
Area: Centro Storico
Address: Via Del Babuino 118
00187 Rome Italy
Phone: +39 06 6790717

#238
Elio Zema
Category: Furniture Store
Average Price: Expensive
Area: Flaminio
Address: Via Del Babuino 31
00187 Rome Italy
Phone: +39 06 3216878

#239
Candle's Store
Category: Home &Garden,
Arts, Crafts, Art Gallery
Average Price: Expensive
Area: San Giovanni
Address: Via Dei Campani 49
00185 Rome Italy
Phone: +39 06 4464849

#240
Antica Manifattura Cappelli
Category: Arts, Crafts
Average Price: Expensive
Area: Prati
Address: Via Degli Scipioni, 46
00192 Rome Italy
Phone: +39 06 39725679

#241
Teichner
Category: Fashion
Average Price: Expensive
Area: San Giovanni
Address: Via Appia Nuova 2
00187 Rome Italy
Phone: +39 06 7000934

#242
Toko
Category: Fashion
Average Price: Expensive
Area: Centro Storico
Address: Via Del Corallo, 32-33
00186 Rome Italy
Phone: +39 06 68210780

#243
Old Soccer
Category: Sports Wear
Average Price: Expensive
Area: Flaminio
Address: Via Di Ripetta, 30
00186 Rome Italy
Phone: +39 06 96846111

#244
Rigasu'
Category: Women's Clothing
Average Price: Expensive
Area: Nomentano
Address: Via Nomentana, 135
00198 Rome Italy
Phone: +39 06 44202214

#245
La Feltrinelli
Category: Bookstore
Average Price: Expensive
Area: Prati
Address: Via Giulio Cesare 88
00192 Rome Italy
Phone: +39 06 37514023

#246
Centro Commerciale I Granai
Category: Shopping Center
Average Price: Expensive
Area: Appia Antica
Address: Via Mario Rigamonti 100
00142 Rome Italy
Phone: +39 06 5034212

#247
Lush Italia
Category: Cosmetics, Beauty Supply
Average Price: Expensive
Area: Centro Storico
Address: Via Del Corso 500
00186 Rome Italy
Phone: +39 06 3612364

#248
Super
Category: Women's Clothing,
Men's Clothing, Accessories
Average Price: Expensive
Area: Monti
Address: Via Leonina 42
00184 Rome Italy
Phone: +39 06 98266450

#249
D-Mail
Category: Toy Store
Average Price: Expensive
Area: Tuscolano
Address: Via Dei Consoli 185
00175 Rome Italy
Phone: +39 06 76910113

#250
Feltrinelli International
Category: Bookstore
Average Price: Expensive
Area: Termini, Centro Storico
Address: Via Vittorio Emanuele
Orlando, 84, 00185 Rome Italy
Phone: +39 06 4827878

#251
Nike Store
Category: Fashion, Active Life
Average Price: Expensive
Area: Centro Storico
Address: Via Del Corso 478
00186 Rome Italy
Phone: +39 06 3214130

#252
Dadada
Category: Women's Clothing
Average Price: Expensive
Area: Centro Storico
Address: Via Del Corso, 500
00186 Rome Italy
Phone: +39 06 3213504

#253
Brandy E Melville
Category: Women's Clothing
Average Price: Expensive
Area: Salario, Parioli
Address: Viale Parioli, 7
00197 Rome Italy
Phone: +39 06 80687853

#254
Libreria Tombolini
Category: Bookstore
Average Price: Expensive
Area: Centro Storico
Address: Via IV Novembre 146
00187 Rome Italy
Phone: +39 06 6785925

#255
Boschetto Tre
Category: Home Decor
Average Price: Expensive
Area: Monti
Address: Via Del Boschetto 3
00184 Rome Italy
Phone: +39 06 48906922

#256
Santini Fausto
Category: Shoe Store
Average Price: Expensive
Area: Monti
Address: Via Di Cavour 106
00185 Rome Italy
Phone: +39 06 4880934

#257
Mondelliani
Category: Eyewear, Opticians
Average Price: Expensive
Area: Centro Storico
Address: Via Dei Bergamaschi 49
00186 Rome Italy
Phone: +39 06 6793481

#258
Gruppo Foto Pennetta
Category: Photography Store
Average Price: Expensive
Area: Trastevere
Address: Via Dandolo 4
00153 Rome Italy
Phone: +39 06 5896648

#259
Spazio IF
Category: Art Gallery, Fashion
Average Price: Expensive
Area: Centro Storico
Address: Via Dei Coronari 44A
00186 Rome Italy
Phone: +39 06 64760639

#260
Mood
Category: Women's Clothing
Average Price: Expensive
Area: Centro Storico
Address: Via Del Corso 344
00186 Rome Italy
Phone: +39 06 6780308

#261
Romeo Bike
Category: Bikes, Bike Rentals
Average Price: Expensive
Area: Flaminio
Address: Via Del Vantaggio 41A
00186 Rome Italy
Phone: +39 06 32609838

#262
El Charro
Category: Shoe Store
Average Price: Expensive
Area: Flaminio
Address: Via Di San Giacomo
00187 Rome Italy
Phone: +39 06 36002209

#263
Lelli
Category: Home Decor,
Interior Design, Carpeting
Average Price: Expensive
Area: Flaminio
Address: Via Margutta 5
00187 Rome Italy
Phone: +39 06 3614000

#264
Pandemonium
Category: Fashion
Average Price: Expensive
Area: Centro Storico
Address: Via Dei Giubbonari, 104
00186 Rome Italy
Phone: +39 06 6868061

#265
The Milk Bar
Category: Baby Gear &Furniture
Average Price: Expensive
Area: Monti
Address: Via Di San Martino Ai Monti 34
00184 Rome Italy
Phone: +39 06 97276418

#266
Herder Editrice E Libreria
Category: Bookstore
Average Price: Expensive
Area: Centro Storico
Address: Piazza Montecitorio, 117/120
00186 Rome Italy
Phone: +39 06 6794628

#267
Gente Rome
Category: Fashion
Average Price: Expensive
Area: Prati
Address: Via Del Babuino, 80
00187 Rome Italy
Phone: +39 06 3207671

#268
Librairie Fran'aise De Rome
Category: Bookstore
Average Price: Expensive
Area: Centro Storico
Address: Piazza San Luigi Dei Francesi
23, 00186 Rome Italy
Phone: +39 06 68307

#269
Hocus Pocus
Category: Music & Dvds
Average Price: Expensive
Area: San Giovanni
Address: Via Marruvio 18
00183 Rome Italy
Phone: +39 06 70497511

#270
Solo Natura
Category: Herbs &Spices,
Cosmetics, Beauty Supply
Average Price: Expensive
Area: Esquilino
Address: Via Emanuele Filiberto 126/128
00185 Rome Italy
Phone: +39 06 70452836

#271
Gioielleria Montagnani
Category: Jewelry, Watches
Average Price: Expensive
Area: Prati
Address: Via Degli Scipioni, 73/75
00192 Rome Italy
Phone: +39 06 39731733

#272
Mondopop
Category: Toy Store,
Art Gallery, Bookstore
Average Price: Expensive
Area: Flaminio, Centro Storico
Address: Via Dei Greci 30
00187 Rome Italy
Phone: +39 06 36005117

#273
Profumeria Gini
Category: Cosmetics, Beauty Supply
Average Price: Expensive
Area: San Giovanni
Address: Via Appia Nuova, 156,
00040 Rome Italy
Phone: +39 06 7081056

#274
Sound's Factory
Category: Vinyl Records
Average Price: Expensive
Area: Prati
Address: Via Crescenzio 41A
00193 Rome Italy
Phone: +39 06 97612860

#275
**Ferramenta Supermercato
Del Legno**
Category: Hardware Store
Average Price: Expensive
Area: San Giovanni
Address: Via Siria 42
00179 Rome Italy
Phone: +39 06 7803039

#276
Batik
Category: Home Decor
Average Price: Expensive
Area: Nomentano
Address: Viale Adriatico, 43
00141 Rome Italy
Phone: +39 06 8183905

#277
Bambusa Garden Center
Category: Furniture Store
Average Price: Expensive
Area: Nomentano, Salario
Address: Via Topino, 13/A
00199 Rome Italy
Phone: +39 06 8554955

#278
Game Stop
Category: Video Game Rental
Average Price: Expensive
Area: San Lorenzo
Address: Viale Ippocrate, 11
00161 Rome Italy
Phone: +39 06 44243739

#279
E.Molinari Emporium
Category: Shopping
Average Price: Expensive
Area: Salario
Address: Viale VAL Padana 26
00141 Rome Italy
Phone: +39 06 886402262

#280
Croppo
Category: Home &Garden
Average Price: Expensive
Area: Appia Antica
Address: Via Mario Rigamonti 100
00142 Rome Italy
Phone: +39 06 51955898

#281
Saccoccio Gioielli
Category: Jewelry
Average Price: Expensive
Area: Casilino
Address: Via Dei Castani 223
00171 Rome Italy
Phone: +39 06 24401113

#282
Farmacia Internazionale
Category: Drugstore, Nutritionists
Average Price: Expensive
Area: Centro Storico
Address: Piazza Barberini 49
00187 Rome Italy
Phone: +39 06 4871195

#283
La Chiave
Category: Furniture Store,
Women's Clothing, Accessories
Average Price: Expensive
Address: Largo Delle Stimmate 28
00186 Rome Italy
Phone: +39 06 68308848

#284
Geppy Shoes
Category: Shoe Store
Average Price: Expensive
Area: Centro Storico
Address: Via Nazionale 6
00184 Rome Italy
Phone: +39 06 4884814

#285
Fabindia
Category: Fashion
Average Price: Expensive
Area: Centro Storico
Address: Via Banco Di Santo Spirito, 40
00186 Rome Italy
Phone: +39 06 68891230

#286
Kaja
Category: Shopping
Average Price: Expensive
Area: Monti
Address: Via Degli Zingari, 62
00184 Rome Italy
Phone: +39 06 4882962

#287
Soul Food
Category: Vinyl Records
Average Price: Expensive
Area: Esquilino, Aventino
Address: Via Di San Giovanni In Laterano
194, 00184 Rome Italy
Phone: +39 06 70452025

#288
Coppelia
Category: Sporting Goods
Average Price: Expensive
Area: Monti
Address: Piazza Dell'esquilino, 29
00185 Rome Italy
Phone: +39 06 47824448

#289
Ruben
Category: Women's Clothing
Average Price: Expensive
Area: Centro Storico
Address: Via Nazionale 10
00184 Rome Italy
Phone: +39 06 4827452

#290
Alcova
Category: Adult
Average Price: Expensive
Area: Centro Storico
Address: Piazza Sforza Cesarini 27
00186 Rome Italy
Phone: +39 06 6864118

#291
Casuccio E Scalera
Category: Shoe Store
Average Price: Expensive
Area: Centro Storico
Address: Via Del Corso, 483/484
00186 Rome Italy
Phone: +39 06 3227094

#292
Mr. Boots
Category: Shoe Store
Average Price: Expensive
Area: San Giovanni
Address: Piazza Dei Re Di Rome10
00183 Rome Italy
Phone: +39 06 77208672

#293
40 Gradi
Category: Shopping
Average Price: Expensive
Area: Prati
Address: Via Virgilio, 1
00193 Rome Italy
Phone: +39 06 68134612

#294
Storia E Magia
Category: Shopping
Average Price: Expensive
Area: Prati
Address: Via Ottaviano 32
00192 Rome Italy
Phone: +39 06 39745528

#295
Vertecchi
Category: Cards, Stationery
Average Price: Expensive
Area: Flaminio
Address: Via Pietro Da Cortona 18
00189 Rome Italy
Phone: +39 06 3322821

#296
Flaminia Computer
Category: Adult Education, Computers
Average Price: Expensive
Area: Flaminio
Address: Via Flaminia 387
00196 Rome Italy
Phone: +39 06 45439818

#297
Leone Limentani
Category: Flowers, Gifts, Kitchen &Bath
Average Price: Expensive
Area: Centro Storico
Address: Via Portico d'Ottavia 47
00186 Rome Italy
Phone: +39 06 68307000

#298
Edo City
Category: Women's Clothing
Average Price: Expensive
Area: Monti
Address: Via Leonina 78
00184 Rome Italy
Phone: +39 06 48071981

#299
B Moda Arte Design
Category: Shopping
Average Price: Expensive
Area: Monti
Address: Piazza Madonna Dei Monti, 1
00184 Rome Italy
Phone: +39 06 47826335

#300
Estremi
Category: Furniture Store
Average Price: Expensive
Area: Monti
Address: Via Del Boschetto 2A
00184 Rome Italy
Phone: +39 06 4744001

#301
Motelsalieri
Category: Men's Clothing, Art Gallery
Average Price: Expensive
Area: Monti
Address: Via Giovanni Lanza, 162
00184 Rome Italy
Phone: +39 06 48989966

#302
Pellicano'
Category: Fashion
Average Price: Expensive
Area: Centro Storico
Address: Via Del Seminario, 93
00186 Rome Italy
Phone: +39 06 69942199

#303
Loco
Category: Shoe Store
Average Price: Expensive
Area: Centro Storico
Address: Via Dei Baullari 22
00186 Rome Italy
Phone: +39 06 68808216

#304
Angeli
Category: Leather Goods
Average Price: Expensive
Area: Centro Storico
Address: Via Dei Baullari, 139
00186 Rome Italy
Phone: +39 06 6875835

#305
Borsalino
Category: Accessories
Average Price: Expensive
Area: Centro Storico
Address: Via Campo Marzio 72A
00186 Rome Italy
Phone: +39 06 6796120

#306
Eurogarden
Category: Nursery, Gardening
Average Price: Expensive
Area: Aventino, Ostiense
Address: Viale Guido Baccelli, 85
00153 Rome Italy
Phone: +39 06 5742157

#307
Banchetti Sport
Category: Sporting Goods
Average Price: Expensive
Area: Centro Storico
Address: Via Campo Marzio, 38
00186 Rome Italy
Phone: +39 06 6871420

#308
Non Solo Bianco
Category: Home Decor
Average Price: Expensive
Area: Centro Storico
Address: Via Fontanella Borghese 38
00186 Rome Italy
Phone: +39 06 6876657

#309
Leam
Category: Fashion
Average Price: Expensive
Area: San Giovanni
Address: Via Appia Nuova, 26-32
00183 Rome Italy
Phone: +39 06 77207204

#310
Non Solo Arte
Category: Tobacco Shop
Average Price: Expensive
Area: Flaminio
Address: Via Di Ripetta, 60
00186 Rome Italy
Phone: +39 06 3216987

#311
Colapietro
Category: Hardware Store
Average Price: Expensive
Area: Trastevere, Ostiense
Address: Via Eugenio Baranti 10
00146 Rome Italy
Phone: +39 06 5561693

#312
Zefiro
Category: Bridal
Average Price: Expensive
Area: Prati
Address: Via Marcantonio Colonna, 18
00192 Rome Italy
Phone: +39 06 3214349

#313
Arya
Category: Jewelry
Average Price: Expensive
Area: Nomentano, Pinciano
Address: Via Bergamo, 44
00198 Rome Italy
Phone: +39 06 98876139

#314
Max &Co.
Category: Women's Clothing
Average Price: Expensive
Area: Pinciano
Address: Via Salaria 59
00198 Rome Italy
Phone: +39 06 85354712

#315
La Calendula
Category: Cosmetics, Beauty Supply
Average Price: Expensive
Area: Nomentano, Salario
Address: Via Corsica, 22
00198 Rome Italy
Phone: +39 06 8559813

#316
Libreria Militare Ares
Category: Bookstore
Average Price: Expensive
Area: San Lorenzo
Address: Via Lorenzo Il Magnifico 46
00162 Rome Italy
Phone: +39 06 44232188

#317
Annie
Category: Women's Clothing
Average Price: Expensive
Area: Trastevere
Address: Viale Trastevere 73
00153 Rome Italy
Phone: +39 06 5800261

#318
Urban Tales
Category: Women's Clothing
Average Price: Expensive
Area: Trastevere
Address: Via Dei Fienaroli 21A
00153 Rome Italy
Phone: +39 06 58301130

#319
De Sanctis 1890
Category: Shopping
Average Price: Expensive
Area: Centro Storico
Address: Piazza Di Pietra 24
00186 Rome Italy
Phone: +44 6688 06810

#320
Laboratorio Marcoaurelio
Category: Jewelry
Average Price: Expensive
Area: Centro Storico
Address: Via Dei Cappellari 21
00186 Rome Italy
Phone: +39 348 2762842

#321
Fantasie Di Fiori
Category: Florist
Average Price: Expensive
Area: Centro Storico
Address: Vicolo Savelli 54
00186 Rome Italy
Phone: +39 06 68809529

#322
Manecchi Shopping Rome
Category: Fashion
Average Price: Expensive
Area: Centro Storico
Address: Via Di Campo Marzio 35
00186 Rome Italy
Phone: +39 06 68301614

#323
Becool
Category: Shopping
Average Price: Expensive
Area: Centro Storico
Address: Via Del Leone 12/A
00186 Rome Italy
Phone: +39 06 68130603

#324
Talarico Cravatte Sartoriali
Category: Men's Clothing
Average Price: Expensive
Area: Centro Storico
Address: Via Dei Coronari 51
00186 Rome Italy
Phone: +39 06 6871257

#325
Timolati For Big
Category: Shoe Store
Average Price: Expensive
Area: Flaminio, Prati
Address: Via Giorgio Vasari 8
00196 Rome Italy
Phone: +39 06 3234933

#326
Delfina
Category: Swimwear
Average Price: Expensive
Area: Centro Storico
Address: Via Dei Banchi Nuovi, 40
00186 Rome Italy
Phone: +39 06 68308775

#327
Manna Music
Category: Musical Instruments
Average Price: Expensive
Area: Prati
Address: Via Germanico, 190
00192 Rome Italy
Phone: +39 06 3242033

#328
Il Sellaio
Category: Accessories
Average Price: Expensive
Area: Prati
Address: Via Caio Mario 14
00192 Rome Italy
Phone: +39 06 3211719

#329
Lush
Category: Cosmetics, Beauty Supply
Average Price: Expensive
Area: Centro Storico
Address: Via Dei Baullari 112
00186 Rome Italy
Phone: +39 06 68301810

#330
Blue Marlin
Category: Women's Clothing
Average Price: Expensive
Area: Salario
Address: Viale Regina Margherita 12
00198 Rome Italy
Phone: +39 06 8558484

#331
Ferramenta Europa
Category: Hardware Store
Average Price: Expensive
Area: Balduina/Montemario
Address: Circonvallazione Cornelia 313
00167 Rome Italy
Phone: +39 06 6621562

#332
Emmal'
Category: Flowers, Gifts
Average Price: Expensive
Area: Appia Antica
Address: Via Andrea Mantegna 32
00147 Rome Italy
Phone: +39 06 5125498

#333
Bianconi Timbri E Targhe
Category: Office Equipment
Average Price: Expensive
Area: Appia Antica
Address: Viale Del Caravaggio 27
00147 Rome Italy
Phone: +39 06 5134586

#334
Blitz
Category: Hobby Shop,
Toy Store, Party Supplies
Average Price: Expensive
Area: Appia Antica
Address: Via Attilio Ambrosini, 186 - 192
00147 Rome Italy
Phone: +39 06 5402568

#335
Centro Carta Pizzino
Category: Flowers, Gifts
Average Price: Expensive
Area: Monteverde
Address: Via Luigi Zambarelli, 40
00152 Rome Italy
Phone: +39 06 5370483

#336
Buffetti - L'ufficio Moderno
Category: Office Equipment
Average Price: Expensive
Area: Eur
Address: Viale Beethoven 18
00144 Rome Italy
Phone: +39 06 5918416

#337
Vivaio San Placido
Category: Nursery, Gardening
Average Price: Expensive
Area: Ardeatina
Address: Via Ardeatina, 620
00178 Rome Italy
Phone: +39 06 5034568

#338
Mercatino Compra Vendita Usato
Category: Thrift Store
Average Price: Expensive
Area: Monteverde
Address: Viale Quattro Venti, 77
00152 Rome Italy
Phone: +39 06 5895258

#339
Libreria Forense
Category: Bookstore
Average Price: Expensive
Address: Via Marianna Dionigi, 28
00193 Rome Italy
Phone: +39 06 3204698

#340
Momento
Category: Women's Clothing
Average Price: Expensive
Area: Centro Storico
Address: Piazza Benedetto Cairoli, 9
00186 Rome Italy
Phone: +39 06 68802044

#341
Arion Montecitorio
Category: Bookstore
Average Price: Expensive
Area: Centro Storico
Address: Piazza Montecitorio, 59
00186 Rome Italy
Phone: +39 06 6781103

#342
Marte's
Category: Shoe Store, Accessories
Average Price: Expensive
Area: Centro Storico
Address: Via Nazionale 14
00184 Rome Italy
Phone: +39 06 4881048

#343
Accessorize
Category: Accessories
Average Price: Expensive
Area: Termini
Address: Via Giovanni Giolitti 34
00185 Rome Italy
Phone: +39 06 47823097

#344
Refuse
Category: Women's Clothing
Average Price: Exclusive
Area: Centro Storico
Address: Via Di Fontanella Borghese 40
00186 Rome Italy
Phone: +39 06 68136975

#345
Campo Marzio Design
Category: Luggage, Leather Goods
Average Price: Exclusive
Area: Centro Storico
Address: Via Del Tritone 211
00187 Rome Italy
Phone: +39 06 6797709

#346
40 Gradi
Category: Men's Clothing,
Women's Clothing
Average Price: Exclusive
Address: Via Virgilio 1
00193 Rome Italy
Phone: +39 06 68134612

#347
Babington
Category: Shopping, Italian
Average Price: Exclusive
Area: Centro Storico
Address: Piazza Di Spagna 23
00187 Rome Italy
Phone: +39 06 6786027

#348
Pifebo Vintage Shop
Category: Vintage
Average Price: Exclusive
Area: Monti
Address: Via Dei Serpenti 141
00184 Rome Italy
Phone: +39 06 89015204

#349
Olimpo Del Fumetto
Category: Comic Books
Average Price: Exclusive
Area: Tuscolano
Address: Via Flavio Stilicone 52
00175 Rome Italy
Phone: +39 06 76965861

#350
Contini
Category: Home &Garden,
Interior Design
Average Price: Exclusive
Area: San Giovanni
Address: Via Appia Nuova, 169
00182 Rome Italy
Phone: +39 06 7016793

#351
Fumetteria
Fumetti UsatiPoket 2000
Category: Bookstore
Average Price: Exclusive
Area: Prati
Address: Via Famagosta 39/41
00192 Rome Italy
Phone: +39 06 37515700

#352
Lion Optical
Category: Eyewear, Opticians
Average Price: Exclusive
Area: Appia Antica
Address: Via Lorenzo Bonincontri 33
00147 Rome Italy
Phone: +39 06 45421860

#353
Bacillario
Category: Fashion
Average Price: Exclusive
Area: Flaminio
Address: Via Laurina 41
00187 Rome Italy
Phone: +39 06 3241687

#354
Zita Fabiani
Category: Fashion
Average Price: Exclusive
Area: Montesacro/Talenti
Address: Via Ugo Ojetti 205
00137 Rome Italy
Phone: +39 06 86802227

#355
Cenci
Category: Sporting Goods,
Men's Clothing
Average Price: Exclusive
Area: Centro Storico
Address: Via Campo Marzio, 4/5/6/7
00186 Rome Italy
Phone: +39 06 6990681

#356
HB Profumerie
Category: Cosmetics, Beauty Supply
Average Price: Exclusive
Address: Via Del Babuino 54
00187 Rome Italy
Phone: +39 06 32651547

#357
Crepida
Category: Shoe Store
Average Price: Exclusive
Area: Centro Storico
Address: Via Arco Della Ciambella 7
00186 Rome Italy
Phone: +39 06 6861733

#358
Et Moi
Category: Lingerie
Average Price: Exclusive
Area: Centro Storico
Address: Via Del Corso, 96
00186 Rome Italy
Phone: +39 06 6991677

#359
Giochi Di Seta
Category: Women's Clothing, Accessories
Average Price: Exclusive
Area: Centro Storico
Address: Via Dei Coronari 152
00186 Rome Italy
Phone: +39 06 68300148

#360
Sabon
Category: Cosmetics, Beauty Supply
Average Price: Exclusive
Area: Prati
Address: Via Cola Di Rienzo, 241
00192 Rome Italy
Phone: +39 06 3208653

#361
Targetti Sankey
Category: Electronics
Average Price: Exclusive
Area: Centro Storico
Address: Via Nazionale, 193
00184 Rome Italy
Phone: +39 06 4744694

#362
**Officina Profumo Farmaceutica
Di Santa Maria Novella**
Category: Cosmetics, Beauty Supply
Average Price: Exclusive
Area: Centro Storico
Address: Corso Del Rinascimento 47
00186 Rome Italy
Phone: +39 06 6879608

#363
Profumeria Parenti
Category: Cosmetics, Beauty Supply
Average Price: Exclusive
Area: Prati
Address: Via Monte Santo, 32
00195 Rome Italy
Phone: +39 06 37352619

#364
Mama Bijoux
Category: Jewelry
Average Price: Exclusive
Area: Centro Storico
Address: Via Del Seminario 88
00186 Rome Italy
Phone: +39 06 6786901

#365
**Boccanera Calzature
Di DE Filippo / Alberto**
Category: Shoe Store
Average Price: Exclusive
Area: Testaccio, Ostiense
Address: Via Luca Della Robbia, 36
00153 Rome Italy
Phone: +39 06 5756804

#366
Futura Grafica S.R.L.
Category: Computers
Average Price: Exclusive
Area: Esquilino
Address: Via Merulana 80
00185 Rome Italy
Phone: +39 06 70495092

#367
G.D.V.
Category: Fashion
Average Price: Exclusive
Area: Centro Storico
Address: Via Del Corso, 150
00186 Rome Italy
Phone: +39 06 6791435

#368
Prada Store
Category: Fashion
Average Price: Exclusive
Area: Centro Storico
Address: Via Condotti, 91
00187 Rome Italy
Phone: +39 06 6794876

#369
I Pinco Pallino
Category: Children's Clothing
Average Price: Exclusive
Area: Centro Storico
Address: Via Del Babuino 115
00187 Rome Italy
Phone: +39 06 69190549

#370
Tarascio
Category: Watches
Average Price: Exclusive
Area: Termini
Address: Via Vittorio Veneto, 134
00187 Rome Italy
Phone: +39 06 42011775

#371
Olfattorio
Category: Bar, Shopping
Average Price: Exclusive
Area: Flaminio
Address: Via Di Ripetta, 34
00186 Rome Italy
Phone: +39 06 3612325

#372
Sezione Aurea
Category: Jewelry
Average Price: Exclusive
Area: Prati
Address: Via Dei Gracchi, 28
00192 Rome Italy
Phone: +39 06 39751300

#373
Ottica Giacomini
Category: Eyewear, Opticians
Average Price: Exclusive
Area: Appia Antica
Address: Via Dei Georgofili 70
00147 Rome Italy
Phone: +39 06 59600791

#374
Stereoland
Category: Electronics
Average Price: Exclusive
Area: Appia Antica
Address: Via Dei Georgofili, 90
00147 Rome Italy
Phone: +39 06 5400479

#375
Sorelle Ferroni
Category: Fashion, Sewing, Alterations
Average Price: Exclusive
Area: Appia Antica
Address: Via Dei Georgofili, 75
00147 Rome Italy
Phone: +39 06 5130039

#376
Blused
Category: Office Equipment,
Building Supplies
Average Price: Exclusive
Area: Appia Antica
Address: Via Ceruso 18
00147 Rome Italy
Phone: +39 336 751340

#377
Arte Profumi
Category: Cosmetics, Beauty Supply
Average Price: Exclusive
Area: Appia Antica
Address: Via A. Mantegna 6
00147 Rome Italy
Phone: +39 06 5138587

#378
La Maison Pour Le Petits
Category: Children's Clothing
Average Price: Exclusive
Area: Salario
Address: Via Di Villa San Filippo 30/32
00197 Rome Italy
Phone: +39 06 8083598

#379
Privilege
Category: Fashion
Average Price: Exclusive
Area: Casilino
Address: Via Dei Castani 120
00172 Rome Italy
Phone: +39 06 2314422

#380
Muscle Shop
Category: Cosmetics, Beauty Supply,
Fitness &Instruction
Average Price: Exclusive
Area: Nomentano
Address: Via Adamello, 21
00141 Rome Italy
Phone: +39 06 8176319

#381
Strigoi
Category: Accessories
Area: San Giovanni
Address: Circonvallazione Appia 98A
00179 Rome Italy
Phone: +39 339 2633250

#382
Il Gatto Con Gli Stivali
Category: Accessories
Area: San Giovanni
Address: Via Dei Marsi 16
00185 Rome Italy
Phone: +39 06 4454746

#383
Penny Lane
Category: Accessories, Men's Clothing
Area: Centro Storico
Address: Via Del Governo Vecchio 4
00186 Rome Italy
Phone: +39 06 68892414

#384
Isola Novecento
Category: Antiques
Area: Monti
Address: Via Madonna Dei Monti 60
00184 Rome Italy
Phone: +39 06 4740804

#385
Art"
Category: Antiques
Area: Aventino, Ostiense
Address: Via Giovanni Miani 24A
00154 Rome Italy
Phone: +39 06 57289707

#386
Antiquas Antiquariato
Category: Antiques
Area: Salario
Address: Viale Parioli 168/170
00197 Rome Italy
Phone: +39 06 8078866

#387
Ex-Novo
Category: Antiques, Vintage
Area: Ostiense
Address: Via Corinto 12
00146 Rome Italy
Phone: +39 06 93570534

#388
Euro Ricambi Elettrodomestici
Category: Appliances
Area: Trastevere
Address: Via Ettore Rolli, 40
00153 Rome Italy
Phone: +39 06 5898548

#389
Ferramenta Castellani
Category: Appliances &Repair,
Hardware Store
Area: Appia Antica
Address: Via Salistri 5
00147 Rome Italy
Phone: +39 338 6759817

#390
Gagosian Gallery
Category: Art Gallery
Area: Centro Storico
Address: Via Francesco Crispi 16
00187 Rome Italy
Phone: +39 06 42086498

#391
The House Of Love &Dissent
Category: Art Gallery
Area: Monti
Address: Via Leonina, 85
00184 Rome Italy
Phone: +39 06 48903661

#392
Fondazione Pastificio Cerere
Category: Art Gallery
Area: San Lorenzo
Address: Via Degli Ausoni, 1
00165 Rome Italy
Phone: +39 06 45422960

#393
Dorothy Circus Gallery
Category: Art Gallery
Area: Centro Storico
Address: Via Dei Pettinari 76
00186 Rome Italy
Phone: +39 06 68805928

#394
Fondazione Volume!
Category: Art Gallery
Area: Borgo
Address: Via S. Francesco Di Sales 86/88,
00165 Rome Italy
Phone: +39 06 6892431

#395
Unosunove
Category: Art Gallery
Area: Centro Storico
Address: Palazzo Santacroce,
Via Degli Specchi 20
00186 Rome Italy
Phone: +39 06 97613810

#396
Galleria Lorcan O'Neill Rome
Category: Art Gallery
Area: Borgo
Address: Via Orti D'Alibert, 1/E
00165 Rome Italy
Phone: +39 06 68892980

#397
Galleria Bonomo
Category: Art Gallery
Area: Centro Storico
Address: Via Del Portico D'Ottavia, 13
00186 Rome Italy
Phone: +39 06 683276

#398
Galleria Edieuropa
Category: Art Gallery
Area: Centro Storico
Address: Piazza Dei Cenci, 56
00186 Rome Italy
Phone: +39 06 68805795

#399
Stamperia Del Tevere
Category: Art Gallery
Area: Trastevere
Address: Via San Francesco A Ripa 69
00153 Rome Italy
Phone: +39 328 2263450

#400
Le Perle
Category: Art Gallery
Area: Centro Storico
Address: Via Dei Chiavari, 56
00186 Rome Italy
Phone: +39 06 6873366

#401
Mostra Dei Bruegel
Category: Art Gallery
Area: Centro Storico
Address: Via Dell'arco Della Pace 5
00186 Rome Italy
Phone: +39 06 68809036

#402
T293
Category: Art Gallery
Area: Centro Storico
Address: Via Dei Leutari 32
00186 Rome Italy
Phone: +39 06 83763242

#403
Affordable Art Fair
Category: Art Gallery
Area: Testaccio, Ostiense
Address: Piazza Orazio Giustiniani 4
00153 Rome Italy
Phone: +39 390 49657401

#404
Mila
Category: Art Gallery
Area: Centro Storico
Address: Via Di Monte Brianzo 49
00186 Rome Italy
Phone: +39 06 68804079

#405
Sala 1
Category: Art Gallery
Area: San Giovanni
Address: Piazza Di Porta San Giovanni 10,
00185 Rome Italy
Phone: +39 06 7008691

#406
Contemporanea
Category: Art Gallery
Area: Centro Storico
Address: Vicolo Sugarelli, 6
00186 Rome Italy
Phone: +39 338 2210224

#407
Endemica Gallery
Category: Art Gallery
Area: Nomentano
Address: Via Mantova 14

00198 Rome Italy
Phone: +39 06 84240140

#408
Mikro
Category: Art Gallery
Area: Nomentano, Salario
Address: Corso Trieste 121
00198 Rome Italy
Phone: +39 06 8417556

#409
Wo-Ma'n Home Gallery
Category: Art Gallery
Area: Pigneto
Address: Via Pietro Ruga 24
00176 Rome Italy
Phone: +39 328 9292135

#410
Li.Boh
Category: Art Gallery, Fashion
Area: San Giovanni
Address: Via Del Pigneto 52
00176 Rome Italy
Phone: +39 06 70304648

#411
Alinari
Category: Art Gallery,
Photography Store
Area: Centro Storico
Address: Via Alibert 16
00187 Rome Italy
Phone: +39 06 69941998

#412
Lo Scriba
Category: Art Supplies, Fashion
Area: Salario
Address: Via Magliano Sabina 44
00199 Rome Italy
Phone: +39 06 86398788

#413
Restauri Squatriti
Category: Arts, Crafts
Area: Flaminio
Address: Via Di Ripetta, 29
00186 Rome Italy
Phone: +39 06 3610232

#414
Gavaudan
Category: Arts, Crafts
Area: Trastevere
Address: Via Dei Vascellari, 19
00153 Rome Italy
Phone: +39 06 5894844

#415
Le Api Operaie
Category: Arts, Crafts
Area: San Giovanni
Address: Via Elvia Recina 13
00183 Rome Italy
Phone: +39 347 8050064

#416
Bricofer
Category: Arts, Crafts
Area: Casilino
Address: Via Collatina Vecchia 412
00155 Rome Italy
Phone: +39 06 225800

#417
Nino Agostini E Figli
Category: Arts, Crafts,
Appliances &Repair
Area: Appia Antica
Address: Piazza Federico Marcello Lante
22, 00147 Rome Italy
Phone: +39 06 5125935

#418
Daidalos
Category: Arts, Crafts, Jewelry
Area: Salario
Address: Viale Somalia, 211
00199 Rome Italy
Phone: +39 06 86215828

#419
Altroquando
Category: Bar, Bookstore
Area: Centro Storico
Address: Via Del Governo Vecchio 82
00186 Rome Italy
Phone: +39 06 68892200

#420
Bar Pepe
Category: Bar, Tobacco Shop
Area: Ostiense
Address: Viale Guglielmo Marconi 39
00146 Rome Italy
Phone: +39 06 55300993

#421
Navona Governo Vecchio
Category: Bed &Breakfast,
Vintage
Area: Centro Storico
Address: Via Del Governo Vecchio 118
00186 Rome Italy
Phone: +39 06 45429400

#422
Collalti
Category: Bikes, Bike Rentals
Area: Centro Storico
Address: Via Del Pellegrino 82
00186 Rome Italy
Phone: +39 06 68801084

#423
Libreria L'Aventure
Category: Books, Mags, Music &Video
Average Price:
Area: Flaminio
Address: Via Del Vantaggio 21
00186 Rome Italy
Phone: +39 06 3202360

#424
Notebook
Category: Bookstore
Area: Flaminio
Address: Viale Pietro De Coubertin 30
00196 Rome Italy
Phone: +39 06 80693461

#425
Borri Books - Libreria Termini
Category: Bookstore
Area: Termini
Address: Piazza Dei Cinquecento
00185 Rome Italy
Phone: +39 06 4828422

#426
Zafari Libreria
Category: Bookstore
Area: Termini, San Giovanni
Address: Via Dei Volsci 62
00185 Rome Italy
Phone: +39 06 89534188

#427
La Fabbrica Dei Giganti
Category: Bookstore
Area: Nomentano
Address: Via Val d'Ossola 99
00141 Rome Italy
Phone: +39 06 45434970

#428
Libreria Kappa
Category: Bookstore
Area: Termini
Address: Via Del Castro Pretorio 22
00185 Rome Italy
Phone: +39 06 4940473

#429
Libreria Della Fronda
Category: Bookstore
Area: Nomentano
Address: Via Enrico Stevenson, 28-30
00162 Rome Italy
Phone: +39 06 86320109

#430
Libreria Griot
Category: Bookstore
Area: Trastevere
Address: Via Di Santa Cecilia
1/A -Trastevere, 00153 Rome Italy
Phone: +39 06 58334116

#431
Libreria Sant'Agostino
Category: Bookstore
Average Price:
Area: Centro Storico
Address: Via Sant'Agostino 17
00186 Rome Italy
Phone: +39 06 6875470

#432
Locus Solus
Category: Bookstore
Area: Termini, San Giovanni
Address: Via Degli Equi 14
00185 Rome Italy
Phone: +39 346 5049842

#433
Libreria La Scaletta
Category: Bookstore
Area: San Lorenzo
Address: Viale Ippocrate, 96/A
00161 Rome Italy
Phone: +39 06 44238852

#434
Libreria La Gru
Category: Bookstore
Area: Monti
Address: Via Del Boschetto 20
00184 Rome Italy
Phone: +39 334 9013091

#435
Libreria M.T. Cicerone
Category: Bookstore
Area: Centro Storico
Address: Largo Chigi
00187 Rome Italy
Phone: +39 06 69941553

#436
Let'sArt
Category: Bookstore
Area: Centro Storico
Address: Via Del Pellegrino 132
00186 Rome Italy
Phone: +39 06 68809860

#437
Libreria Cruccu
Category: Bookstore
Area: Ostiense
Address: Circonvallazione
Ostiense 243, 00154 Rome Italy
Phone: +39 06 57300514

#438
Simon Tanner
Category: Bookstore
Area: San Giovanni, Appia Antica
Address: Via Lidia 58
00179 Rome Italy
Phone: +39 06 78347908

#439
Doppiagi
Category: Bookstore
Area: Eur
Address: Via Duccio Di Buoninsegna
30/32, 00142 Rome Italy
Phone: +39 06 5034129

#440
Book'Bar
Category: Bookstore, Café
Area: Centro Storico
Address: Via Milano 15
00184 Rome Italy
Phone: +39 06 48913361

#441
Libreria Tara
Category: Bookstore, Library
Area: Centro Storico
Address: Piazza Del Teatro Di Pompeo 41,
00186 Rome Italy
Phone: +39 06 68808227

#442
Libreria Kappa
Category: Bookstore, Library
Area: Pinciano
Address: Via Salaria 121E
00198 Rome Italy
Phone: +39 06 85357042

#443
Libreria Amore E Psiche
Category: Bookstore, Vintage
Area: Centro Storico
Address: Via Santa Caterina Da Siena 61,
00186 Rome Italy
Phone: +39 06 6783908

#444
Carlotta Rio
Category: Bridal
Area: Centro Storico
Address: ViaDell' Arco Della Ciambella
19A, 00186 Rome Italy
Phone: +39 06 6872308

#445
Perla Bomboniere
Category: Bridal, Party Supplies
Area: Nomentano
Address: Via Val Di Non, 27
00141 Rome Italy
Phone: +39 06 8863834

#446
Cartaria Appia
Category: Cards, Stationery
Area: San Giovanni
Address: Piazza Zama, 27
00183 Rome Italy
Phone: +39 06 70495557

#447
Marionette
Category: Children's Clothing
Area: Testaccio, Ostiense
Address: Via Mastro Giorgio 62/64
00153 Rome Italy
Phone: +39 06 5779048

#448
Bompoint Alta Moda
Category: Children's Clothing
Area: Centro Storico
Address: Piazza San Lorenzo In Lucina
25, 00186 Rome Italy
Phone: +39 06 6871548

#449
Pure Sermoneta
Category: Children's Clothing
Area: Centro Storico
Address: Via Frattina 111
00187 Rome Italy
Phone: +39 06 6794555

#450
Neko Rome
Category: Comic Books
Area: San Giovanni
Address: Via Niso 44
00181 Rome Italy
Phone: +39 06 64011486

#451
Computime
Category: Computers
Area: San Lorenzo
Address: Via Giovanni Battista Morgagni,
30/G 00161 Rome Italy
Phone: +39 06 44254833

#452
Primo Piano
Category: Men's Clothing
Area: Eur
Address: Viale Beethoven 86
00144 Rome Italy
Phone: +39 00 390654280862

#453
Eddie's Fun Tours Rome
Category: Shopping, Active Life
Area: Esquilino
Address: Via Aleardo Aleardi 16
00185 Rome Italy
Phone: +39 00 390694365460

#454
At Claraluna
Category: Women's Clothing
Area: Borgo
Address: Via Alcide De Gasperi 39
00193 Rome Italy
Phone: +39 03 07768238

#455
De Angelis
Category: Furniture Store, Mattresses
Area: Casilino
Address: Via Della Vaccheria Gianni 100
00155 Rome Italy
Phone: +39 06 2285251

#456
Tulli
Category: Electronics
Area: Tuscolano, Casilino
Address: Via Francesco Baracca, 74
00177 Rome Italy
Phone: +39 06 2412600

#457
Pelletteria Vanda
Category: Leather Goods
Area: Tuscolano
Address: Via Di Torpignattara 13
00177 Rome Italy
Phone: +39 06 2413400

#458
Gienne Ottica
Category: Eyewear, Opticians
Area: Tuscolano
Address: Via Di Torpignattara, 98
00177 Rome Italy
Phone: +39 06 2414121

#459
Musetti Color
Category: Home Decor
Area: Tuscolano
Address: Via Ciro Da Urbino 57
00176 Rome Italy
Phone: +39 06 2414150

#460
New York Jeans
Category: Fashion
Area: Casilino
Address: Via Tor De Schiavi, 387
00171 Rome Italy
Phone: +39 06 2594480

#461
A.D. Luzi
Category: Fabric Store
Area: Monti
Address: Via Tor De' Schiavi 39
00172 Rome Italy
Phone: +39 06 2598395

#462
Casa Del Cronometro
Category: Jewelry
Area: Prati
Address: Via Silla, 80
00192 Rome Italy
Phone: +39 06 3210971

#463
Ottica Cavour
Category: Eyewear, Opticians
Area: Prati
Address: Piazza Cavour 17
00193 Rome Italy
Phone: +39 06 3211698

#464
Remix
Category: Vinyl Records, Comic Books
Area: Flaminio
Address: Via Del Fiume 8
00186 Rome Italy
Phone: +39 06 3216514

#465
La Bottega Dell'artigiano
Category: Fashion
Area: Prati
Address: Via Settembrini, 41/43
00195 Rome Italy
Phone: +39 06 3217446

#466
Hennes &Mauritz
Category: Fashion
Area: Flaminio
Address: Via Del Corso 512
00186 Rome Italy
Phone: +39 06 3233450

#467
Barracuda
Category: Women's Clothing
Area: Flaminio
Address: Piazza Dei Carracci 5
00196 Rome Italy
Phone: +39 06 3236226

#468
Indri Sport
Category: Shopping
Area: Flaminio
Address: Via Fracassini, 62-66
00196 Rome Italy
Phone: +39 06 3236368

#469
Arte 3
Category: Shopping
Area: Flaminio
Address: Via Del Fiume 3a
00186 Rome Italy
Phone: +39 06 3244414

#470
Leml'
Category: Fashion
Area: Corso Francia
Address: Via Della Farnesina 12b/36
00135 Rome Italy
Phone: +39 06 33218734

#471
Le Flaneur
Category: Florist
Area: Corso Francia
Address: Via Flaminia 730
00191 Rome Italy
Phone: +39 06 33221127

#472
Toy Center
Category: Toy Store
Area: Cassia
Address: Via Della Stazione Di Grottarossa
1060 00189 Rome Italy
Phone: +39 06 33221793

#473
Il Telecomando
Category: Electronics
Area: Corso Francia
Address: Viale Tor Di Quinto 5
00191 Rome Italy
Phone: +39 06 3330166

#474
Eureka
Category: Electronics, Mobile Phones
Area: Corso Francia
Address: Via Flaminia Vecchia 694
00191 Rome Italy
Phone: +39 06 3340027

#475
Horti Di Veio
Category: Florist,
Nursery, Gardening
Area: Cassia
Address: Via Oriolo Romeno 10
00189 Rome Italy
Phone: +39 06 33710258

#476
Scarpe Diem
Category: Women's Clothing
Area: Balduina/Montemario
Address: Via A.Friggeri 154/156
00136 Rome Italy
Phone: +39 06 35402121

#477
Valentino
Category: Women's Clothing
Area: Flaminio, Centro Storico
Address: Via Del Babuino 61
00187 Rome Italy
Phone: +39 06 36001906

#478
Lazio 100
Category: Sporting Goods
Area: Flaminio
Address: Via Calderini 66C
00196 Rome Italy
Phone: +39 06 36003969

#479
Adidas Italy
Category: Sports Wear
Average Price:
Area: Centro Storico
Address: Via Del Corso, 475
00186 Rome Italy
Phone: +39 06 36006308

#480
Mastrofini
Category: Shoe Store
Area: Flaminio
Address: Via Angelo Brunetti 15
00186 Rome Italy
Phone: +39 06 3610204

#481
Farmacia Guarnacci
Category: Drugstore
Area: Flaminio
Address: Via Flaminia 5
00196 Rome Italy
Phone: +39 06 3610905

#482
Duca
Category: Jewelry, Watches
Area: Corso Francia
Address: Via Di Vigna Stelluti 151
00191 Rome Italy
Phone: +39 06 36300173

#483
Glocal Accessories
Category: Jewelry
Area: Prati
Address: Via Monte Zebio 15
00195 Rome Italy
Phone: +39 06 37350686

#484
Candia Profumi
Category: Cosmetics, Beauty Supply
Area: Prati
Address: Via Candia
00192 Rome Italy
Phone: +39 06 39723390

#485
Rome Shop
Category: Sports Wear
Area: Prati
Address: Via Leone IV 55
00192 Rome Italy
Phone: +39 06 39745679

#486
Farmacia Colli Aniene
Category: Drugstore
Area: Tiburtino
Address: Viale Palmiro Togliatti 1583
00155 Rome Italy
Phone: +39 06 40800586

#487
**Vanity...Non Solo Magre
Taglie Comode**
Category: Plus Size Fashion
Area: San Lorenzo
Address: Via Cave Di Pietralata 62
00157 Rome Italy
Phone: +39 06 41735496

#488
Petrone Gioielli
Category: Shopping
Area: Centro Storico
Address: Via Dei Servi 24
00187 Rome Italy
Phone: +39 06 42012593

#489
IT Point
Category: Computers,
IT Services &Computer Repair
Area: San Lorenzo
Address: Via Luigi Arnaldo Vassallo 25
00100 Rome Italy
Phone: +39 06 43599887

#490
Cusinelli
Category: Home Decor
Area: Nomentano
Address: Via Nomentana, 283
00161 Rome Italy
Phone: +39 06 4402208

#491
Sologiochi
Category: Toy Store
Area: Nomentano
Address: Via Val Travaglia 32
00141 Rome Italy
Phone: +39 06 44202579

#492
Decoupage E Arti Manuali
Category: Home Decor
Area: San Lorenzo
Address: Via Padova 19A
00161 Rome Italy
Phone: +39 06 44239840

#493
Roberto Giansanti
Category: Jewelry
Area: San Lorenzo, Nomentano
Address: Via Livorno 21
00162 Rome Italy
Phone: +39 06 44244915

#494
L'Aquilotto
Category: Toy Store
Area: Nomentano
Address: Viale Regina Margherita 240
00198 Rome Italy
Phone: +39 06 44250718

#495
Pc Quadro
Category: Computers,
IT Services &Computer Repair
Area: San Lorenzo
Address: Viale Delle Provincie, 87-89
00162 Rome Italy
Phone: +39 06 44254373

#496
Email Shop
Category: Fashion
Area: San Lorenzo
Address: Via Tiburtina 146
00185 Rome Italy
Phone: +39 06 4441269

#497
Ottica Castri
Category: Eyewear, Opticians
Area: Termini
Address: Via Dei Salentini 16
00185 Rome Italy
Phone: +39 06 4453636

#498
Not Your Dolls
Category: Women's Clothing
Area: Termini, San Giovanni
Address: Via Dei Latini 33
00185 Rome Italy
Phone: +39 06 4464256

#499
Stereoimmagine
Category: Electronics
Area: Esquilino
Address: Via Dello Statuto 39
00185 Rome Italy
Phone: +39 06 4465623

#500
Claudio San'
Category: Leather Goods
Area: Termini
Address: Largo Degli Osci 67A
00185 Rome Italy
Phone: +39 06 4469284

TOP 500 RESTAURANTS

Most Recommended by Locals & Trevelers
Ranking (from #1 to #500)

#1
Tazza d'Oro
Category: Bar, Café
Average Price: Under €7
Area: Centro Storico
Address: Via Degli Orfani 84
00186 Rome Italy
Phone: +39 06 6789792

#2
Pizzarium
Category: Pizza
Average Price: €8-20
Area: Balduina/Montemario, Prati
Address: Via Della Meloria 43
00136 Rome Italy
Phone: +39 06 39745416

#3
Da Francesco
Category: Romen
Average Price: €8-20
Area: Centro Storico
Address: Piazza Del Fico 29
00186 Rome Italy
Phone: +39 06 6864009

#4
Sant'Eustachio Il Caff'
Category: Bar, Café
Average Price: Under €7
Area: Centro Storico
Address: Piazza Sant'Eustachio 81
00186 Rome Italy
Phone: +39 06 68802048

#5
Open Baladin
Category: Brewerie, Burgers
Average Price: €8-20
Area: Centro Storico
Address: Via Degli Specchi 6
00186 Rome Italy
Phone: +39 06 6838989

#6
Felice A Testaccio
Category: Romen
Average Price: €21-40
Area: Testaccio, Ostiense
Address: Via Mastro Giorgio 29
00153 Rome Italy
Phone: +39 06 5746800

#7
Frigidarium
Category: Ice Cream, Desserts
Average Price: Under €7
Area: Centro Storico
Address: Via Del Governo Vecchio 112
00186 Rome Italy
Phone: +39 334 9951184

#8
Pinsere
Category: Pizza
Average Price: Under €7
Area: Termini
Address: Via Flavia 98
00187 Rome Italy
Phone: +39 06 42020924

#9
Antica Osteria Brunetti
Category: Italian
Average Price: €8-20
Area: Flaminio
Address: Via Angelo Brunetti 10
00186 Rome Italy
Phone: +39 06 64521062

#10
That's Amore
Category: Italian
Average Price: €8-20
Area: Centro Storico
Address: Via In Arcione 115
00187 Rome Italy
Phone: +39 667 90302

#11
Ai Tre Scalini
Category: Wine Bar, Tapas Bar
Average Price: €8-20
Area: Monti
Address: Via Panisperna 251
00184 Rome Italy
Phone: +39 06 48907495

#12
Etabl'
Category: Wine Bar, Café
Average Price: €8-20
Area: Centro Storico
Address: Vicolo Delle Vacche 9
00186 Rome Italy
Phone: +39 06 97616694

#13
Hang Zhou
Category: Chinese
Average Price: €8-20
Area: Esquilino
Address: Via Principe Eugenio 82
00185 Rome Italy
Phone: +39 06 4872732

#14
Duecento Gradi
Category: Sandwiches, Fast Food
Average Price: €8-20
Area: Citt'Del Vaticano, Prati
Address: Piazza Risorgimento 3
00192 Rome Italy
Phone: +39 06 39754239

#15
Dar Poeta
Category: Pizza
Average Price: €8-20
Area: Trastevere
Address: Vicolo Del Bologna 45
00153 Rome Italy
Phone: +39 06 5880516

#16
Cul De Sac
Category: Italian, Beer, Wine, Spirits
Average Price: €8-20
Area: Centro Storico
Address: Piazza Pasquino 73
00186 Rome Italy
Phone: +39 06 68801094

#17
Da Tonino
Category: Italian
Average Price: €8-20
Area: Centro Storico
Address: Via Del Governo Vecchio 18
00186 Rome Italy
Phone: +39 06 6877002

#18
Cantina Cantarini
Category: Romen
Average Price: €8-20
Area: Termini
Address: Piazza Sallustio 12
00187 Rome Italy
Phone: +39 06 485528

#19
Ai Marmi
Category: Pizza, Italian
Average Price: €8-20
Area: Trastevere
Address: Viale Trastevere 53
00153 Rome Italy
Phone: +39 06 5810919

#20
The Library
Category: Italian
Average Price: €21-40
Area: Centro Storico
Address: Vicolo Della Cancelleria 7
00186 Rome Italy
Phone: +39 334 8061200

#21
Navona Notte
Category: Italian, Pizza
Average Price: Under €7
Area: Centro Storico
Address: Via Del Teatro Pace 44
00186 Rome Italy
Phone: +39 06 6869278

#22
Cacio E Pepe
Category: Italian
Average Price: €8-20
Area: Prati
Address: Via Giuseppe Avezzana 11
00195 Rome Italy
Phone: +39 06 3217268

#23
Eataly
Category: Food, Italian
Average Price: €21-40
Area: Ostiense
Address: Piazzale XII Ottobre 1492
00154 Rome Italy
Phone: +39 06 90279201

#24
Al Duello
Category: Italian
Average Price: €21-40
Area: Centro Storico
Address: Vicolo Vaccarella 11A
00186 Rome Italy
Phone: +39 06 68891816

#25
Osteria Barberini
Category: Italian
Average Price: €21-40
Area: Centro Storico
Address: Via Della Purificazione 20
00187 Rome Italy
Phone: +39 06 4743325

#26
Mekong
Category: Vietnamese
Average Price: €21-40
Area: Tuscolano
Address: Via Enea 56A
00181 Rome Italy
Phone: +39 06 7825247

#27
Luzzi
Category: Pizza, Italian
Average Price: €8-20
Area: Esquilino, Aventino
Address: Via Di San Giovanni In Laterano
88 00184 Rome Italy
Phone: +39 06 7096332

#28
Sora Margherita
Category: Romen
Average Price: €21-40
Area: Centro Storico
Address: Piazza Delle Cinque Scole 30
00186 Rome Italy
Phone: +39 06 6874216

#29
Trattoria Vecchia Rome
Category: Italian
Average Price: €8-20
Area: Esquilino
Address: Via Ferruccio 12B
00185 Rome Italy
Phone: +39 06 4467143

#30
Roscioli
Category: Romen, Grocery
Average Price: €21-40
Area: Centro Storico
Address: Via Dei Giubbonari 21
00186 Rome Italy
Phone: +39 06 6875287

#31
Life
Category: Wine Bar, Italian
Average Price: €8-20
Area: Centro Storico
Address: Via Della Vite 28
00187 Rome Italy
Phone: +39 06 69380948

#32
Sora Lella
Category: Romen
Average Price: €21-40
Area: Trastevere, Centro Storico
Address: Via Di Ponte Quattro Capi 16
00186 Rome Italy
Phone: +39 06 6861601

#33
Obik' Mozzarella Bar
Category: Italian, Pizza
Average Price: €8-20
Area: Centro Storico
Address: Via Dei Prefetti 28
00186 Rome Italy
Phone: +39 06 6832630

#34
Taverna Trilussa
Category: Romen
Average Price: €21-40
Area: Trastevere
Address: Via Del Politeama 23
00153 Rome Italy
Phone: +39 06 5818918

#35
L'Oasi Della Birra
Category: Beer, Wine, Spirits, Brewerie
Average Price: €8-20
Area: Testaccio, Ostiense
Address: Piazza Testaccio 38
00153 Rome Italy
Phone: +39 06 5746122

#36
Soul Kitchen
Category: Apulian, Café
Average Price: €8-20
Area: San Lorenzo, San Giovanni
Address: Via Dei Sabelli 193
00185 Rome Italy
Phone: +39 06 64871016

#37
Sisini La Casa Del Suppl'
Category: Pizza
Average Price: Under €7
Area: Trastevere
Address: Via San Francesco A Ripa 137
00153 Rome Italy
Phone: +39 06 5897110

#38
Osteria Quarantaquattro
Category: Italian
Average Price: €21-40
Area: Termini
Address: Via Aureliana 42 Rome,
Rome Italy
Phone: +39 04 4642013318

#39
Pizza Rustica Da Giustina
Category: Pizza
Average Price: Under €7
Area: Casilino
Address: Viale Della Primavera 221
00172 Rome Italy
Phone: +39 06 2426161

#40
La Taverna Dei Fori Imperiali
Category: Italian
Average Price: €8-20
Area: Monti, Centro Storico
Address: Via Della Madonna Dei Monti 9
00184 Rome Italy
Phone: +39 06 6798643

#41
Da Vito E Dina
Category: Romen
Average Price: €8-20
Area: Prati
Address: Via Degli Scipioni 50
00192 Rome Italy
Phone: +39 06 39723293

#42
Corallo
Category: Pizza, Italian
Average Price: €8-20
Area: Centro Storico
Address: Via Corallo 10
00186 Rome Italy
Phone: +39 06 68307703

#43
Da Baffetto
Category: Pizza
Average Price: €8-20
Area: Centro Storico
Address: Via Del Governo Vecchio 114
00186 Rome Italy
Phone: +39 06 6861617

#44
Mamma Angela's Trattoria
Category: Italian
Average Price: €8-20
Area: Termini
Address: Via Palestro 53
00185 Rome Italy
Phone: +39 06 44341317

#45
Da Enzo Al 29
Category: Romen
Average Price: €21-40
Area: Trastevere
Address: Via Dei Vascellari 29
00153 Rome Italy
Phone: +39 06 5812260

#46
Grandma Bistrot
Category: Wine Bar,
Breakfast &Brunch
Average Price: €8-20
Area: Tuscolano
Address: Via Dei Corneli 25
00175 Rome Italy
Phone: +39 377 2649540

#47
La Carbonara
Category: Italian
Average Price: €8-20
Area: Monti
Address: Via Panisperna 214
00184 Rome Italy
Phone: +39 06 4825176

#48
Ditirambo
Category: Italian
Average Price: €21-40
Address: Piazza Della Cancelleria 74
00186 Rome Italy
Phone: +39 06 6871626

#49
Baccano
Category: Wine Bar, Italian
Average Price: €21-40
Area: Centro Storico
Address: Via Delle Muratte 23
00187 Rome Italy
Phone: +39 06 69941166

#50
Pizza R'
Category: Italian, Pizza
Average Price: €8-20
Area: Flaminio
Address: Via Di Ripetta 14
00186 Rome Italy
Phone: +39 06 3211468

#51
Sofia
Category: Italian
Average Price: €21-40
Area: Centro Storico
Address: Via Di Capo Le Case 51
00187 Rome Italy
Phone: +39 06 89873857

#52
Dar Filettaro
Category: Italian, Specialty Food
Average Price: €8-20
Area: Centro Storico
Address: Largo Dei Librari 88
00186 Rome Italy
Phone: +39 06 6864018

#53
Pastificio
Category: Italian, Specialty Food
Average Price: Under €7
Area: Centro Storico
Address: Via Della Croce 8
00187 Rome Italy
Phone: +39 06 6793102

#54
Marzapane
Category: Italian, Desserts
Average Price: €8-20
Area: Pinciano
Address: Via Velletri 39
00198 Rome Italy
Phone: +39 06 64781692

#55
Antica Taverna
Category: Romen
Average Price: €8-20
Area: Centro Storico
Address: Via Di Monte Giordano 12
00186 Rome Italy
Phone: +39 06 68801053

#56
Burro E Sugo
Category: Romen
Average Price: €8-20
Area: Ostiense
Address: Via Elvio Pertinace 1
00145 Rome Italy
Phone: +39 06 59606244

#57
Ba' Ghetto
Category: Kosher, Jewish
Average Price: €21-40
Area: Centro Storico
Address: Via Del Portico d'Ottavia 57
00186 Rome Italy
Phone: +39 06 68892868

#58
Maccheroni
Category: Romen
Average Price: €8-20
Area: Centro Storico
Address: Piazza Delle Coppelle 44
00186 Rome Italy
Phone: +39 06 68307895

#59
Mondo Arancina
Category: Pizza, Specialty Food
Average Price: Under €7
Area: Prati
Address: Via Marcantonio Colonna 38
00192 Rome Italy
Phone: +39 06 97619213

#60
Bartocci
Category: Ice Cream, Gluten-Free
Average Price: €8-20
Area: Nomentano
Address: Via Alessandria 145
00198 Rome Italy
Phone: +39 06 99695535

#61
'Gusto
Category: Italian, Breakfast &Brunch
Average Price: €8-20
Area: Flaminio, Centro Storico
Address: Piazza Augusto Imperatore 9
00196 Rome Italy
Phone: +39 06 3226273

#62
Piccolo Arancio
Category: Romen
Average Price: €8-20
Area: Centro Storico
Address: Vicolo Scanderbeg 112
00187 Rome Italy
Phone: +39 06 6786139

#63
Hostaria Romena
Category: Italian
Average Price: €8-20
Area: Centro Storico
Address: Via Del Boccaccio 1
00187 Rome Italy
Phone: +39 06 4745284

#64
Fabrica
Category: Breakfast &Brunch
Average Price: €21-40
Area: Prati
Address: Via Gerolamo Savonarola 8
00195 Rome Italy
Phone: +39 06 39725514

#65
Tre Scalini
Category: Italian, Café
Average Price: Above €41
Area: Centro Storico
Address: Piazza Navona 28
00186 Rome Italy
Phone: +39 06 6861234

#66
Armando Al Pantheon
Category: Romen
Average Price: €21-40
Area: Centro Storico
Address: Salita Dei Crescenti 31
00186 Rome Italy
Phone: +39 06 68803034

#67
Caf' Caf'
Category: Mediterranean, Italian
Average Price: €8-20
Area: Aventino
Address: Via De' SS. Quattro 44
00184 Rome Italy
Phone: +39 06 7008743

#68
Il Buchetto
Category: Pizza
Average Price: €8-20
Area: Flaminio
Address: Via Flaminia 119
00196 Rome Italy
Phone: +39 06 3201707

#69
Pizzeria Formula 1
Category: Pizza
Average Price: Under €7
Area: Termini, San Giovanni
Address: Via Degli Equi 13
00185 Rome Italy
Phone: +39 06 4453866

#70
Metamorfosi
Category: Italian, Mediterranean
Average Price: Above €41
Area: Parioli
Address: Via Giovanni Antonelli 30
00197 Rome Italy
Phone: +39 06 8076839

#71
Qui Se Magna
Category: Italian
Average Price: Under €7
Area: Pigneto
Address: Via Del Pigneto 307
00176 Rome Italy
Phone: +39 06 274803

#72
Colline Emiliane
Category: Italian
Average Price: €8-20
Area: Centro Storico
Address: Via Degli Avignonesi 22
00187 Rome Italy
Phone: +39 06 4817538

#73
00100 Pizza Trapizzino Testaccio
Category: Pizza
Average Price: €8-20
Area: Testaccio, Ostiense
Address: Via Giovanni Branca 88
00153 Rome Italy
Phone: +39 06 43419624

#74
Sabatini
Category: Italian
Average Price: Above €41
Area: Trastevere
Address: Vicolo San Maria In Trastevere
18, 00153 Rome Italy
Phone: +39 06 5818307

#75
Antico Arco
Category: Wine Bar, Italian
Average Price: Above €41
Area: Monteverde
Address: Piazzale Aurelio 7
00152 Rome Italy
Phone: +39 06 5815274

#76
Moma
Category: Wine Bar, Italian
Average Price: €21-40
Area: Centro Storico
Address: Via San Basilio 42
00187 Rome Italy
Phone: +39 06 42011798

#77
Ristochicco
Category: Italian
Average Price: €8-20
Area: Prati
Address: Borgo Pio 186
00193 Rome Italy
Phone: +39 06 68308360

#78
Giuda Ballerino
Category: Italian
Average Price: Above €41
Area: Tuscolano
Address: Largo Appio Claudio 346
00174 Rome Italy
Phone: +39 06 71584807

#79
La Gensola
Category: Romen, Seafood
Average Price: €21-40
Area: Trastevere
Address: Piazza Della Gensola 15
00153 Rome Italy
Phone: +39 06 5816312

#80
I Clementini
Category: Romen
Average Price: €8-20
Area: Esquilino, Aventino
Address: Via Di San Giovanni In Laterano
106 00184 Rome Italy
Phone: +39 06 45426395

#81
Bella Napoli
Category: Italian
Average Price: €8-20
Area: Prati
Address: Via Simone De Saint Bon 57
00195 Rome Italy
Phone: +39 06 37518016

#82
Al Forno Della Soffitta
Category: Pizza
Average Price: €8-20
Area: Termini
Address: Via Piave 62
00187 Rome Italy
Phone: +39 06 45439765

#83
Al Grottino
Category: Pizza
Average Price: €8-20
Area: San Giovanni
Address: Via Orvieto 6
00182 Rome Italy
Phone: +39 06 7024440

#84
Il Timoniere
Category: Romen
Average Price: €21-40
Area: Ostiense
Address: Via Francesco Orazio Da
Pennabilli 5, 00154 Rome Italy
Phone: +39 06 5110007

#85
Trattoria Der Pallaro
Category: Romen
Average Price: €8-20
Area: Centro Storico
Address: Largo Del Pallaro 15
00186 Rome Italy
Phone: +39 06 68801488

#86
Babette
Category: Italian, Mediterranean
Average Price: €21-40
Area: Flaminio
Address: Via Margutta 1D
00187 Rome Italy
Phone: +39 06 3211559

#87
Zerozero100
Category: Italian, Lounge
Average Price: €8-20
Area: San Lorenzo, San Giovanni
Address: Via Del Verano 27
00185 Rome Italy
Phone: +39 06 44702346

#88
Il Caminetto
Category: Italian
Average Price: €21-40
Area: Salario, Parioli
Address: Viale Dei Parioli 89
00197 Rome Italy
Phone: +39 06 8083946

#89
Trattoria Da Cesare
Category: Romen
Average Price: €21-40
Area: Ostiense
Address: Via Del Casaletto 45
00151 Rome Italy
Phone: +39 06 536015

#90
L'idillio
Category: Italian
Average Price: €8-20
Area: Pigneto
Address: Via Augusto Dulceri 29
00176 Rome Italy
Phone: +39 06 297089

#91
Hostaria Da Pietro
Category: Romen
Average Price: €21-40
Area: Flaminio
Address: Via Ges'E Maria, 18
00187 Rome Italy
Phone: +39 06 3208816

#92
L'Archetto
Category: Italian
Average Price: €21-40
Area: Centro Storico
Address: Via Dell'archetto 26
00187 Rome Italy
Phone: +39 06 6789064

#93
Pietro Valentini
Category: Italian
Average Price: €21-40
Area: Centro Storico
Address: Via Dei Pianellari 19
00186 Rome Italy
Phone: +39 06 6868565

#94
Marco G
Category: Italian
Average Price: €21-40
Area: Borgo
Address: Via Garibaldi 56
00153 Rome Italy
Phone: +39 06 5809289

#95
Grazia &Graziella
Category: Italian
Average Price: €8-20
Area: Trastevere
Address: Largo Fumasoni Biondi 5
00153 Rome Italy
Phone: +39 06 5880398

#96
Pescheria Osteria Sor Duilio
Category: Seafood, Live/Raw Food
Average Price: €8-20
Area: Montesacro/Talenti
Address: Via Delle Cave Di Pietralata 44
00157 Rome Italy
Phone: +39 06 41787439

#97
Antica Schiacciata Romena
Category: Pizza
Average Price: €21-40
Area: Ostiense
Address: Via Folco Portinari 38
00151 Rome Italy
Phone: +39 06 536112

#98
Flavio Al Velavevodetto
Category: Romen
Average Price: €21-40
Area: Testaccio, Ostiense
Address: Via Di Monte Testaccio 97
00153 Rome Italy
Phone: +39 06 5744194

#99
Da Manolo
Category: Sandwiches, Burgers
Average Price: Under €7
Area: Prati
Address: Via Di Porta Castello 7
00193 Rome Italy
Phone: +39 06 68134249

#100
Momart Caf'
Category: Buffet, Wine Bar
Average Price: €8-20
Area: Nomentano
Address: Viale XXI Aprile 19
00162 Rome Italy
Phone: +39 06 86391656

#101
Sciu' Sciu'
Category: Italian
Average Price: €21-40
Area: Monti
Address: Via Urbana 56
00184 Rome Italy
Phone: +39 06 48906038

#102
Cantina E Cucina
Category: Italian
Average Price: €21-40
Area: Centro Storico
Address: Via Del Governo Vecchio 87
00186 Rome Italy
Phone: +39 06 6892574

#103
Mazzo
Category: Italian
Average Price: €8-20
Area: Casilino
Address: Via Delle Rose 54
00171 Rome Italy
Phone: +39 06 64962847

#104
Makasar Caf'
Category: Tea Room, Brasserie
Average Price: €8-20
Area: Prati
Address: Via Plauto 33
00193 Rome Italy
Phone: +39 06 6874602

#105
Fa-B'o
Category: Juice Bar, Organic Store
Average Price: €8-20
Area: Prati
Address: Via Germanico 43
00192 Rome Italy
Phone: +39 06 64525810

#106
Tat'
Category: Italian, Pizza
Average Price: €8-20
Area: Eur
Address: Piazza Guglielmo Marconi 11
00144 Rome Italy
Phone: +39 06 5920105

#107
Forno La Renella
Category: Pizza
Average Price: Under €7
Area: Trastevere
Address: Via Del Moro 15/16
00153 Rome Italy
Phone: +39 06 5817265

#108
Mez' Bistrot
Category: Middle Eastern, Mediterranean
Average Price: €21-40
Area: Monteverde, Ostiense
Address: Via Di Monteverde 9B
00152 Rome Italy
Phone: +39 06 58204749

#109
Nonna Betta
Category: Kosher, Jewish
Average Price: €21-40
Area: Centro Storico
Address: Via Del Portico d'Ottavia 16
00186 Rome Italy
Phone: +39 06 68806263

#110
Genkai 2
Category: Chinese, Japanese
Average Price: €21-40
Area: Balduina/Montemario, Prati
Address: Via Marcantonio Bragadin 80
00136 Rome Italy
Phone: +39 06 39720056

#111
Trattoria De Gli Amici
Category: Italian
Average Price: €21-40
Area: Trastevere
Address: Piazza Sant'Egidio 6
00153 Rome Italy
Phone: +39 06 5806033

#112
Berzitello
Category: Romen
Average Price: €21-40
Area: Centro Storico
Address: Via Delle Quattro
Fontane 32 B, 00184 Rome Italy
Phone: +39 06 47824714

#113
Casa &Bottega
Category: Bakery, Juice Bar
Average Price: €8-20
Area: Centro Storico
Address: Via Dei Coronari 183
00186 Rome Italy
Phone: +39 06 6864358

#114
Rome Sparita
Category: Pizza, Romen
Average Price: €8-20
Area: Trastevere
Address: Piazza Santa Cecilia 24
00153 Rome Italy
Phone: +39 06 5800757

#115
PagaRome
Category: Seafood
Average Price: Above €41
Area: Parioli
Address: Viale Bruno Buozzi 31
00197 Rome Italy
Phone: +39 06 80663155

#116
Ai Piani
Category: Seafood
Average Price: Above €41
Area: Parioli
Address: Via Francesco Denza 35
00197 Rome Italy
Phone: +39 06 8079704

#117
Il Giardino Dei Ciliegi
Category: Café, Italian
Average Price: €8-20
Area: Trastevere
Address: Via Dei Fienaroli 4
00153 Rome Italy
Phone: +39 06 5803423

#118
La Pentolaccia
Category: Italian
Average Price: €21-40
Area: Termini
Address: Via Flavia 38
00187 Rome Italy
Phone: +39 06 483477

#119
Cru.Dop
Category: Italian, Live/Raw Food
Average Price: €21-40
Area: Tuscolano
Address: Via Tuscolana 898
00174 Rome Italy
Phone: +39 06 76909916

#120
Pompi
Category: Café, Desserts
Average Price: €8-20
Area: San Giovanni
Address: Via Albalonga 7
00183 Rome Italy
Phone: +39 06 7000418

#121
Old Bear
Category: Romen
Average Price: €8-20
Area: Centro Storico
Address: Via Gigli d'Oro 3
00186 Rome Italy
Phone: +39 06 68210009

#122
Nerone
Category: Pizza
Average Price: €8-20
Area: Trastevere
Address: Via Del Moro 43
00153 Rome Italy
Phone: +39 06 58301756

#123
Lagan'
Category: Romen
Average Price: €21-40
Area: Centro Storico
Address: Via Dell'orso 44
00186 Rome Italy
Phone: +39 06 68301161

#124
Il Quinto Quarto
Category: Romen
Average Price: €21-40
Area: Corso Francia
Address: Via Della Farnesina 13
00135 Rome Italy
Phone: +39 06 3338768

#125
Que Te Pongo
Category: Sandwiches
Average Price: €8-20
Area: Flaminio
Address: Via Di Ripetta 40
00186 Rome Italy
Phone: +39 06 32652670

#126
La Cuccuma
Category: Pizza
Average Price: Under €7
Area: Esquilino
Address: Via Merulana, 221
00185 Rome Italy
Phone: +39 06 77201361

#127
Bisteak
Category: Steakhouse, Italian
Average Price: €21-40
Area: Montesacro/Talenti
Address: Via Di Pietralata 141
00158 Rome Italy
Phone: +39 06 41792126

#128
Fish Market
Category: Seafood, Live/Raw Food
Average Price: €21-40
Area: Montesacro/Talenti
Address: Via Di Pietralata 149B
00158 Rome Italy
Phone: +39 347 0095009

#129
Vulcano
Category: Pizza
Average Price: €8-20
Area: Pigneto
Address: Via Del Pigneto 189
00176 Rome Italy
Phone: +39 06 64801485

#130
Tribeca Caf'
Category: Café, Coffee &Tea
Average Price: €8-20
Area: Nomentano
Address: Via Messina 29
00198 Rome Italy
Phone: +39 06 44250923

#131
Andirivieni
Category: Bar, Italian
Average Price: €8-20
Area: Balduina/Montemario, Prati
Address: Via Della Meloria 80
00136 Rome Italy
Phone: +39 06 39735305

#132
Brasserie 4:20
Category: Brasserie, Pub
Average Price: €8-20
Area: Trastevere
Address: Via Portuense 82
00153 Rome Italy
Phone: +39 06 58310737

#133
Trattoria Da Lucia
Category: Romen
Average Price: €8-20
Area: Trastevere
Address: Vicolo Del Mattonato 2B
00153 Rome Italy
Phone: +39 06 5803601

#134
Il Fornaio
Category: Bakery, Italian
Average Price: €8-20
Area: Centro Storico
Address: Via Dei Baullari 5
00186 Rome Italy
Phone: +39 06 68803947

#135
Ginger
Category: Breakfast &Brunch
Average Price: €8-20
Area: Centro Storico
Address: Via Borgognona 43
00187 Rome Italy
Phone: +39 06 96036390

#136
Settimio All'arancio
Category: Italian
Average Price: €21-40
Area: Centro Storico
Address: Via Arancio 50
00186 Rome Italy
Phone: +39 06 6876119

#137
Circus
Category: Juice Bar, Sandwiches
Average Price: Under €7
Area: Centro Storico
Address: Via Della Vetrina 15
00186 Rome Italy
Phone: +39 06 97619258

#138
Pourquoi!
Category: Brasserie, Pub
Average Price: €8-20
Area: San Lorenzo, San Giovanni
Address: Via Dei Volsci 82
00185 Rome Italy
Phone: +39 06 44361955

#139
'Mpare
Category: Desserts, Sicilian
Average Price: €8-20
Area: San Lorenzo
Address: Via Catania 29
00161 Rome Italy
Phone: +39 06 44252368

#140
Lasagnam
Category: Romen
Average Price: €8-20
Area: Monti
Address: Via Frangipane 15
00184 Rome Italy
Phone: +39 06 69940625

#141
Dar Sor Olimpio Al Drago
Category: Italian
Average Price: €8-20
Area: Trastevere
Address: Piazza Del Drago, 2
00153 Rome Italy
Phone: +39 339 8857574

#142
Baires
Category: Argentine
Average Price: €21-40
Area: Centro Storico
Address: Corso Rinascimento, 1
00186 Rome Italy
Phone: +39 06 6861293

#143
Osteria Da Fortunata
Category: Romen
Average Price: €8-20
Area: Centro Storico
Address: Via Del Pellegrino 11
00186 Rome Italy
Phone: +39 06 60667391

#144
Santa Lucia
Category: Italian
Average Price: €21-40
Area: Centro Storico
Address: Largo Febo 12
00186 Rome Italy
Phone: +39 06 68802427

#145
Enosteria Capolecase
Category: Mediterranean, Italian
Average Price: €21-40
Area: Centro Storico
Address: Via Di Capo Le Case 53
00187 Rome Italy
Phone: +39 06 6786115

#146
Trattoria Da Alfredo E Ada
Category: Italian
Average Price: Under €7
Area: Centro Storico
Address: Via Banchi Nuovi, 14
00186 Rome Italy
Phone: +39 06 6878842

#147
El Norteno
Category: Latin American
Average Price: €8-20
Area: Termini
Address: Via Del Castro Pretorio 26
00185 Rome Italy
Phone: +39 06 49381722

#148
Ippokrates
Category: Greek
Average Price: €8-20
Area: Termini
Address: Via Piave 30
00187 Rome Italy
Phone: +39 06 64824179

#149
Marinari
Category: Desserts, Fast Food
Average Price: €21-40
Area: Nomentano, Salario
Address: Corso Trieste 95
00198 Rome Italy
Phone: +39 06 8551045

#150
Alla Rampa
Category: Romen
Average Price: €21-40
Area: Centro Storico
Address: Piazza Mignanelli 18
00187 Rome Italy
Phone: +39 06 6782621

#151
Hostaria Capo De Fero
Category: Italian, Pizza
Average Price: €21-40
Area: Trastevere
Address: Via San Cosimato 16
00153 Rome Italy
Phone: +39 06 5818038

#152
Mezzo
Category: Italian
Average Price: €21-40
Area: Salario
Address: Via Di Priscilla 25A
00199 Rome Italy
Phone: +39 06 86399017

#153
Piccolo Abruzzo
Category: Italian
Average Price: €21-40
Area: Termini
Address: Via Sicilia 237
00187 Rome Italy
Phone: +39 06 42820176

#154
Joseph
Category: Italian
Average Price: €8-20
Area: Balduina/Montemario
Address: Via Accursio 12
00165 Rome Italy
Phone: +39 06 6623887

61

#155
Pierluigi
Category: Italian
Average Price: Above €41
Area: Centro Storico
Address: Piazza De' Ricci 144
00186 Rome Italy
Phone: +39 06 6861302

#156
Taverna Sacchetti
Category: Italian
Average Price: €21-40
Area: Balduina/Montemario
Address: Via Della Pineta Sacchetti 436A,
00168 Rome Italy
Phone: +39 06 3012352

#157
La Taverna Dei Monti
Category: Italian
Average Price: €8-20
Area: Monti, Centro Storico
Address: Via Del Boschetto 41
00184 Rome Italy
Phone: +39 06 4817724

#158
Aristocampo
Category: Italian
Average Price: €21-40
Area: Trastevere
Address: Via Della Lungaretta 75
00153 Rome Italy
Phone: +39 06 58335530

#159
Assaggi d'Autore
Category: Italian
Average Price: €8-20
Area: Centro Storico
Address: Via Dei Lucchesi 28
00187 Rome Italy
Phone: +39 06 6990949

#160
Karalis
Category: Seafood, Sardinian
Average Price: €21-40
Area: Montesacro/Talenti
Address: Via Carlo Lorenzini 71
00137 Rome Italy
Phone: +39 06 822040

#161
Acqua E Farina
Category: Pizza
Average Price: €8-20
Area: Testaccio, Ostiense
Address: Piazza Orazio Giustiniani 2
00153 Rome Italy
Phone: +39 06 5741382

#162
Trattoria Nuova Stella
Category: Romen
Average Price: €21-40
Area: Termini
Address: Via Daniele Manin 54
00185 Rome Italy
Phone: +39 06 4875390

#163
Romena Mente
Category: Bar, Café
Average Price: €8-20
Area: Ostiense
Address: Circonvallazione Ostiense 136
00154 Rome Italy
Phone: +39 06 51605131

#164
Il Chianti
Category: Italian
Average Price: €21-40
Area: Centro Storico
Address: Via Del Lavatore 81
00187 Rome Italy
Phone: +39 06 6787550

#165
Il Fico
Category: Italian
Average Price: €8-20
Area: Centro Storico
Address: Via Di Monte Giordano 49
00186 Rome Italy
Phone: +39 06 6875568

#166
Baccanale Trastevere
Category: Pub, Italian
Average Price: €8-20
Area: Trastevere
Address: Via Della Lungaretta 81
00153 Rome Italy
Phone: +39 06 45448268

#167
La Vecchia Locanda
Category: Italian
Average Price: €8-20
Area: Centro Storico
Address: Vicolo Sinibaldi 2
00186 Rome Italy
Phone: +39 06 68802831

#168
Maranega
Category: Bar, Café
Average Price: €8-20
Area: Centro Storico
Address: Piazza Campo De' Fiori 48
00186 Rome Italy
Phone: +39 06 68300331

#169
Eleonora d'Arborea
Category: Seafood
Average Price: €21-40
Area: Nomentano
Address: Corso Trieste 23
00198 Rome Italy
Phone: +39 06 44250943

#170
Ciccia Bomba
Category: Italian
Average Price: €8-20
Area: Centro Storico
Address: Via Del Governo Vecchio 76
00186 Rome Italy
Phone: +39 06 68802108

#171
Dao
Category: Chinese
Average Price: €21-40
Area: Nomentano, Salario
Address: Viale Jonio 328
00141 Rome Italy
Phone: +39 06 87197573

#172
Voy
Category: Breakfast &Brunch, Italian
Average Price: €8-20
Area: Corso Francia
Address: Via Flaminia 496
00191 Rome Italy
Phone: +39 06 33222179

#173
Vero
Category: Juice Bar,
Fast Food
Average Price: €8-20
Area: Prati
Address: Via Vittoria Colonna 7
00193 Rome Italy
Phone: +39 06 3202086

#174
Mam'
Category: Italian, Food
Average Price: €21-40
Address: Via Sforza Pallavicini 19
00193 Rome Italy
Phone: +39 06 68139095

#175
Arancia Blu
Category: Vegetarian, Vegan
Average Price: €21-40
Area: Flaminio
Address: Via Cesare Beccaria 3
00196 Rome Italy
Phone: +39 06 3610801

#176
Vivi Bistrot
Category: Italian, Bistro
Average Price: €21-40
Area: Monteverde, Aurelia
Address: Via Vitellia 102
00152 Rome Italy
Phone: +39 06 5827540

#177
Laboratorio 3
Category: Italian, Pizza
Average Price: €8-20
Area: Montesacro/Talenti
Address: Via Di Pietralata 180
00158 Rome Italy
Phone: +39 06 4501288

#178
Urbana 47
Category: Italian, Food Delivery Service
Average Price: €21-40
Area: Monti
Address: Via Urbana 47
00184 Rome Italy
Phone: +39 06 47884006

#179
T-Bone Station
Category: American, Burgers
Average Price: €21-40
Area: Centro Storico
Address: Via Francesco Crispi 29
00187 Rome Italy
Phone: +39 06 6787650

#180
Splendor Parthenopes
Category: Pizza, Italian
Average Price: €21-40
Area: Centro Storico, Prati
Address: Via Vittoria Colonna 32C
00193 Rome Italy
Phone: +39 06 6833710

#181
Buono
Category: Italian, Pizza
Average Price: €8-20
Area: San Giovanni
Address: Via Albenga 1
00183 Rome Italy
Phone: +39 06 77204453

#182
Bla Kongo
Category: Scandinavian, African
Average Price: €8-20
Area: Pinciano
Address: Via Ofranto 6
00198 Rome Italy
Phone: +39 06 8546705

#183
Augusto
Category: Italian
Average Price: €8-20
Area: Trastevere
Address: Piazza De' Renzi 15
00153 Rome Italy
Phone: +39 06 5803798

#184
Scilla E Cariddi
Category: Specialty Food, Sicilian
Average Price: €8-20
Area: Centro Storico
Address: Via IV Novembre 145
00187 Rome Italy
Phone: +39 06 89767230

#185
Da Michele
Category: Italian
Average Price: €8-20
Area: Esquilino
Address: Via Merulana 237
00185 Rome Italy
Phone: +39 06 4872672

#186
Ai Due Ponti
Category: Italian
Average Price: €8-20
Area: Corso Francia
Address: Via Flaminia 858
00191 Rome Italy
Phone: +39 06 3332518

#187
Il Leoncino
Category: Pizza
Average Price: €8-20
Area: Centro Storico
Address: Via Del Leoncino 28
00186 Rome Italy
Phone: +39 06 6867757

#188
Rosti Al Pigneto
Category: Italian, Burgers
Average Price: €8-20
Area: Pigneto
Address: Via Bartolomeo d'Alviano 65
00176 Rome Italy
Phone: +39 06 2752608

#189
Osteria Dei Pontefici
Category: Italian, Pizza
Average Price: €21-40
Area: Borgo, Prati
Address: Via Gregorio VII 53
00165 Rome Italy
Phone: +39 06 635206

#190
Er Caffettiere
Category: Café, Bar
Average Price: €8-20
Area: Monti
Address: Via Urbana 72
00184 Rome Italy
Phone: +39 320 4168532

#191
Taverna Romena Monti 79
Category: Italian
Average Price: €8-20
Area: Monti
Address: Via Della Madonna Dei Monti 79,
00184 Rome Italy
Phone: +39 06 4745325

#192
Assunta Madre
Category: Seafood
Average Price: Above €41
Area: Centro Storico
Address: Via Giulia 14
00186 Rome Italy
Phone: +39 06 68806972

#193
Osteria Del Pegno
Category: Italian
Average Price: €21-40
Area: Centro Storico
Address: Vicolo Di Montevecchio 8
00186 Rome Italy
Phone: +39 06 68807025

#194
Doney
Category: Italian
Average Price: €21-40
Area: Termini
Address: Via Vittorio Veneto 141
00187 Rome Italy
Phone: +39 06 47082783

#195
Il Cuore Di Napoli
Category: Italian, Pizza
Average Price: €8-20
Area: Termini
Address: Via Cernaia 31
00185 Rome Italy
Phone: +39 06 44340252

#196
Trattoria Pommidoro
Category: Italian
Average Price: €8-20
Area: San Lorenzo, San Giovanni
Address: Piazza Dei Sanniti 44
00185 Rome Italy
Phone: +39 06 4452692

#197
Bar Hungaria
Category: Bar, Burgers
Average Price: €21-40
Area: Salario
Address: Piazza Ungheria 7
00198 Rome Italy
Phone: +39 06 8551432

#198
Foodoo
Category: Italian
Average Price: €8-20
Area: Balduina/Montemario
Address: Viale Delle Medaglie d'Oro 342
00136 Rome Italy
Phone: +39 06 45436730

#199
Lo Zodiaco
Category: Bar, Italian
Average Price: €21-40
Area: Balduina/Montemario
Address: Viale Del Parco Mellini 88
00136 Rome Italy
Phone: +39 06 35496744

#200
Ferro E Ghisa
Category: Italian, Steakhouse
Average Price: €8-20
Area: Balduina/Montemario, Aurelia
Address: Circonvalazione Aurelia 11
00165 Rome Italy
Phone: +39 06 66032638

#201
L'Asino d'Oro
Category: Romen
Average Price: €8-20
Area: Monti
Address: Via Del Boschetto 73
00184 Rome Italy
Phone: +39 06 48913832

#202
Bar Lillo
Category: Café, Bar
Average Price: Under €7
Area: Trastevere
Address: Via Dei Genovesi 39
00153 Rome Italy
Phone: +39 06 5817142

#203
Il Bocconcino
Category: Italian
Average Price: €21-40
Area: Aventino
Address: Via Ostilia 23
00184 Rome Italy
Phone: +39 06 77079175

#204
Taverna Urbana
Category: Italian
Average Price: €21-40
Area: Monti
Address: Via Urbana 137
00184 Rome Italy
Phone: +39 06 4884439

#205
Trattoria Perilli Luigi E Bernardino
Category: Italian
Average Price: €21-40
Area: Testaccio, Ostiense
Address: Via Marmorata, 39
00100 Rome Italy
Phone: +39 06 5742415

#206
Clemente Alla Maddalena
Category: Venues &Events, Italian
Average Price: Above €41
Area: Centro Storico
Address: Piazza Della Maddalena 4
00186 Rome Italy
Phone: +39 06 6833633

#207
Taverna Barberini
Category: Gluten-Free, Vegetarian
Average Price: €8-20
Area: Centro Storico
Address: Via Delle Quattro Fontane 160
00184 Rome Italy
Phone: +39 06 4883619

#208
La Botticella
Category: Italian
Average Price: €8-20
Area: Trastevere
Address: Vicolo Del Leopardo 39A
00153 Rome Italy
Phone: +39 06 5814738

#209
Baguetteria Del Fico
Category: Sandwiches
Average Price: Under €7
Area: Centro Storico
Address: Via Della Fossa 12
00197 Rome Italy
Phone: +39 388 1246590

#210
Il Drappo
Category: Sardinian
Average Price: €21-40
Area: Centro Storico
Address: Vicolo Del Malpasso 9
00186 Rome Italy
Phone: +39 06 6877365

#211
Mamar'
Category: Pizza
Average Price: €8-20
Area: Termini, San Giovanni
Address: Via Dei Sabelli 26A
00185 Rome Italy
Phone: +39 06 44340944

#212
Trattoria Da Teo
Category: Romen
Average Price: €21-40
Area: Trastevere
Address: Piazza Dei Ponziani 7A
00153 Rome Italy
Phone: +39 06 5818355

#213
Pizzeria Florida
Category: Pizza
Average Price: Under €7
Area: Centro Storico
Address: Via Florida 25
00186 Rome Italy
Phone: +39 06 68803236

#214
Isidoro
Category: Italian
Average Price: €8-20
Area: Esquilino, Aventino
Address: Via Di San Giovanni In Laterano
59A 00184 Rome Italy
Phone: +39 06 7008266

#215
L'Antico Forno
Category: Bakery, Pizza
Average Price: €8-20
Area: Centro Storico
Address: Via Delle Muratte 8
00187 Rome Italy
Phone: +39 06 6792866

#216
Da Fortunato
Category: Italian
Average Price: €21-40
Area: Centro Storico
Address: Via Del Pantheon 55
00186 Rome Italy
Phone: +39 06 6792788

#217
L'Orso 80
Category: Italian
Average Price: €21-40
Area: Centro Storico
Address: Via Dell'orso 33
00186 Rome Italy
Phone: +39 06 6864904

#218
Uve E Forme
Category: Winery, Italian
Average Price: €21-40
Area: San Lorenzo
Address: Via Padova 6
00161 Rome Italy
Phone: +39 06 44236801

#219
Ottavio
Category: Seafood, Italian
Average Price: Above €41
Area: San Giovanni
Address: Via Di Santa Croce In
Gerusalemme 9
00185 Rome Italy
Phone: +39 06 7020520

#220
Doppiozero 2
Category: Specialty Food, Italian
Average Price: €8-20
Area: Testaccio, Ostiense
Address: Via Ostiense, 68
00154 Rome Italy
Phone: +39 06 57301961

#221
Pepe Verde
Category: Italian
Average Price: €21-40
Area: Nomentano
Address: Viale Gorizia 38
00198 Rome Italy
Phone: +39 06 85301181

#222
Enoteca Barberini
Category: Winery, Pizza
Average Price: €8-20
Area: Centro Storico
Address: Via Del Tritone 123
00187 Rome Italy
Phone: +39 06 62205971

#223
Al Mattarello d'Oro
Category: Pizza
Average Price: Under €7
Area: Bufalotta
Address: Via Della Bufalotta 292
00137 Rome Italy
Phone: +39 06 87141390

#224
Pizzeria San Marino
Category: Pizza
Average Price: €8-20
Area: Nomentano
Address: Corso Trieste 161
00198 Rome Italy
Phone: +39 06 86203479

#225
Betto E Mary
Category: Italian
Average Price: €21-40
Area: Tuscolano
Address: Via Dei Savorgnan 99
00176 Rome Italy
Phone: +39 06 45421780

#226
Tiepolo
Category: Brasserie
Average Price: €21-40
Area: Flaminio
Address: Via Giovanni Battista Tiepolo 3
00196 Rome Italy
Phone: +39 06 3227449

#227
La Locanda Dei Girasoli
Category: Italian, Pizza
Average Price: €8-20
Area: Tuscolano
Address: Via Dei Sulpici 117H
00174 Rome Italy
Phone: +39 06 7610194

#228
Ai Spaghettari
Category: Pizza
Average Price: €8-20
Area: Trastevere
Address: Piazza Di San Cosimato 58
00153 Rome Italy
Phone: +39 06 5800450

#229
Osteria Mavi
Category: Italian
Average Price: €21-40
Area: Ostiense
Address: Via Enrico Fermi 71
00146 Rome Italy
Phone: +39 06 5584801

#230
Trattoria Cadorna
Category: Italian
Average Price: €21 40
Area: Termini
Address: Via Raffaele Cadorna 12
00187 Rome Italy
Phone: +39 06 4827061

#231
Locanda Dei Massimi
Category: Italian
Average Price: €8-20
Area: Aurelia
Address: Via Portuense 863
00148 Rome Italy
Phone: +39 06 6550684

#232
Le Mani In Pasta
Category: Italian
Average Price: €21-40
Area: Trastevere
Address: Via Dei Genovesi 37
00153 Rome Italy
Phone: +39 06 5816017

#233
Li Rioni
Category: Pizza, Italian
Average Price: €8-20
Area: Esquilino, Aventino
Address: Via Dei Santissimi Quattro 24
00184 Rome Italy
Phone: +39 06 70450605

#234
Duke's
Category: Bar, American
Average Price: Above €41
Area: Salario
Address: Viale Parioli 200
00197 Rome Italy
Phone: +39 06 80662455

#235
Sorpasso
Category: Italian
Average Price: €21-40
Area: Prati
Address: Via Properzio 31
00193 Rome Italy
Phone: +39 06 89024554

#236
Il Giardino Romeno
Category: Romen
Average Price: €21-40
Area: Centro Storico
Address: Via Del Portico d'Ottavia 18
00186 Rome Italy
Phone: +39 06 68809661

#237
Osteria Pucci
Category: Romen
Average Price: €21-40
Area: Trastevere
Address: Piazza Mastai, 2
00153 Rome Italy
Phone: +39 06 5819870

#238
Alba Dolce
Category: Breakfast &Brunch, Desserts
Average Price: Under €7
Area: San Giovanni
Address: Via Albalonga 64
00183 Rome Italy
Phone: +39 06 70490093

#239
Tanto Pe' Magn'
Category: Italian
Average Price: €21-40
Area: Ostiense
Address: Via Giustino De Jacobis 9
00154 Rome Italy
Phone: +39 06 51607422

#240
I Butteri
Category: Italian, Steakhouse
Average Price: €21-40
Area: Nomentano
Address: Piazza Regina Margherita 28
00198 Rome Italy
Phone: +39 06 8548130

#241
Ad Hoc
Category: Italian
Average Price: Above €41
Area: Flaminio
Address: Via Di Ripetta 43
00186 Rome Italy
Phone: +39 06 3233040

#242
Casa Mangiacotti
Category: Beer, Wine, Spirits
Average Price: €8-20
Area: Pigneto
Address: Via Gentile Da Mogliano 180
00176 Rome Italy
Phone: +39 392 4319477

#243
Aristocampo
Category: Fast Food, Sandwiches
Average Price: €8-20
Area: Centro Storico
Address: Piazza Campo De' Fiori 30
00186 Rome Italy
Phone: +39 06 6864897

#244
Angelo E Simonetta
Category: Pizza
Average Price: €21-40
Area: Nomentano
Address: Via Nomentana 581
00141 Rome Italy
Phone: +39 06 87188853

#245
Angelino Ai Fori
Category: Romen, Pizza
Average Price: €8-20
Area: Monti, Centro Storico
Address: Largo Corrado Ricci 42
00184 Rome Italy
Phone: +39 06 6791121

#246
Ciampini
Category: Café, Coffee &Tea
Average Price: Above €41
Area: Centro Storico
Address: Piazza Di San Lorenzo In Lucina
29 Rome, Rome Italy
Phone: +39 06 68135108

#247
Tullio
Category: Italian
Average Price: Above €41
Area: Centro Storico
Address: Via San Nicola Da
Talentino 26, 00187 Rome Italy
Phone: +39 06 4745560

#248
Otello Alla Concordia
Category: Italian
Average Price: €21-40
Area: Centro Storico
Address: Via Della Croce 81
00187 Rome Italy
Phone: +39 06 6791178

#249
Fernanda Osteria
Category: Italian
Average Price: €21-40
Area: Trastevere
Address: Via Ettore Rolli 1
00153 Rome Italy
Phone: +39 06 5894333

#250
Strabbioni
Category: Café, Italian
Average Price: €21-40
Area: Termini
Address: Via Servio Tullio 2
00187 Rome Italy
Phone: +39 06 4873965

#251
Ombre E Cicheti
Category: Italian
Average Price: €8-20
Area: Borgo
Address: Via Del Largo Terrione 18
00165 Rome Italy
Phone: +39 06 633280

#252
Ai Bozzi Da Giovanni
Category: Italian
Average Price: €21-40
Area: Trastevere
Address: Piazza Giuditta
Tavani Arquati 107
00153 Rome Italy
Phone: +39 06 5816640

#253
La Fontana
Category: Wine Bar, Italian
Average Price: €8-20
Area: Centro Storico
Address: Vicolo De' Modelli 56
00187 Rome Italy
Phone: +39 390 669924087

#254
L'Emporio Alla Pace
Category: Café, Bar
Average Price: Under €7
Area: Centro Storico
Address: Via Della Pace 28
00186 Rome Italy
Phone: +39 06 68802938

#255
Il Pagliaccio
Category: Italian
Average Price: Above €41
Area: Centro Storico
Address: Via Dei Banchi Vecchi 129A
00186 Rome Italy
Phone: +39 06 68809595

#256
Pasta Imperiale
Category: Italian
Average Price: €8-20
Area: Centro Storico
Address: Via Dei Coronari 160
00186 Rome Italy
Phone: +39 320 1587421

#257
La Piazzetta San Lorenzo
Category: Fast Food, Pizza
Average Price: Under €7
Area: Termini
Address: Largo Degli Osci 15
00185 Rome Italy
Phone: +39 06 4454951

#258
Al Gran Sasso
Category: Italian
Average Price: €8-20
Area: Flaminio
Address: Via Ripetta 32
00186 Rome Italy
Phone: +39 06 3214883

#259
Da Marcello
Category: Italian, Bistro
Average Price: €8-20
Area: San Giovanni
Address: Via Dei Campani 12
00185 Rome Italy
Phone: +39 06 4463311

#260
Trattoria Pizzeria Micci
Category: Italian, Pizza
Average Price: €8-20
Area: Prati
Address: Via Andrea Doria, 55/A
00192 Rome Italy
Phone: +39 06 39733208

#261
Alle Fratte Di Trastevere
Category: Romen
Average Price: €8-20
Area: Trastevere
Address: Via Delle Fratte Di Trastevere 49,
00153 Rome Italy
Phone: +39 06 5835775

#262
La Fraschetta
Category: Romen, Pizza
Average Price: €8-20
Area: Trastevere
Address: Via Di San Francesco A Ripa
134, 00153 Rome Italy
Phone: +39 06 5816012

#263
La Fraschetta Di Mastro Giorgio
Category: Italian
Average Price: €21-40
Area: Testaccio, Ostiense
Address: Via Alessandro Volta 36
00153 Rome Italy
Phone: +39 06 5741369

#264
Pimm's Good
Category: Italian
Average Price: €8-20
Area: Trastevere
Address: Via Di Santa Dorotea 8
00153 Rome Italy
Phone: +39 06 97277979

#265
Osteria Dell'ingegno
Category: Italian, Wine Bar
Average Price: €21-40
Area: Centro Storico
Address: Piazza Di Pietra 45
00186 Rome Italy
Phone: +39 06 6780662

#266
Bali
Category: Indonesian, Lounge
Average Price: €8-20
Area: Trastevere
Address: Via Del Mattonato 29
00153 Rome Italy
Phone: +39 06 5896089

#267
La Silviana
Category: Italian
Average Price: Under €7
Area: Ostiense
Address: Via P. Venturi 84
00149 Rome Italy
Phone: +39 06 55264908

#268
Hostaria Pizzeria Giacomelli
Category: Pizza, Romen
Average Price: €8-20
Area: Prati
Address: Via Emilio Faa' Di Bruno 25
00195 Rome Italy
Phone: +39 06 3725910

#269
Perilli
Category: Romen
Average Price: €21-40
Area: Testaccio, Ostiense
Address: Via Marmorata 39
00153 Rome Italy
Phone: +39 06 5755100

#270
Coso Wine
Category: Italian, Wine Bar
Average Price: €8-20
Area: Centro Storico
Address: Via In Lucina 16L
00186 Rome Italy
Phone: +39 06 68210420

#271
Pizzeria San Marco
Category: Pizza, Italian
Average Price: €21-40
Area: Termini
Address: Via Sardegna 38D
00187 Rome Italy
Phone: +39 06 42012620

#272
Il Peperoncino Dispettoso
Category: Pizza
Average Price: €8-20
Area: Balduina/Montemario
Address: Viale Delle Medaglie
D'Oro 158, 00136 Rome Italy
Phone: +39 06 35498451

#273
Trattoria Monti
Category: Italian
Average Price: €8-20
Area: Esquilino, Termini
Address: Via Di San Vito 13
00185 Rome Italy
Phone: +39 06 4466573

#274
Settembrini
Category: Wine Bar, Italian
Average Price: €21-40
Area: Prati
Address: Via Luigi Settembrini 25
00195 Rome Italy
Phone: +39 06 3232617

#275
Dulcamara
Category: Italian, Wine Bar
Average Price: €21-40
Area: Corso Francia
Address: Via Flaminia 449
00191 Rome Italy
Phone: +39 06 3332108

#276
Trattoria Da Danilo
Category: Romen
Average Price: €21-40
Area: Esquilino
Address: Via Petrarca 13
00185 Rome Italy
Phone: +39 06 77200111

#277
Peppe Ai Gerani
Category: Pizza
Average Price: €8-20
Area: Aurelia
Address: Via Della Pisana 192
00163 Rome Italy
Phone: +39 06 66151944

#278
El Pueblo
Category: Mexican
Average Price: €21-40
Area: Balduina/Montemario
Address: Via Giacinto De Vecchi Pieralice
34 00167 Rome Italy
Phone: +39 06 631855

#279
Akbar
Category: Cocktail Bar, Jazz &Blues
Average Price: €8-20
Area: Trastevere
Address: Piazza In Piscinula 51
00153 Rome Italy
Phone: +39 06 5800681

#280
Spirito Divino
Category: Romen
Average Price: €21-40
Area: Trastevere
Address: Via Dei Genovesi 31
00153 Rome Italy
Phone: +39 06 5896689

#281
L'Arcano
Category: Italian
Average Price: €21-40
Area: Centro Storico
Address: Via Delle Paste 102
00186 Rome Italy
Phone: +39 06 6786929

#282
La Matriciana Dal 1870
Category: Italian
Average Price: €21-40
Area: Centro Storico
Address: Via Del Viminale 40
00184 Rome Italy
Phone: +39 06 4881775

#283
Da Olimpio
Category: Italian
Average Price: €8-20
Area: Centro Storico
Address: Via Degli Avignonesi 37
00187 Rome Italy
Phone: +39 06 4885225

#284
Estrobar
Category: Italian
Average Price: €21-40
Area: Testaccio, Ostiense
Address: Via Matteucci 10
00154 Rome Italy
Phone: +39 06 57289141

#285
Lilli
Category: Romen
Average Price: €21-40
Area: Centro Storico
Address: Via Tor Di Nona 23
00186 Rome Italy
Phone: +39 06 6861916

#286
Da Giovanni
Category: Italian
Average Price: €21-40
Area: Termini
Address: Via Antonio Salandra 1
00187 Rome Italy
Phone: +39 06 485950

#287
Alice Pizza Point
Category: Pizza
Average Price: €8-20
Area: Termini
Address: Via Flavia 91
00187 Rome Italy
Phone: +39 06 42743445

#288
Osteria Le Coq
Category: Italian
Average Price: €21-40
Area: Monteverde
Address: Viale Di Villa Pamphili 35C
00152 Rome Italy
Phone: +39 06 58335146

#289
Sahara
Category: African, Italian
Average Price: €8-20
Area: San Lorenzo
Address: Viale Ippocrate 43
00161 Rome Italy
Phone: +39 06 44242063

#290
Yasashi Sa
Category: Japanese, Chinese
Average Price: €8-20
Area: Tiburtino
Address: Via Dei Durantini 12
00157 Rome Italy
Phone: +39 06 4386910

#291
I Vascellari
Category: Romen
Average Price: €8-20
Area: Trastevere
Address: Via Vascellari 21
00153 Rome Italy
Phone: +39 06 58334628

#292
Er Buchetto
Category: Sandwiches
Average Price: €21-40
Area: Termini, Centro Storico
Address: Via Del Viminale 2F
00184 Rome Italy
Phone: +39 06 4883031

#293
Casina Valadier
Category: Italian, Lounge
Average Price: Above €41
Area: Pinciano, Flaminio
Address: Piazza Bucarest
00187 Rome Italy
Phone: +39 06 69922090

#294
La Bottega Del Caff'
Category: Coffee &Tea, Café
Average Price: €21-40
Area: Monti
Address: Piazza Madonna Dei Monti 5
00184 Rome Italy
Phone: +39 06 4741578

#295
La Carbonara
Category: Romen
Average Price: €8-20
Area: Centro Storico
Address: Campo De' Fiori 23
00186 Rome Italy
Phone: +39 06 6864783

#296
Pizzeria Ternana
Category: Pizza
Average Price: €8-20
Area: Nomentano
Address: Via Alessandria 170
00198 Rome Italy
Phone: +39 06 44250384

#297
Bistro By Linda
Category: Mexican
Average Price: €21-40
Area: San Lorenzo
Address: Via Eleonora d'Arborea 15
00162 Rome Italy
Phone: +39 06 44244889

#298
Tiger Tandoori
Category: Indian
Average Price: €8-20
Area: Pigneto
Address: Via Del Pigneto 193
00176 Rome Italy
Phone: +39 06 97610172

#299
Melograno
Category: Pizza, Gelato
Average Price: Under €7
Area: Centro Storico
Address: Piazza Di Trevi 101
00187 Rome Italy
Phone: +39 06 6792802

#300
Mexico All'aventino
Category: Mexican
Average Price: Above €41
Area: Aventino
Address: Viale Aventino 83
00153 Rome Italy
Phone: +39 06 57289447

#301
Madame Baguette
Category: French, Sandwiches
Average Price: €8-20
Area: Termini
Address: Via Boncompagni 81
00187 Rome Italy
Phone: +39 06 42013072

#302
Cave Canem
Category: Pizza, Italian
Average Price: €8-20
Area: Trastevere
Address: Piazza San Calisto 11
00153 Rome Italy
Phone: +39 06 5898217

#303
Osteria Pistoia
Category: Italian
Average Price: €21-40
Area: Monteverde
Address: Piazza Madonna Della
Salette 13, 00152 Rome Italy
Phone: +39 06 58203381

#304
Spirito Di Vino
Category: Italian
Average Price: €8-20
Area: Trastevere
Address: Via Dei Genovesi 31A
00153 Rome Italy
Phone: +39 06 5896689

#305
Zia Rosetta
Category: Sandwiches
Average Price: €8-20
Area: Monti
Address: Via Urbana 54
00184 Rome Italy
Phone: +39 06 31052516

#306
La Vacca 'Mbriaca
Category: Italian
Average Price: €8-20
Area: Monti
Address: Via Urbana 29
00184 Rome Italy
Phone: +39 06 48907118

#307
Time Piadina Artigianale
Category: Fast Food, Specialty Food
Average Price: €8-20
Area: Centro Storico
Address: Piazza Del Teatro Di Pompeo 3
00186 Rome Italy
Phone: +39 06 45504430

#308
Bar Viminale
Category: Bar, Café
Average Price: €8-20
Area: Centro Storico
Address: Via Del Viminale 47
00184 Rome Italy
Phone: +39 06 486941

#309
Bar Brunori
Category: Café, Bar
Average Price: €8-20
Area: Aventino, Ostiense
Address: Largo Giovanni Chiarini 2
00154 Rome Italy
Phone: +39 06 5746418

#310
Er Faciolaro
Category: Romen
Average Price: €8-20
Area: Centro Storico
Address: Via Dei Pastino 122
00186 Rome Italy
Phone: +39 06 6783896

#311
Dobar
Category: Italian, Café
Average Price: €8-20
Area: Centro Storico
Address: Via Delle Carrozze 61
00187 Rome Italy
Phone: +39 06 69797096

#312
Da Giggi
Category: Italian
Average Price: Under €7
Area: Centro Storico
Address: Via Belsiana 94A
00187 Rome Italy
Phone: +39 06 6791130

#313
Taverna Rossini
Category: Pizza, Italian
Average Price: €21-40
Area: Parioli
Address: Viale Gioacchhino Rossini 54
00198 Rome Italy
Phone: +39 06 84242903

#314
Ai Vespri Siciliani
Category: Sicilian
Average Price: €21-40
Area: Balduina/Montemario
Address: Piazzale Delle Medaglie
d'Oro 22, 00138 Rome Italy
Phone: +39 06 35340324

#315
Gianni 3
Category: Italian
Average Price: €8-20
Area: Nomentano, Salario
Address: Via Lago Di Lesina, 81
00199 Rome Italy
Phone: +39 06 8601593

#316
Pasticceria Rosticceria Salentina
Category: Desserts, Apulian
Average Price: €8-20
Area: Salario
Address: Via Lago Tana 51
00199 Rome Italy
Phone: +39 06 86203994

#317
La Mucca Bischera
Category: Italian, Pizza
Average Price: €21-40
Area: Termini, San Giovanni
Address: Via Degli Equi 56
00185 Rome Italy
Phone: +39 06 4469349

#318
Taverna Egeo
Category: Greek
Average Price: €21-40
Area: Pigneto
Address: Via Augusto Dulceri 99
00176 Rome Italy
Phone: +39 06 273807

#319
Hostaria Del Moro
Category: Italian
Average Price: €8-20
Area: Trastevere
Address: Vicolo Del Cinque 36
00153 Rome Italy
Phone: +39 06 5809165

#320
ARometicus
Category: Salad, Juice Bar
Average Price: €8-20
Area: Monti
Address: Via Urbana 134
00184 Rome Italy
Phone: +39 06 4881355

#321
Trattoria Da Olindo
Category: Italian
Average Price: €8-20
Area: Trastevere
Address: Vicolo Della Scala 8
00153 Rome Italy
Phone: +39 06 5818835

#322
Illy Espressamente
Category: Café, Italian
Average Price: €21-40
Area: Centro Storico
Address: Via Degli Uffici Del Vicario 31
00186 Rome Italy
Phone: +39 06 87782701

#323
I Due Ciccioni
Category: Italian
Average Price: €21-40
Area: Trastevere
Address: Vicolo Del Cedro 3
00153 Rome Italy
Phone: +39 339 4775805

#324
433 Next Bar
Category: European
Average Price: €8-20
Area: Centro Storico
Address: Via Del Governo Vecchio 123
00186 Rome Italy
Phone: +39 06 68308796

#325
Osteria Della Vite
Category: Italian
Average Price: €8-20
Area: Centro Storico
Address: Via Della Vite 96
00187 Rome Italy
Phone: +39 06 69797680

#326
Da Roberto E Loretta
Category: Italian
Average Price: €8-20
Area: San Giovanni
Address: Via Saturnia 18
00183 Rome Italy
Phone: +39 06 77201037

#327
Il Pomodorino
Category: Italian, Pizza
Average Price: €8-20
Area: Termini
Address: Via Campania 45E
00187 Rome Italy
Phone: +39 06 42011356

#328
Il Tempio Di Minerva
Category: Italian
Average Price: €8-20
Area: Termini
Address: Viale Manzoni, 64, 66, 68
00185 Rome Italy
Phone: +39 06 44704714

#329
Lancelot
Category: Pub, Italian
Average Price: Under €7
Area: Termini, San Giovanni
Address: Via Dei Volsci 77
00185 Rome Italy
Phone: +39 06 4454675

#330
Ambasciata
Category: Pizza
Average Price: €21-40
Area: Prati
Address: Via Ennio Quirino Visconti 52
00193 Rome Italy
Phone: +39 06 89928794

#331
La Grotta Azzurra
Category: Seafood
Average Price: €21-40
Area: Prati
Address: Via Cicerone 62A
00193 Rome Italy
Phone: +39 06 3234586

#332
I San Pietrini
Category: Mediterranean, Deli
Average Price: €8-20
Area: Borgo
Address: Via Delle Fornaci 89
00165 Rome Italy
Phone: +39 06 43418462

#333
Tram Tram
Category: Italian
Average Price: €21-40
Area: San Lorenzo, San Giovanni
Address: Via Dei Reti 44
00185 Rome Italy
Phone: +39 06 490416

#334
Da Benito E Gilberto Al Falco
Category: Seafood, Italian
Average Price: Above €41
Area: Prati
Address: Via Del Falco 19
00193 Rome Italy
Phone: +39 06 6867769

#335
Fratelli La Bufala
Category: Pizza, Italian
Average Price: €8-20
Area: Pinciano
Address: Via Velletri 22
00198 Rome Italy
Phone: +39 06 853044696

#336
L'Archetto
Category: Pizza
Average Price: €8-20
Area: Prati
Address: Via Germanico 105
00192 Rome Italy
Phone: +39 06 3231163

#337
Sciascia Caff'
Category: Café, Desserts
Average Price: €8-20
Area: Prati
Address: Via Fabio Massimo 80A
00192 Rome Italy
Phone: +39 06 3211580

#338
Osteria Di Monteverde
Category: Romen, Seafood
Average Price: €8-20
Area: Monteverde
Address: Via Pietro Cartoni 163
00152 Rome Italy
Phone: +39 06 53273887

#339
Buffi Bistrot
Category: Brasserie, Deli
Average Price: €8-20
Area: Pigneto
Address: Via Braccio Da Montone 3
00176 Rome Italy
Phone: +39 06 96035820

#340
Vanni
Category: Desserts, Ice Cream
Average Price: Above €41
Area: Prati
Address: Via Col Di Lana 10
00195 Rome Italy
Phone: +39 06 45425075

#341
Ginza
Category: Japanese
Average Price: Above €41
Area: Esquilino
Address: Via Emanuele Filiberto 251
00185 Rome Italy
Phone: +39 06 7005739

#342
La Gallina Capricciosa
Category: Peruvian
Average Price: €8-20
Area: Flaminio
Address: Via Giuseppe Sacconi 53
00196 Rome Italy
Phone: +39 06 3236234

#343
Kilo
Category: Steakhouse
Average Price: €21-40
Area: Pinciano, Salario
Address: Via Tirso 30
00198 Rome Italy
Phone: +39 06 64781752

#344
Zoc
Category: Italian
Average Price: €21-40
Area: Centro Storico
Address: Via Delle Zoccolette 22
00186 Rome Italy
Phone: +39 06 68192515

#345
Libreria Giuf'
Category: Bookstore, Organic Store
Average Price: €8-20
Area: San Giovanni
Address: Via Degli Aurunci 38
00185 Rome Italy
Phone: +39 06 44361406

#346
La Pariolina
Category: Pizza, Italian
Average Price: €21-40
Area: Salario, Parioli
Address: Viale Parioli 93
00197 Rome Italy
Phone: +39 06 8086002

#347
Fuji
Category: Japanese, Chinese
Average Price: €8-20
Area: Tiburtino
Address: Via Tiburtina 717
00159 Rome Italy
Phone: +39 06 89026299

#348
A Casa Di Alice
Category: Italian
Average Price: €8-20
Area: Nomentano, Pinciano
Address: Via Bergamo 34
00198 Rome Italy
Phone: +39 06 8549737

#349
Acquolina
Category: Seafood, Italian
Average Price: Above €41
Area: Corso Francia
Address: Via Antonio Serra 60
00191 Rome Italy
Phone: +39 06 3337192

#350
La Cicala E La Formica
Category: Mediterranean, Italian
Average Price: €8-20
Area: Monti
Address: Via Leonina 17
00186 Rome Italy
Phone: +39 06 4817490

#351
Ciuri Ciuri
Category: Desserts, Café
Average Price: €8-20
Area: Esquilino
Address: Via Labicana 126
00184 Rome Italy
Phone: +39 06 45424856

#352
Antico Caff' Del Moro
Category: Beer, Wine, Spirits, Café
Average Price: €8-20
Area: Trastevere
Address: Via Del Moro 38
00153 Rome Italy
Phone: +39 06 5806885

#353
Chocolat
Category: Café, Italian
Average Price: €8-20
Area: Centro Storico
Address: Via Della Dogana Vecchia 12
00186 Rome Italy
Phone: +39 06 68135545

#354
Sangallo
Category: Romen
Average Price: Above €41
Area: Centro Storico
Address: Via Dei Coronari 180
00186 Rome Italy
Phone: +39 06 68134055

#355
Oishi
Category: Japanese, Chinese
Average Price: €21-40
Area: Testaccio, Ostiense
Address: Via Del Gazometro 40B
00154 Rome Italy
Phone: +39 06 57302376

#356
Brassai
Category: Café
Average Price: €8-20
Area: Centro Storico
Address: Via Di Panico 28
00186 Rome Italy
Phone: +39 06 68210325

#357
Lo Stil Novo
Category: Italian
Average Price: €21-40
Area: Termini
Address: Via Sicilia 66B
00187 Rome Italy
Phone: +39 06 43411810

#358
La Taverna Dei Mercanti
Category: Italian
Average Price: €21-40
Area: Trastevere
Address: Piazza Dei Mercanti 3
00153 Rome Italy
Phone: +39 06 5881693

#359
Jenny A San Lorenzo
Category: Italian
Average Price: €8-20
Area: San Giovanni
Address: Piazza Dei Campani 14
00185 Rome Italy
Phone: +39 339 6930203

#360
Il Pasticciaccio
Category: Lounge, Café
Average Price: €8-20
Area: Esquilino
Address: Via Merulana 34
00185 Rome Italy
Phone: +39 06 4826928

#361
Caff' Scolastici
Category: Café
Average Price: €8-20
Area: Ostiense
Address: Via Guglielmo Marconi 98
00146 Rome Italy
Phone: +39 06 5584366

#362
Al Casale
Category: Pizza
Average Price: €8-20
Area: Montesacro/Talenti
Address: Via Del Casale Rocchi 27A
00158 Rome Italy
Phone: +39 06 41730599

#363
Pizzeria Goose
Category: Pizza
Average Price: €8-20
Area: Borgo, Prati
Address: Via Gregorio Vii 34
00165 Rome Italy
Phone: +39 06 39366269

#364
Dal Toscano
Category: Tuscan
Average Price: Above €41
Area: Prati
Address: Via Germanico 58
00192 Rome Italy
Phone: +39 06 39725717

#365
Pizzeria Leonina
Category: Pizza, Fast Food
Average Price: €8-20
Area: Monti
Address: Via Leonina 84
00184 Rome Italy
Phone: +39 06 4827744

#366
Carrot's
Category: Italian, Sports Bar
Average Price: €8-20
Area: Parioli
Address: Piazza Euclide 1
00197 Rome Italy
Phone: +39 06 8074594

#367
I Tre Pupazzi
Category: Portuguese, Italian
Average Price: €8-20
Area: Prati
Address: Via Dei Tre Pupazzi 1
00193 Rome Italy
Phone: +39 06 68803220

#368
Ai Balestrari
Category: Romen
Average Price: €8-20
Area: Centro Storico
Address: Via Dei Balestrari 41
00186 Rome Italy
Phone: +39 06 6865377

#369
Il Duca
Category: Romen
Average Price: €8-20
Area: Trastevere
Address: Vicolo De' Cinque 52
00153 Rome Italy
Phone: +39 06 5817706

#370
Luna Caprese
Category: Pizza
Average Price: €8-20
Area: Nomentano
Address: Via Val Pellice 1
00141 Rome Italy
Phone: +39 06 88643049

#371
The Gallery Caf'
Category: Café
Average Price: €8-20
Area: Centro Storico
Address: Via Del Tritone 36
00187 Rome Italy
Phone: +39 06 89682434

#372
Serafini Alla Pace
Category: Italian
Average Price: €21-40
Area: Centro Storico
Address: Via Di Tor Millina 1
00186 Rome Italy
Phone: +39 06 68809843

#373
Ricomincio Da Tre
Category: Pizza, Italian
Average Price: €8-20
Area: San Giovanni
Address: Via Amiterno 56
00183 Rome Italy
Phone: +39 06 7081150

#374
Il Bosco Degli Elfi
Category: Italian
Average Price: €8-20
Area: Tuscolano
Address: Via Tuscolana 822
00174 Rome Italy
Phone: +39 06 7140382

#375
Il Maritozzaro
Category: Bar, Café
Average Price: €8-20
Area: Trastevere
Address: Via Ettore Rolli 50
00153 Rome Italy
Phone: +39 06 5810781

#376
Sukhothai
Category: Thai
Average Price: €21-40
Area: Monteverde
Address: Via Andrea Busiri Vici 48
00152 Rome Italy
Phone: +39 06 55263993

#377
Da Ezio - Le Scalette
Category: Italian
Average Price: €21-40
Area: Salario
Address: Via Chiana 89
00198 Rome Italy
Phone: +39 06 8551109

#378
Spaccanapoli
Category: Pizza, Italian
Average Price: €21-40
Area: San Giovanni
Address: Via Eurialo 10D
00181 Rome Italy
Phone: +39 06 7847147

#379
Dar Moschino
Category: Italian
Average Price: €21-40
Area: Ostiense
Address: Piazza Benedetto Brin 5
00154 Rome Italy
Phone: +39 06 5139473

#380
Conte Staccio
Category: Music Venues, Lounge
Average Price: €8-20
Area: Testaccio, Ostiense
Address: Via Di Monte Testaccio 65B
00153 Rome Italy
Phone: +39 06 57289712

#381
Sicilia In Bocca
Category: Italian
Average Price: €21-40
Area: Prati
Address: Via Emilio Faa' Di Bruno 26
00195 Rome Italy
Phone: +39 06 37358400

#382
La Sagra Del Vino
Category: Italian
Average Price: €8-20
Area: Balduina/Montemario
Address: Via Marziale 5
00136 Rome Italy
Phone: +39 06 39737015

#383
San Marco
Category: Pizza
Average Price: €8-20
Area: Prati
Address: Via Tacito 29
00193 Rome Italy
Phone: +39 06 3235398

#384
Mamma Angelina
Category: Italian
Average Price: €21-40
Area: Salario
Address: Via Arrigo Boito 65
00199 Rome Italy
Phone: +39 06 8608928

#385
0,75 - Zerosettantacinque
Category: Wine Bar, Italian
Average Price: €8-20
Area: Aventino
Address: Via Dei Cerchi 65
00186 Rome Italy
Phone: +39 06 6875706

#386
Yoshi
Category: Japanese
Average Price: Above €41
Area: Testaccio, Ostiense
Address: Via Ostiense 64
00154 Rome Italy
Phone: +39 06 5745227

#387
Iari The Vino
Category: Italian
Average Price: €8-20
Area: Monti
Address: Via Del Colosseo, 5
00184 Rome Italy
Phone: +39 06 69191069

#388
Il Buttero
Category: Romen
Average Price: €8-20
Area: Trastevere
Address: Via Della Lungaretta 156
00153 Rome Italy
Phone: +39 06 5800517

#389
Broccoletti
Category: Romen
Average Price: €8-20
Area: Monti
Address: Via Urbana 104
00184 Rome Italy
Phone: +39 06 4742772

#390
Dolce Amaro
Category: Café
Average Price: €8-20
Area: Centro Storico
Address: Via Delle Quattro Fontane 38
00184 Rome Italy
Phone: +39 06 48903344

#391
Da Trani
Category: Seafood, Romen
Average Price: €8-20
Area: Centro Storico
Address: Via Genova 22
00184 Rome Italy
Phone: +39 06 4881396

#392
Leon D'Oro
Category: Italian
Average Price: €8-20
Area: Centro Storico
Address: Via Sistina 9
00187 Rome Italy
Phone: +39 06 42020326

#393
Antica Norcineria
Category: Deli
Average Price: €8-20
Area: Centro Storico
Address: Via Della Scrofa 100
00186 Rome Italy
Phone: +39 06 68801074

#394
Osteria Dell'antiquario
Category: Italian
Average Price: €21-40
Area: Centro Storico
Address: Piazzetta Di San Simeone,
26/27, 00186 Rome Italy
Phone: +39 06 6879694

#395
Addo' Masto
Category: Italian
Average Price: Under €7
Area: Ostiense
Address: Via Giacomo Bove 43
00154 Rome Italy
Phone: +39 06 5746372

#396
Brunello
Category: Wine Bar, Italian
Average Price: Above €41
Area: Termini, Centro Storico
Address: Via Vittorio Veneto 70A
00187 Rome Italy
Phone: +39 06 48902867

#397
Gaetano Costa
Category: Italian
Average Price: Above €41
Area: Termini
Address: Via Sicilia 45
00187 Rome Italy
Phone: +39 06 42016731

#398
Osteria Pesce Fritto E Baccal'
Category: Romen
Average Price: €8-20
Area: Termini
Address: Via Dei Falisci 4
00185 Rome Italy
Phone: +39 06 64501183

#399
Al Forno Della Soffitta
Category: Italian
Average Price: €8-20
Area: Termini
Address: Via Piave 62
00187 Rome Italy
Phone: +39 06 42011164

#400
Osteria Del Cavaliere
Category: Italian
Average Price: €8-20
Area: San Giovanni
Address: Via Alba, 32
00182 Rome Italy
Phone: +39 06 64850434

#401
La Soffitta Renovatio
Category: Pizza, Italian
Average Price: €8-20
Area: Prati
Address: Piazza Del Risorgimento 46A
00192 Rome Italy
Phone: +39 06 68892977

#402
Il Quagliaro
Category: Italian
Average Price: €8-20
Area: Casilino
Address: Largo Mola Di Bari 17
00171 Rome Italy
Phone: +39 06 25210875

#403
Pizzeria Est Est Est Ricci
Category: Pizza
Average Price: €8-20
Area: Centro Storico
Address: Via Genova 32
00184 Rome Italy
Phone: +39 06 4881107

#404
Trattoria Da Carlo
Category: Italian
Average Price: €8-20
Area: Pigneto
Address: Via Di Acqua Bullicante 106
00177 Rome Italy
Phone: +39 06 45597925

#405
Peperino
Category: Food Delivery Service, Pizza
Average Price: €8-20
Area: Tiburtino
Address: Via C. Facchinetti 54
00159 Rome Italy
Phone: +39 06 43253291

#406
Giuseppe Tornatora
Category: Desserts, Cafè
Average Price: €8-20
Area: Balduina/Montemario
Address: Via Igea 14
00135 Rome Italy
Phone: +39 06 35501816

#407
Il Secchio E L'Olivaro
Category: Pizza
Average Price: €8-20
Area: Aurelia
Address: Via Portuense 958
00148 Rome Italy
Phone: +39 06 6552192

#408
Al Gallo Rosso
Category: Italian, Pizza
Average Price: €8-20
Area: Nomentano
Address: Via Di Vigna Mangani 13
00158 Rome Italy
Phone: +39 338 7410147

#409
Gaudeo
Category: Sandwiches
Average Price: €8-20
Area: Monti
Address: Via Del Boschetto 12
00184 Rome Italy
Phone: +39 06 98183689

#410
Miscellanea
Category: Italian
Average Price: €8-20
Area: Centro Storico
Address: Via Della Palombella 34
00186 Rome Italy
Phone: +39 06 68135318

#411
Pizzeria Nuovo Mondo
Category: Pizza
Average Price: Under €7
Area: Testaccio, Ostiense
Address: Via Amerigo Vespucci 15
00153 Rome Italy
Phone: +39 06 5746004

#412
Retro
Category: Italian
Average Price: €21-40
Area: Ostiense
Address: Via Enrico Dal Pozzo 5
00146 Rome Italy
Phone: +39 00 39065574370

#413
InRome
Category: Italian
Average Price: €21-40
Area: Centro Storico
Address: Via Dei Fienili 56
00186 Rome Italy
Phone: +39 06 69191024

#414
La Taverna Del Ghetto
Category: Italian
Average Price: €21-40
Area: Centro Storico
Address: Via Portico D'ottavia 8
00186 Rome Italy
Phone: +39 06 68809771

#415
Renato E Luisa
Category: Romen
Average Price: €21-40
Area: Centro Storico
Address: Via Dei Barbieri 25
00186 Rome Italy
Phone: +39 06 6869660

#416
Terrazza Barberini
Category: Cucina Campana
Average Price: €8-20
Area: Centro Storico
Address: Via Barberini 16
00187 Rome Italy
Phone: +39 06 42010644

#417
Caff' Domiziano
Category: Pizza, Italian
Average Price: €21-40
Area: Centro Storico
Address: Piazza Navona 88
00186 Rome Italy
Phone: +39 06 68806845

#418
Birrifugio
Category: Pub, Romen
Average Price: €8-20
Area: Trastevere
Address: Via Federico Rosazza 6
00153 Rome Italy
Phone: +39 06 58303189

#419
Crostaceria Sa Tanca
Category: Italian
Average Price: €21-40
Area: Monti, Centro Storico
Address: Via Palermo 57
00184 Rome Italy
Phone: +39 06 48913347

#420
Taverna Le Coppelle
Category: Italian
Average Price: €8-20
Area: Centro Storico
Address: Via Delle Coppelle 38
00186 Rome Italy
Phone: +39 06 68806557

#421
Dolce Vita
Category: Bar, Italian
Average Price: €8-20
Area: Centro Storico
Address: Piazza Navona 70
00186 Rome Italy
Phone: +39 06 68806221

#422
Pasticceria Crochon
Category: Desserts, Café
Average Price: €8-20
Area: Testaccio, Ostiense
Address: Via Del Gazometro 11
00154 Rome Italy
Phone: +39 06 5741326

#423
Orsini Pizza
Category: Pizza
Average Price: €8-20
Area: San Giovanni
Address: Via Magnagrecia, 38
00183 Rome Italy
Phone: +39 06 77208770

#424
Mandaloun
Category: Middle Eastern
Average Price: €21-40
Area: Termini, Pinciano, Centro Storico
Address: Via Porta Pinciana 16B
00187 Rome Italy
Phone: +39 06 64824507

#425
Divin Peccato
Category: Italian
Average Price: Above €41
Area: Borgo
Address: Piazza Della Rovere 84
00165 Rome Italy
Phone: +39 06 97605991

#426
Ferrovecchio
Category: Burgers
Average Price: €8-20
Area: Termini, San Giovanni
Address: Via Dei Sabelli 32
00185 Rome Italy
Phone: +39 06 446002

#427
I Quattro Mori
Category: Italian
Average Price: €8-20
Area: Borgo
Address: Via Delle Fornaci 8
00165 Rome Italy
Phone: +39 06 632609

#428
Pizzeria Gaudi
Category: Pizza
Average Price: €8-20
Area: Pinciano
Address: Via Ruggero Giovannelli, 8/12
00198 Rome Italy
Phone: +39 06 8845451

#429
Celebrit'
Category: Chinese
Average Price: €8-20
Area: Tiburtino
Address: Via Igino Giordani 53
00159 Rome Italy
Phone: +39 06 4064005

#430
Cu Mangia Crisci
Category: Sicilian
Average Price: Under €7
Area: Ostiense
Address: Via Chiabrera 162
00145 Rome Italy
Phone: +39 06 5415720

#431
Trattoria Moderna
Category: Italian
Average Price: €8-20
Area: Centro Storico
Address: Vicolo Dei Chiodaroli 16
00186 Rome Italy
Phone: +39 06 68803423

#432
Il Ciak
Category: Italian
Average Price: €21-40
Area: Trastevere
Address: Vicolo Del Cinque 21
00153 Rome Italy
Phone: +39 06 5894774

#433
Ciro Kebab Pizza
Category: Kebab, Pizza
Average Price: Under €7
Area: Casilino
Address: Via Dei Castani 251A
00171 Rome Italy
Phone: +39 06 4384173

#434
La Sandwicheria
Category: Sandwiches
Average Price: €8-20
Area: Centro Storico
Address: Largo Del Nazareno 16
00187 Rome Italy
Phone: +39 06 69797805

#435
Il Baretto
Category: Coffee &Tea, Café
Average Price: €8-20
Area: Monteverde
Address: Via Garibaldi 28
00153 Rome Italy
Phone: +39 06 58205716

#436
Antica Trattoria Polese
Category: Italian
Average Price: €21-40
Area: Centro Storico
Address: Piazza Sforza Cesarini 40
00186 Rome Italy
Phone: +39 06 6861709

#437
Rosso
Category: Italian
Average Price: €21-40
Area: Aventino
Address: Viale Aventino 32
00153 Rome Italy
Phone: +39 06 64420656

#438
Trattoria Da Bucatino
Category: Italian
Average Price: €8-20
Area: Testaccio, Ostiense
Address: Via Luca Della Robbia 84
00153 Rome Italy
Phone: +39 06 5746886

#439
I Capperi
Category: Pizza
Average Price: €21-40
Area: Balduina/Montemario
Address: Via Damiano Chiesa 12
00136 Rome Italy
Phone: +39 06 35340085

#440
T &T Caff'
Category: Café, Italian
Average Price: €8-20
Area: Ostiense
Address: Piazzale Eugenio Morelli 33
00151 Rome Italy
Phone: +39 06 65793241

#441
'O Famo Strano
Category: Sandwiches
Average Price: Under €7
Area: San Giovanni
Address: Viale Dello Scalo San
Lorenzo 11, 00185 Rome Italy
Phone: +39 327 0040637

#442
Er Panonto
Category: Pizza
Average Price: €8-20
Area: Ostiense
Address: Via Enrico Cravero 10
00154 Rome Italy
Phone: +39 06 5135022

#443
Go Thai
Category: Vietnamese, Thai
Average Price: €21-40
Area: Appia Antica
Address: Via Cesare Baronio 141
00179 Rome Italy
Phone: +39 06 78384683

#444
Le Tavernelle
Category: Italian
Average Price: €8-20
Area: Monti
Address: Via Panisperna 48
00184 Rome Italy
Phone: +39 06 4740724

#445
Insalata Ricca
Category: Italian
Average Price: €8-20
Area: Aventino
Address: Piazza Albania 3
00153 Rome Italy
Phone: +39 06 5743877

#446
Montecaruso
Category: Italian
Average Price: €21-40
Area: Termini
Address: Via Farini 12
00185 Rome Italy
Phone: +39 06 483549

#447
Il Condor
Category: Italian, Pizza
Average Price: €8-20
Area: Termini
Address: Via Daniele Manin 50
00185 Rome Italy
Phone: +39 06 4880805

#448
Taverna Pretoriana
Category: Italian
Average Price: Under €7
Area: Termini
Address: Via Palestro 46
00185 Rome Italy
Phone: +39 390 64450273

#449
San Lollo
Category: Italian
Average Price: €8-20
Area: Termini, San Giovanni
Address: Via Dei Sabelli 51
00185 Rome Italy
Phone: +39 06 4940726

#450
Grand Dragon
Category: Chinese
Average Price: €8-20
Area: Nomentano
Address: Via Nomentana 49
00161 Rome Italy
Phone: +39 06 44250314

#451
Cantiani
Category: Café, Coffee &Tea
Average Price: €8-20
Area: Prati
Address: Via Cola Di Rienzo 234
00192 Rome Italy
Phone: +39 06 6874164

#452
Osteria Dei Pazzi
Category: Romen
Average Price: €21-40
Area: Ostiense
Address: Via Enrico Cravero 22
00154 Rome Italy
Phone: +39 06 97613866

#453
Quei Bravi Ragazzi
Category: Café
Average Price: €8-20
Area: San Giovanni
Address: Via Enna 2
00182 Rome Italy
Phone: +39 328 8677836

#454
Hostaria Natalino E Maurizio
Category: Italian
Average Price: €21-40
Area: Corso Francia
Address: Corso Francia 115
00191 Rome Italy
Phone: +39 06 3332730

#455
Sacco
Category: Pizza, Italian
Average Price: €21-40
Area: Tuscolano, San Giovanni
Address: Via Amelia 77
00181 Rome Italy
Phone: +39 06 7808007

#456
Da Francesco
Category: Italian
Average Price: €8-20
Area: Tuscolano, Casilino
Address: Via Casilina 493
00177 Rome Italy
Phone: +39 06 2413229

#457
Tbar
Category: Lounge, Wine Bar
Average Price: €8-20
Area: Ostiense
Address: Viale Ostiense 182A
00154 Rome Italy
Phone: +39 06 5740009

#458
Pigneto Quarantuno
Category: Italian
Average Price: €8-20
Area: San Giovanni
Address: Via Del Pigneto 41
00176 Rome Italy
Phone: +39 06 70399483

#459
Inka's Grill
Category: Peruvian
Average Price: €21-40
Area: Balduina/Montemario
Address: Via Del Forte Boccea 96
00167 Rome Italy
Phone: +39 06 97270531

#460
29 Metri Quadri
Category: Lounge, Wine Bar
Average Price: Under €7
Area: Corso Francia
Address: Piazzale Di Ponte Milvio 31
00191 Rome Italy
Phone: +39 06 33219542

#461
Da Brando
Category: Italian
Average Price: €8-20
Area: Corso Francia
Address: Via Flaminia 534
00191 Rome Italy
Phone: +39 06 33225327

#462
Crazy Bull
Category: American, Burgers
Average Price: €8-20
Area: Corso Francia
Address: Via Riano 1
00191 Rome Italy
Phone: +39 06 3338432

#463
Istanbul Kebab
Category: Kebab
Average Price: €8-20
Area: Nomentano
Address: Via Nomentana Nuova 43
00141 Rome Italy
Phone: +39 06 88973688

#464
Al Basha Yaser Kebabbaro
Category: Kebab, Fast Food
Average Price: Under €7
Area: Nomentano
Address: Via Val Di Cogne 46
00141 Rome Italy
Phone: +39 349 4587650

#465
Ilocale
Category: Italian, Beer, Wine, Spirits
Average Price: €8-20
Area: Nomentano
Address: Via Peralba 2A
00141 Rome Italy
Phone: +39 06 8182620

#466
Hostaria Mamutones
Category: Italian
Average Price: €21-40
Area: Bufalotta
Address: Piazza Monte Gennaro 29
00139 Rome Italy
Phone: +39 06 8185237

#467
Giggetto Il Re Della Pizza
Category: Pizza
Average Price: €8-20
Area: Nomentano, Pinciano
Address: Via Alessandria 43
00198 Rome Italy
Phone: +39 06 8412527

#468
Insalata Ricca
Category: Pizza, Italian
Average Price: €8-20
Area: Citt'Del Vaticano, Prati
Address: Piazza Risorgimento 4
00192 Rome Italy
Phone: +39 06 39730387

#469
Haus Garten Bagel Bar
Category: Bar, Bagels
Average Price: €8-20
Area: Prati
Address: Piazza Monte Grappa 1
00195 Rome Italy
Phone: +39 06 32120073

#470
I Gladiatori
Category: Italian, Pizza
Average Price: €8-20
Area: Bufalotta
Address: Via Della Bufalotta, 131
00139 Rome Italy
Phone: +39 06 87202090

#471
Tor Cervara 109
Category: Romen
Average Price: €8-20
Area: Tiburtino
Address: Via Di Tor Cervara 109
00155 Rome Italy
Phone: +39 334 8912475

#472
Mejo De Betto E Mary
Category: Romen
Average Price: €21-40
Area: Montesacro/Talenti
Address: Via Di Pietralata 150
00158 Rome Italy
Phone: +39 06 606662318

#473
Bottiglieria Pigneto
Category: Breakfast &Brunch, Café
Average Price: €8-20
Area: Pigneto
Address: Via Del Pigneto 106A
00176 Rome Italy
Phone: +39 06 272362

#474
Enoteca Corsi
Category: Italian
Average Price: €8-20
Area: Centro Storico
Address: Via Del Ges'87
00186 Rome Italy
Phone: +39 06 6790821

#475
La Limonaia
Category: Pizza
Average Price: €21-40
Area: Nomentano
Address: Via Spallanziani 1
00161 Rome Italy
Phone: +39 06 4404021

#476
Mangiafuoco
Category: Italian
Average Price: €21-40
Area: Salario
Address: Via Chiana 37
00198 Rome Italy
Phone: +39 06 85357255

#477
Makoto
Category: Japanese
Average Price: €8-20
Area: San Lorenzo
Address: Via Beniamino De Ritis 10
00157 Rome Italy
Phone: +39 06 4383754

#478
Wiener House
Category: Austrian, European
Average Price: €8-20
Area: Bufalotta
Address: Via Alberto Lionello 201
00139 Rome Italy
Phone: +39 06 87070802

#479
Pizzeria Amalfi
Category: Pizza
Average Price: Under €7
Area: Prati
Address: Via Dei Gracchi 12
00192 Rome Italy
Phone: +39 06 39733165

#480
Porca Vacca
Category: Italian
Average Price: €8-20
Area: San Giovanni
Address: Via Dei Sabelli 99
00185 Rome Italy
Phone: +39 06 44361167

#481
Somo
Category: Japanese, Asian Fusion
Average Price: Above €41
Area: Trastevere
Address: Via Goffredo Mameli 5
00153 Rome Italy
Phone: +39 06 5882060

#482
Da Meo Patacca
Category: Italian
Average Price: €21-40
Area: Trastevere
Address: Piazza Dei Mercanti 30
00153 Rome Italy
Phone: +39 06 58331086

#483
Novecento
Category: Italian, European
Average Price: €8-20
Area: Testaccio, Ostiense
Address: Via Dei Conciatori, 10
00154 Rome Italy
Phone: +39 06 57250445

#484
Mare
Category: Seafood
Average Price: €8-20
Area: Flaminio
Address: Via Di Ripetta 242
00186 Rome Italy
Phone: +39 06 89017481

#485
Dal Pollarolo 1936
Category: Italian
Average Price: €8-20
Area: Flaminio
Address: Via Di Ripetta 4
00186 Rome Italy
Phone: +39 06 3610276

#486
Dar Bruttone
Category: Italian
Average Price: €8-20
Area: San Giovanni
Address: Via Taranto 118
00182 Rome Italy
Phone: +39 06 89024870

#487
Ris Caf'
Category: Pub, Italian
Average Price: €8-20
Area: Prati
Address: Piazza Risorgimento 16
00192 Rome Italy
Phone: +39 06 39754330

#488
Pizza Geg'
Category: Pizza
Average Price: Under €7
Area: Cassia
Address: Via Cassia 927
00189 Rome Italy
Phone: +39 06 30362548

#489
Ambasciata d'Abruzzo
Category: Romen
Average Price: €21-40
Area: Parioli
Address: Via Pietro Tacchini 26
00197 Rome Italy
Phone: +39 06 8078256

#490
I Due Leoni
Category: Pizza
Average Price: €8-20
Area: Montesacro/Talenti
Address: Via Ugo Ojetti 416
00137 Rome Italy
Phone: +39 06 8292169

#491
La Barrique
Category: Italian
Average Price: €8-20
Area: Monti, Centro Storico
Address: Via Del Boschetto 41B
00184 Rome Italy
Phone: +39 06 47825953

#492
Gustosito
Category: Bar, Café
Average Price: Under €7
Area: Ostiense
Address: Via Libetta 25
00154 Rome Italy
Phone: +39 06 5781367

#493
Specialit' Pizza Il Kebabbaro
Category: Turkish, Ethnic Food
Average Price: Under €7
Area: Prati
Address: Viale Giulio Cesare 126
00192 Rome Italy
Phone: +39 328 7640359

#494
El Puerto Latino
Category: Food, Fast Food
Average Price: Under €7
Area: San Giovanni
Address: Via L'Aquila 31
00176 Rome Italy
Phone: +39 331 8326538

#495
Mangia M'
Category: Sandwiches, Juice Bar
Average Price: Under €7
Area: Trastevere
Address: Via Benedetta 3
00153 Rome Italy
Phone: +39 06 58303360

#496
Pizza Design
Category: Kebab, Pizza
Average Price: Under €7
Area: Balduina/Montemario
Address: Via Cornelia 17
00165 Rome Italy
Phone: +39 06 6624284

#497
Sushime
Category: Japanese, Sushi Bar
Average Price: Under €7
Area: Pinciano
Address: Via Rieti 5
00198 Rome Italy
Phone: +39 06 85387331

#498
Pizza Magi
Category: Pizza
Average Price: Under €7
Area: Balduina/Montemario
Address: Piazza Carlo Mazzaresi 27
00136 Rome Italy
Phone: +39 06 35400321

#499
Trattoria Vaticano Giggi
Category: Italian
Average Price: Under €7
Area: Prati
Address: Via Catone 10
00192 Rome Italy
Phone: +39 06 39730551

#500
Il Bello Della Pizza
Category: Pizza
Average Price: Under €7
Area: San Lorenzo
Address: Via Di Portonaccio 33A
00159 Rome Italy
Phone: +39 06 43253144

TOP 100 ATTRACTIONS

Most Recommended by Locals & Trevelers
Ranking (from #1 to #100)

#1
Pantheon
Landmark/Historic
Area: Centro Storico
Address: Piazza Della Rotonda 2
00186 Rome Italy
Phone: +39 06 68300230

#2
Colosseo
Landmark/Historic, Train Stations,
Public Transportation
Area: Aventino
Address: Piazza Del Colosseo 1
00184 Rome Italy
Phone: +39 06 39967700

#3
Fontana Di Trevi
Landmark/Historic
Area: Centro Storico
Address: Piazza Di Trevi
00187 Rome Italy

#4
Piazza Navona
Landmark
Area: Centro Storico
Address: Piazza Navona
00186 Rome Italy

#5
Piazza San Pietro
Landmark
Area: Borgo
Address: Piazza San Pietro
00165 Rome Italy

#6
Foro Romeno
Museum
Area: Monti, Centro Storico
Address: Via Dei Fori Imperiali Rome,
Rome Italy

#7
**Museo Nazionale Castel
Sant'Angelo**
Museum
Area: Prati
Address: Lungotevere Castello 50
00186 Rome Italy
Phone: +39 06 6819111

#8
Piazza Del Popolo
Landmark
Area: Flaminio
Address: Piazza Del Popolo
00187 Rome Italy
Phone: +39 06 32651438

#9
Ponte Sant'Angelo
Landmark
Area: Centro Storico, Prati
Address: Piazza Ponte Sant'Angelo
00186 Rome Italy

#10
Piazza Campidoglio
Landmark
Area: Centro Storico
Address: Piazza Campidoglio
00186 Rome Italy

#11
Piazza Di Spagna
Landmark
Area: Centro Storico
Address: Piazza Di Spagna
00187 Rome Italy
Phone: +39 06 95557417

#12
Gianicolo
Landmark
Area: Monteverde
Address: Piazzale Giuseppe Garibaldi
00165 Rome Italy

#13
Arco Di Costantino
Landmark
Area: Aventino
Address: Piazza Del Colosseo
00100 Rome Italy

#14
Ara Pacis
Museum
Area: Flaminio
Address: Lungotevere In Augusta
00186 Rome Italy
Phone: +39 06 0608

#15
Gazometro
Landmark
Area: Testaccio, Ostiense
Address: Via Del Commercio
00154 Rome Italy

#16
Largo Di Torre Argentina
Landmark
Area: Centro Storico
Address: Via Di Torre Argentina
00186 Rome Italy
Phone: +39 06 45425240

#17
Cimitero Monumentale Del Verano
Landmark/Historic
Area: San Lorenzo
Address: Piazzale Del Verano, 1
00185 Rome Italy
Phone: +39 06 492361

#18
Pontificio Santuario Scala Santa
Church
Area: San Giovanni
Address: Piazza Di San Giovanni In
Laterano 14
00184 Rome Italy
Phone: +39 06 7726641

#19
Scuderie Del Quirinale
Area: Centro Storico
Address: Via XXIV Maggio 16
00184 Rome Italy
Phone: +39 06 39967500

#20
**Mercati Di Traiano
Museo Dei Fori Imperiali**
Museum
Area: Centro Storico
Address: Via IV Novembre 94
00187 Rome Italy
Phone: +39 06 0608

#21
Scalinata Di Trinit' Dei Monti
Landmark
Area: Centro Storico
Address: Piazza Di Spagna
00187 Rome Italy

#22
Palazzo Farnese
Landmark
Area: Centro Storico
Address: Piazza Farnese, 67
00186 Rome Italy
Phone: +39 06 686011

#23
Chiesa Di Sant'Ivo Alla Sapienza
Church
Area: Centro Storico
Address: Corso Del Rinascimento 40
00186 Rome Italy
Phone: +39 06 6864987

#24
Tempietto Del Bramante
Funeral Service, Cemetery
Area: Trastevere
Address: P.Zza S. Pietro In Montorio 2
00153 Rome Italy

#25
Piazza Mincio
Landmark
Area: Salario
Address: Piazza Mincio
00198 Rome Italy

#26
Catacombe S. Sebastiano
Museum, Church
Area: Appia Antica
Address: Via Appia Antica, 136
00178 Rome Italy
Phone: +39 06 7887035

#27
Basilica San Paolo Fuori Le Mura
Landmark/Historic
Area: Ostiense
Address: Piazzale Di San Paolo
00154 Rome Italy
Phone: +39 06 69880800

#28
Pyramid Of Cestius
Landmark/Historic
Area: Testaccio, Ostiense
Address: Piazzale Ostiense Rome,
Rome Italy

#29
**Basilica Di San Pietro In Vincoli
Al Colle Oppio**
Landmark, Church
Area: Monti
Address: Piazza Di San Pietro In Vincoli
4A, 00184 Rome Italy
Phone: +39 06 97844952

#30
Buco Della Serratura
Landmark/Historic
Area: Aventino
Address: Piazza De Cavalieri Di Malta
00153 Rome Italy

#31
Schl'sselloch
Landmark/Historic
Area: Aventino
Address: Piazza Dei Cavalieri Di Malta
00153 Rome Italy

#32
La Citt' Dell'acqua
Landmark/Historic
Area: Centro Storico
Address: Vicolo Del Puttarello 25
00187 Rome Italy
Phone: +39 339 7786192

#33
Pincio
Landmark/Historic
Area: Flaminio
Address: Piazza Del Popolo Rome,
Rome Italy

#34
Foro Traiano
Landmark/Historic
Area: Monti, Centro Storico
Address: Via Dei Fori Imperiali Rome,
Rome Italy

#35
Palazzo Del Quirinale
Landmark/Historic
Area: Centro Storico
Address: Piazza Del Quirinale
00187 Rome Italy
Phone: +39 06 46911

#36
Salone Delle Fontane
Landmark/Historic
Area: Eur
Address: Via Ciro Il Grande 10/12
00144 Rome Italy
Phone: +39 06 45497500

#37
Terme Di Caracalla
Museum, Landmark/Historic,
Funeral Service, Cemetery
Area: Aventino, San Giovanni
Address: Viale Terme Di Caracalla 52
00153 Rome Italy
Phone: +39 06 39967700

#38
Museo Del Risorgimento
Landmark/Historic
Area: Centro Storico
Address: Complesso Del Vittoriano P.Zza
Venezia - Rome
00187 Rome Italy
Phone: +39 06 6793598

#39
Casa Di Augusto
Historical Building
Area: Aventino
Address: Palatino
00186 Rome Italy

#40
The Catacombs Of Calictus
Landmark/Historic
Area: Appia Antica
Address: Via Appia Antica 110/126
00178 Rome Italy
Phone: +39 06 51301580

#41
Ex Gil
Museum
Area: Trastevere
Address: Largo Ascianghi 5
00153 Rome Italy

#42
Chiesa San Silvestro
Church
Area: Centro Storico
Address: Piazza San Silvestro
00187 Rome Italy
Phone: +39 06 6797775

#43
Piazza Della Madonna Di Monti
Landmark/Historic
Area: Monti
Address: Piazza Della Madonna
Di Monti, 00184 Rome Italy

#44
Santo Stefano Rotondo
Landmark/Historic, Religious Organization
Area: Aventino
Address: Via Montagne Rocciose 41
00144 Rome Italy
Phone: +39 06 5917746

#45
RomeDal Cielo
Landmark/Historic
Area: Centro Storico
Address: Piazza Venezia
00187 Rome Italy

#46
Palazzo Giustiniani
Landmark/Historic
Area: Centro Storico
Address: Via Della Dogana Vecchia 29
00186 Rome Italy
Phone: +39 06 67061

#47
San Pietro In Montorio
Landmark/Historic
Area: Trastevere
Address: Piazza San Pietro In Montorio
00153 Rome Italy

#48
Casa Di Fiammetta
Landmark/Historic
Area: Centro Storico
Address: Via De Coronari 156
00186 Rome Italy

#49
**L'orto Di Piazza Santa Croce
In Gerusalemme**
Landmark/Historic
Area: San Giovanni
Address: Piazza Santa Croce In
Gerusalemme 9a 00185 Rome Italy
Phone: +39 06 7014769

#50
Piazza Cavour
Landmark
Address: Piazza Cavour
00193 Rome Italy

#51
Piazza Della Libert'
Landmark
Area: Prati
Address: Piazza Della Libert'
00100 Rome Italy

#52
Museo Pietro Canonica
Museum
Area: Pinciano
Address: Viale Pietro Canonica 2
00197 Rome Italy
Phone: +39 06 8845702

#53
**Basilica Di San Lorenzo
Fuori Le Mura**
Landmark/Historic
Area: San Lorenzo
Address: Piazzale Di San Lorenzo
00185 Rome Italy

#54
Casa Dei Cavalieri Di Rodi
Landmark/Historic
Area: Phone Number
Address: Via Salita Del Grillo1 Rome,
Rome Italy

#55
Garbatella
Landmark/Historic
Area: Phone Number
Address: Rome, Rome Italy

#56
Fontana Dell'Aqua Paola
Landmark/Historic
Area: Ostiense
Address: Via Garibaldi
00149 Rome Italy

#57
Piazza Sempione
Landmark
Area: Nomentano
Address: Via Delle Alpi Apuane 2
00141 Rome Italy

#58
La Sedia Del Diavolo
Landmark/Historic
Area: Nomentano
Address: Piazza Elio Callistio
00199 Rome Italy

#59
**Palazzo Della Civilt' Italiana
Colosseo Quadrato**
Landmark/Historic
Area: Eur
Address: Quadrato Della Concordia
00144 Rome Italy

#60
Kali Temple
Landmark, Hindu Temples
Area: Phone Number
Address: Via Oreste Ranelletti 52
00166 Rome Italy

#61
Circo Massimo
Landmark/Historic
Area: Aventino
Address: Via Dell'ara Massima Di Ercole
Rome, Rome Italy

#62
**Chiesa Di Sant'Ignazio
Di Loyola**
Church
Area: Centro Storico
Address: Piazza Sant'Ignazio
00186 Rome Italy

#63
Palazzo San Macuto
Historical Building
Area: Centro Storico
Address: Via Del Seminario, 76
00186 Rome Italy
Phone: +39 06 67601

#64
Piazza Di Santa Maria
Church, Landmark
Area: Trastevere
Address: Piazza Di Santa Maria In
Trastevere,00153 Rome Italy

#65
Palazzo Montecitorio
Historical Building
Area: Centro Storico
Address: Piazza Montecitorio
00186 Rome Italy
Phone: +39 06 67601

#66
Palazzo Madama
Historical Building
Area: Centro Storico
Address: Piazza Madama
00186 Rome Italy
Phone: +39 06 67061

#67
Piazza Della Repubblica
Landmark
Area: Termini, Centro Storico
Address: Piazza Della Repubblica
Rome, Rome Italy

#68
Hotel Sant'Angelo
Hotel, Historical Building
Area: Prati
Address: Via Marianna Dionigi 16
00193 Rome Italy
Phone: +39 06 3242000

#69
**Basilica Di Santa Croce In
Gerusalemme**
Landmark/Historic
Area: San Giovanni
Address: Piazza Santa Croce In
Gerusalemme 12, 00185 Rome Italy

#70
Piazza Fiume
Landmark
Area: Pinciano
Address: Piazza Fiume
00198 Rome Italy

#71
Piazzale Degli Eroi
Landmark/Historic
Area: Balduina/Montemario, Prati
Address: Piazzale Degli Eroi
00136 Rome Italy

#72
Mausoleo Santa Costanza
Landmark/Historic
Area: Nomentano
Address: Via Di San Agnese
00198 Rome Italy
Phone: +39 06 86205456

#73
Circus Maximus
Landmark/Historic
Area: Phone Number
Address: Rome, Rome Italy

#74
Basilica Di Massenzio
Landmark/Historic
Area: Monti, Aventino
Address: Clivo Di Venere Felice
00186 Rome Italy

#75
Katakomben
Landmark/Historic
Area: Appia Antica, Ardeatina
Address: Via Appia Antica Rome,
Rome Italy

#76
Piazza Della Rotonda
Landmark/Historic
Area: Centro Storico
Address: Piazza Della Rotonda
00186 Rome Italy

#77
Piazza Barberini
Landmark
Area: Centro Storico
Address: Junction Of Via Del Tritone Via
Veneto Via Quattro Fontane Rome, Rome
Italy

#78
Fontana Del Tritone
Landmark/Historic
Area: Centro Storico
Address: Piazza Barberini
00187 Rome Italy

#79
Statua Di Giovanni Paolo II
Landmark
Area: Termini
Address: Piazza Dei Cinquecento
00185 Rome Italy

#80
Piazza Mancini
Landmark/Historic
Area: Flaminio, Parioli
Address: 00100 Rome Italy

#81
Piazza Annibaliano
Landmark
Area: Nomentano
Address: Piazza Annibaliano Rome,
Rome Italy

#82
Corviale
Landmark/Historic
Area: Aurelia
Address: Via Poggio Verde
00148 Rome Italy

#83
Portico d'Ottavia
Area: Centro Storico
Address: Via Del Portico d'Ottavia 29
00186 Rome Italy
Phone: +39 06 06068

#84
Palazzo Mattei Di Giove
Area: Centro Storico
Address: Via Michelangelo Caetani 32
00186 Rome Italy

#85
Palazzo Valentini
Area: Centro Storico
Address: Via IV Novembre 119
00187 Rome Italy
Phone: +39 06 32810

#86
Quartiere Copped'
Area: Salario
Address: Piazza Mincio
00198 Rome Italy

#87
Campo De' Fiori
Landmark/Historic
Area: Centro Storico
Address: Piazza Campo De' Fiori
00186 Rome Italy

#88
Bocca Della Verit'
Landmark/Historic
Area: Aventino
Address: Piazza Della Bocca Della Verita
Rome, Rome Italy

#89
Complesso Del Vittoriano
Museum, Landmark/Historic,
Funeral Service, Cemetery
Area: Centro Storico
Address: Via Di San Pietro In Carcere
00186 Rome Italy
Phone: +39 06 6780664

#90
Scavi Di Ostia
Landmark/Historic
Area: Ostia
Address: Viale Dei Romegnoli
Ostia Antica, Rome Italy
Phone: +39 06 56358099

#91
Caelius
Landmark/Historic
Area: Aventino
Address: Via Claudia
00100 Rome Italy

#92
Quirinal-H'gel
Landmark/Historic
Area: Centro Storico
Address: Piazza Del Quirinale 1
00100 Rome Italy

#93
Viminal-H'gel
Landmark/Historic
Area: Centro Storico
Address: Piazza Del Viminale 1
00100 Rome Italy

#94
Esquilin-H'gel
Landmark/Historic
Area: Termini
Address: Piazza Di Santa Maria Maggiore
1, 00100 Rome Italy

#95
Rome
Landmark/Historic
Area: Centro Storico
Address: Piazza Capranica 76
00186 Rome Italy
Phone: +39 06 69921720

#96
Comune
Landmark/Historic
Area: Phone Number
Address: Piazza Guglielmo Marconi 3
00044 Frascati Italy

#97
Ponte Della Musica
Armando Trovajoli
Landmark/Historic
Area: Centro Storico
Address: Lungotevere Maresciallo
Cadorna 1
00196 Rome Italy

#98
Villa Maria- Regina
Landmark/Historic
Area: Pineta Sacchetti
Address: Della Camilluccia 687
00135 Rome Italy

#99
Castel Gandolfo
Landmark/Historic
Area: Phone Number
Address: Castelli Romeni
00040 Castel Gandolfo Italy

#100
Accademia Di Francia
Villa Medici
Landmark/Historic, Cultural Center
Area: Centro Storico
Address: Viale Trinit'Dei Monti 1
00187 Rome Italy
Phone: +39 06 67611

TOP 400 ENTERTAINMENT

Most Recommended by Locals & Trevelers
Ranking (from #1 to #400)

#1
Piazza San Pietro
Category: Landmark/Historic,
Arts/Entertainment
Area: Borgo
Address: Piazza San Pietro
00165 Rome Italy

#2
Foro Romeno
Category: Landmark/Historic, Museum
Area: Monti, Centro Storico
Address: Via Dei Fori Imperiali Rome,
Rome Italy

#3
Musei Vaticani
Category: Museum
Area: Citt' Del Vaticano, Prati
Address: Viale Vaticano
00165 Rome Italy
Phone: +39 06 69883333

#4
Palazzo Delle Esposizioni
Category: Museum, Art Gallery
Average Price: Modest
Area: Centro Storico
Address: Via Nazionale 194
00184 Rome Italy
Phone: +39 06 39967200

#5
**Museo Nazionale Castel
Sant'Angelo**
Category: Museum,
Area: Prati
Address: Lungotevere Castello 50
00186 Rome Italy
Phone: +39 06 6819111

#6
Auditorium Parco Della Musica
Category: Opera, Ballet, Music Venues
Average Price: Inexpensive
Area: Flaminio
Address: Viale Pietro De Coubertin 30
00196 Rome Italy
Phone: +39 06 802411

#7
Palatin
Category: Cultural Center
Area: Centro Storico
Address: Via Dei Fori Imperiali
00186 Rome Italy

#8
Silvano Toti Globe Theatre
Category: Performing Arts
Area: Pinciano
Address: Largo Acqua Felix
00197 Rome Italy
Phone: +39 06 0608

#9
**Gregory's Live Jazz
&Dinner Club**
Category: Jazz &Blues, Beer,
Wine, Spirits
Average Price: Inexpensive
Area: Centro Storico
Address: Via Gregoriana 54A
00187 Rome Italy
Phone: +39 327 8263770

#10
Musei Capitolini
Category: Museum
Area: Centro Storico
Address: Piazza Del Campidoglio 1
00186 Rome Italy
Phone: +39 06 0608

#11
Teatro Argentina
Category: Performing Arts
Area: Centro Storico
Address: Largo Di Torre Argentina 52
00186 Rome Italy
Phone: +39 06 6840001

#12
Nuovo Olimpia
Category: Cinema
Area: Centro Storico
Address: Via In Lucina 16G
00186 Rome Italy
Phone: +39 06 6861068

#13
Centrale Montemartini
Category: Museum, Music Venues
Average Price: Inexpensive
Area: Testaccio, Ostiense
Address: Via Ostiense 106
00154 Rome Italy
Phone: +39 06 0608

#14
Stadio Flaminio
Category: Stadium/Arena
Area: Flaminio
Address: Viale Dello Stadio Flaminio
00196 Rome Italy
Phone: +39 06 3212885

#15
Locanda Atlantide
Category: Dance Club, Music Venues
Area: San Giovanni
Address: Via Dei Lucani 22B
00185 Rome Italy
Phone: +39 06 44704540

#16
Multisala Barberini
Category: Cinema
Area: Centro Storico
Address: Piazza Barberini 24
00187 Rome Italy
Phone: +39 06 4821082

#17
Ara Pacis
Category: Landmark/Historic, Museum
Area: Flaminio
Address: Lungotevere In Augusta
00186 Rome Italy
Phone: +39 06 0608

#18
Galleria Nazionale d'Arte Antica
Category: Art Gallery, Museum
Average Price: Inexpensive
Area: Centro Storico
Address: Via Delle Quattro Fontane 13
00184 Rome Italy
Phone: +39 06 4814591

#19
Cinema Dei Piccoli
Category: Cinema
Area: Pinciano
Address: Viale Della Pineta 15
00197 Rome Italy
Phone: +39 06 8553485

#20
Cinematografo Farnese
Category: Cinema
Area: Centro Storico
Address: Piazza Campo De' Fiori, 56
00186 Rome Italy
Phone: +39 06 6864395

#21
Museo Nazionale Etrusco Di Villa Giulia
Category: Museum
Area: Flaminio, Parioli
Address: Piazzale Di Villa Giulia, 9
00196 Rome Italy
Phone: +39 06 3226571

#22
Cinema Adriano
Category: Cinema
Area: Prati
Address: Piazza Cavour 16
00193 Rome Italy
Phone: +39 06 36004988

#23
Angelo Mai Altrove
Category: Music Venues, Dance Club
Average Price: Inexpensive
Area: Aventino, San Giovanni
Address: Via Delle Terme Di
Caracalla 55, 00153 Rome Italy

#24
Terme Di Caracalla
Category: Museum, Landmark/Historic,
Funeral Service, Cemetery
Area: Aventino, San Giovanni
Address: Viale Terme Di Caracalla 52
00153 Rome Italy
Phone: +39 06 39967700

#25
Stadio Olimpico
Category: Soccer, Stadium/Arena
Area: Foro Italico
Address: Viale Dei Gladiatori 2
00135 Rome Italy
Phone: +39 06 36851

#26
MACRO - Museo d'Arte Contemporanea
Category: Museum
Area: Nomentano
Address: Via Nizza 138
00198 Rome Italy
Phone: +39 06 671070428

#27
Cinecitt'
Category: Museum
Area: Tuscolano
Address: Via Tuscolana 1055
00173 Rome Italy
Phone: +39 06 722931

#28
GNAM - Galleria Nazionale d'Arte Moderna
Category: Art Gallery, Museum
Average Price: Inexpensive
Area: Flaminio, Parioli
Address: Viale Delle Belle Arti 131
00196 Rome Italy
Phone: +39 06 3224157

#29
Le Mura Live Club
Category: Wine Bar, Music Venues
Average Price: Inexpensive
Area: Termini, San Giovanni
Address: Via Di Porta Labicana, 24
00185 Rome Italy

#30
The Space Cinema
Category: Cinema
Area: Eur
Address: Parco De' Medici 135
00148 Rome Italy
Phone: +39 06 892111

#31
Casa Bleve
Category: Italian, Winery
Area: Centro Storico
Address: Via Teatro Valle 48
00186 Rome Italy
Phone: +39 06 6865970

#32
Chiostro Del Bramante
Category: Museum
Area: Centro Storico
Address: Arco Della Pace 5
00186 Rome Italy
Phone: +39 06 68809036

#33
Forte Fanfulla
Category: Music Venues
Average Price: Inexpensive
Area: Pigneto
Address: Via Fanfulla Da Lodi 5
00176 Rome Italy

#34
**Explora - Museo Dei
Bambini Di Rome**
Category: Museum
Area: Flaminio
Address: Via Flaminia 80
00196 Rome Italy
Phone: +39 06 3613776

#35
Ombre Rosse
Category: Jazz &Blues, Bar
Average Price: Inexpensive
Area: Trastevere
Address: Piazza Sant'Egidio 12-13
00153 Rome Italy
Phone: +39 06 5884155

#36
Kino
Category: Cinema
Average Price:
Area: San Giovanni
Address: Via Perugia 34
00176 Rome Italy
Phone: +39 06 96525810

#37
Conte Staccio
Category: Music Venues,
Lounge, Italian
Average Price: Inexpensive
Area: Testaccio, Ostiense
Address: Via Di Monte Testaccio 65B
00153 Rome Italy
Phone: +39 06 57289712

#38
Scuderie Del Quirinale
Category: Art Gallery, Museum,
Landmark/Historic
Average Price: Inexpensive
Area: Centro Storico
Address: Via XXIV Maggio 16
00184 Rome Italy
Phone: +39 06 39967500

#39
Casa Del Jazz
Category: Jazz &Blues
Average Price: Inexpensive
Area: Ostiense
Address: Viale Di Porta Ardeatina 55
00154 Rome Italy
Phone: +39 06 704731

#40
Mondo Bizzarro Gallery
Category: Art Gallery, Street Art
Average Price: Inexpensive
Area: Termini
Address: Via Sicilia 251
00187 Rome Italy
Phone: +39 06 44247451

#41
Jailbreak
Category: Music Venues, Pub
Average Price: Modest
Area: Tiburtino
Address: Via Tiburtina 870
00155 Rome Italy
Phone: +39 00 39064063155

#42
Roseto Comunale
Category: Botanical Garden, Park
Area: Aventino
Address: Via Di Valle Murcia 6
00153 Rome Italy
Phone: +39 06 5746810

#43
MercatiDi Traiano
Museo Dei Fori Imperiali
Category: Landmark/Historic, Museum
Area: Centro Storico
Address: Via IV Novembre 94
00187 Rome Italy
Phone: +39 06 0608

#44
Keats-Shelley House
Category: Museum
Area: Centro Storico
Address: Piazza Di Spagna 26
00187 Rome Italy
Phone: +39 06 6784235

#45
Uve E Forme
Category: Winery, Italian
Average Price: Modest
Area: San Lorenzo
Address: Via Padova 6
00161 Rome Italy
Phone: +39 06 44236801

#46
Enoteca Barberini
Category: Winery, Pizza
Average Price: Inexpensive
Area: Centro Storico
Address: Via Del Tritone 123
00187 Rome Italy
Phone: +39 06 62205971

#47
Nuovo Cinema Aquila
Category: Cinema
Area: San Giovanni
Address: Via l'Aquila 68
00176 Rome Italy
Phone: +39 06 70399408

#48
Teatro Ygramul - Ludici Manierati
Category: Performing Arts
Area: Montesacro/Talenti
Address: Via N. M. Nicolai 14
00156 Rome Italy
Phone: +39 327 1974360

#49
Forte Prenestino
Area: Casilino
Address: Via Federico Delpino
00171 Rome Italy
Phone: +39 06 21807855

#50
Uci
Category: Cinema
Area: Bufalotta
Address: Centro Commerciale
Porta Di Rome, 00139 Rome Italy
Phone: +39 06 899788678

#51
Brancaleone
Category: Music Venues
Area: Nomentano, Montesacro/Talenti
Address: Via Levanna 13
00141 Rome Italy
Phone: +39 06 82004382

#52
Lanificio 159
Category: Music Venues
Average Price: Inexpensive
Area: Montesacro/Talenti
Address: Via Di Pietralata 159
00157 Rome Italy
Phone: +39 06 41780081

#53
Big Mama
Category: Jazz &Blues, Music Venues
Average Price: Modest
Area: Trastevere
Address: Vicolo Di San Francesco A Ripa
18, 00153 Rome Italy
Phone: +39 06 5812551

#54
Casa Del Cinema
Category: Cinema
Area: Pinciano
Address: Largo Marcello Mastroianni 1
00197 Rome Italy
Phone: +39 06 0608

#55
Villa Farnesina
Category: Museum, Castle
Area: Borgo
Address: Via Della Lungara 230
00165 Rome Italy
Phone: +39 06 06060884

#56
Officine Fotografiche Rome
Category: Art Gallery
Area: Ostiense
Address: Via Giuseppe Libetta 1
00154 Rome Italy
Phone: +39 06 97274721

#57
Cinema Tibur
Category: Cinema
Area: Termini, San Giovanni
Address: Via Degli Etruschi, 36
00185 Rome Italy
Phone: +39 06 86391361

#58
Alexanderplatz Jazz Club
Category: Jazz &Blues
Average Price: Modest
Area: Prati
Address: Via Ostia 9
00192 Rome Italy
Phone: +39 06 39742171

#59
Mercatino Conca d'Oro
Category: Shopping, Festival
Average Price: Inexpensive
Area: Nomentano
Address: Via Conca d'Oro 113
00141 Rome Italy
Phone: +39 06 88644327

#60
Greenwich
Category: Cinema
Area: Testaccio, Ostiense
Address: Via Giovanni Battista
Bodoni 59, 00153 Rome Italy
Phone: +39 06 5745825

#61
Akbar
Category: Cocktail Bar, Jazz &Blues,
Lounge, Italian, Café
Average Price: Inexpensive
Area: Trastevere
Address: Piazza In Piscinula 51
00153 Rome Italy
Phone: +39 06 5800681

#62
Palazzo Massimo Alle Terme
Museo Nazionale Romeno
Category: Museum
Area: Termini
Address: Largo Di Villa Peretti, 1
00185 Rome Italy
Phone: +39 06 39967700

#63
Il Tiaso
Category: Winery
Average Price: Inexpensive
Area: San Giovanni
Address: Via Ascoli Piceno 20
00176 Rome Italy
Phone: +39 06 45474625

#64
Arte5
Category: Art Gallery, Jazz &Blues
Average Price: Modest
Area: Centro Storico
Address: Corso Vittorio Emanuele II 5
00186 Rome Italy
Phone: +39 06 69921298

#65
Cinema Nuovo Sacher
Category: Cinema
Area: Trastevere
Address: Largo Ascianghi 1
00153 Rome Italy
Phone: +39 06 5818116

#66
Orto Botanico
Category: Botanical Garden, Park
Area: Borgo
Address: Largo Cristina Di Svezia 24
00165 Rome Italy
Phone: +39 06 49912436

#67
Notti Di Cinema A Piazza Vittorio
Category: Cinema, Festival
Area: Esquilino
Address: Piazza Vittorio Emanuele II
00185 Rome Italy
Phone: +39 06 4453685

#68
Casina Delle Civette
Category: Museum
Area: Nomentano
Address: Via Nomentana 70
00161 Rome Italy
Phone: +39 06 44250072

#69
Fandango Incontro
Category: Wine Bar, Museum
Average Price: Inexpensive
Area: Centro Storico
Address: Via Dei Prefetti 22
00186 Rome Italy
Phone: +39 06 97601104

#70
Domus Aurea
Category: Museum
Area: Esquilino, Aventino
Address: Via Della Domus Aurea 1
00184 Rome Italy
Phone: +39 06 39967700

#71
Musei Di San Salvatore In Lauro
Category: Museum
Area: Centro Storico
Address: P.Zza San Salvatore In Lauro,
15, 00186 Rome Italy
Phone: +39 06 68805651

#72
**Accademia Tedesca
Rome Villa Massimo**
Category: Arts/Entertainment
Area: Nomentano
Address: Largo Di Villa Massimo 1-2
00161 Rome Italy
Phone: +39 06 4425931

#73
UCI Cinemas Parco Leonardo
Category: Cinema
Area: Phone Number
Address: Via Gian Lorenzo Bernini 20
00100 Rome Italy

#74
Galleria Spada
Category: Museum
Area: Centro Storico
Address: Piazza Capo Di Ferro, 3
00186 Rome Italy
Phone: +39 06 6861158

#75
La Citt' Dell'utopia
Category: Arts/Entertainment
Area: Ostiense
Address: Via Valeriano 3F
00145 Rome Italy
Phone: +39 06 59648311

#76
Cinema Lux
Category: Cinema
Area: Salario
Address: Via Massaciuccoli, 39
00199 Rome Italy
Phone: +39 06 86391361

#77
Be Bop
Category: Jazz &Blues
Average Price: Inexpensive
Area: Testaccio, Ostiense
Address: Via Giuseppe Giulietti 14
00154 Rome Italy
Phone: +39 06 5755582

#78
Filmstudio
Category: Cinema
Area: Borgo
Address: Via Degli Orti d'Alibert 1/C
00165 Rome Italy
Phone: +39 334 1780632

#79
Bibenda Wine Concept
Category: Wine Bar, Winery
Average Price: Modest
Area: Aventino
Address: Via Capo d'Africa 21
00184 Rome Italy
Phone: +39 06 77206673

#80
Nuovo Cinema Palazzo
Category: Performing Arts, Cinema
Area: San Lorenzo, San Giovanni
Address: Piazza Dei Sanniti
00185 Rome Italy

#81
Esc Atelier Occupato
Category: Music Venues, Social Club
Area: San Lorenzo
Address: Via Dei Volsci 159
00185 Rome Italy

#82
Hula Hoop Club
Category: Cultural Center
Area: Pigneto
Address: Via Luigi Filippo De
Magistris 91, 00176 Rome Italy
Phone: +39 349 3191935

#83
Cinema Madison
Category: Cinema
Area: Ostiense
Address: Via Gabriello Chiabrera 121
00145 Rome Italy
Phone: +39 06 55383193

#84
Azzurro Scipioni
Category: Cinema
Area: Prati
Address: Via Degli Scipioni 82
00192 Rome Italy
Phone: +39 06 39737161

#85
Teatro Studio Uno
Category: Performing Arts
Area: Tuscolano
Address: Via Carlo Della Rocca 6
00177 Rome Italy
Phone: +39 349 4356219

#86
Museo Della Civilt' Romena
Category: Museum
Area: Eur
Address: Piazza G. Agnelli, 10
00144 Rome Italy
Phone: +39 06 0608

#87
Eurcine
Category: Cinema
Area: Eur
Address: Via Liszt, 32
00144 Rome Italy
Phone: +39 06 5910986

#88
Galleria Doria Pamphilj,
Category: Art Gallery
Area: Centro Storico
Address: Via Della Reginella 26
00186 Rome Italy
Phone: +39 06 87452131

#89
Cinema America Occupato
Category: Cinema
Area: Trastevere
Address: Via Natale Del Grande 52
00153 Rome Italy

#90
Altare Della Patria
Category: Museum
Area: Centro Storico
Address: Next To Piazza Venezia Around
Via Del Corso 00186 Rome Italy
Phone: +39 06 0608

#91
Historisches Rom
Category: Arts/Entertainment
Address: Rome, Rome Italy

#92
Soverdi Catacombe Domitilla
Category: Museum
Area: Appia Antica
Address: Via Delle Sette Chiese 282
00147 Rome Italy
Phone: +39 06 5110342

#93
Catacombe S. Sebastiano
Category: Museum, Church,
Landmark/Historic
Area: Appia Antica
Address: Via Appia Antica, 136
00178 Rome Italy
Phone: +39 06 7887035

#94
Stardust Village
Category: Cinema
Area: Eur
Address: Via Di Decima 72
00144 Rome Italy
Phone: +39 06 52244119

#95
Black Out Rock Club
Category: Dance Club, Music Venues
Average Price: Inexpensive
Area: Casilino
Address: Via Casilina 713
00177 Rome Italy
Phone: +39 06 2415047

#96
The Space - Cinema Moderno
Category: Cinema
Area: Termini, Centro Storico
Address: Piazza Della Repubblica 44
00185 Rome Italy
Phone: +39 06 47824665

#97
Teatro Stabile Del Giallo
Category: Performing Arts
Area: Cassia
Address: Via Al Sesto Miglio 78
00189 Rome Italy
Phone: +39 06 33262799

#98
Sinister Noise
Category: Music Venues
Area: Testaccio, Ostiense
Address: Via Dei Magazzini Generali 4b
00154 Rome Italy
Phone: +39 00 393473310648

#99
L'Asino Che Vola
Category: Arts/Entertainment
Area: Appia Antica
Address: Via Antonio Coppi 12D
00179 Rome Italy
Phone: +39 06 7851028

#100
Qube
Category: Dance Club, Music Venues
Average Price: Inexpensive
Area: Pigneto
Address: Via Di Portonaccio 212
00159 Rome Italy
Phone: +39 06 4385445

#101
Cineclub Detour
Category: Cinema
Area: Monti
Address: Via Urbana 107
00184 Rome Italy
Phone: +39 06 4747874

#102
Rising Love
Category: Music Venues
Average Price: Inexpensive
Area: Testaccio, Ostiense
Address: Via Delle Conce 14
00154 Rome Italy
Phone: +39 06 89520643

#103
Bar ' Book
Category: Winery, Café
Average Price: Modest
Area: San Giovanni
Address: Via Dei Piceni 23
00185 Rome Italy
Phone: +39 06 96043014

#104
Antica Vineria
Category: Winery
Average Price: Inexpensive
Area: Centro Storico
Address: Via Monte Della Farina 38
00186 Rome Italy
Phone: +39 06 68806989

#105
Villa Celimontana
Category: Opera, Ballet,
Music Venues, Park
Average Price: Inexpensive
Area: Aventino
Address: Via Della Navicella 12
00184 Rome Italy
Phone: +39 06 5897807

#106
INIT Club
Category: Bar, Dance Club,
Music Venues
Average Price: Inexpensive
Area: San Giovanni
Address: Via Della Stazione
Tuscolana 133, 00182 Rome Italy
Phone: +39 06 97277724

#107
Gagosian Gallery
Category: Art Gallery
Area: Centro Storico
Address: Via Francesco Crispi 16
00187 Rome Italy
Phone: +39 06 42086498

#108
Teatro Sala Uno
Category: Performing Arts
Area: San Giovanni
Address: Piazza Di Porta San
Giovanni 10, 00185 Rome Italy
Phone: +39 06 88976626

#109
Candle's Store
Category: Home &Garden,
Arts, Crafts, Art Gallery
Average Price: Modest
Area: San Giovanni
Address: Via Dei Campani 49
00185 Rome Italy
Phone: +39 06 4464849

#110
Fonderia Delle Arti Ass. Culturale
Category: Performing Arts,
Education, Cultural Center
Area: San Giovanni
Address: Via Assisi 31
00181 Rome Italy
Phone: +39 06 7842112

#111
Intrastevere
Category: Cinema
Area: Trastevere
Address: Vicolo Moroni 3
00153 Rome Italy
Phone: +39 06 5884230

#112
Buccone
Category: Winery, Beer,
Wine, Spirits, Italian
Average Price: Modest
Area: Flaminio
Address: Via Di Ripetta 19
00186 Rome Italy
Phone: +39 06 3612154

#113
Auditorium Conciliazione
Category: Opera, Ballet
Area: Prati
Address: Via Della Conciliazione 4
00193 Rome Italy
Phone: +39 06 684391

#114
C.V.A. Centro Vini Arcioni
Category: Flowers, Gifts, Winery
Area: Salario
Address: Via Nemorense, 57/57A
00199 Rome Italy
Phone: +39 06 86206616

#115
Teatro Palladium
Category: Performing Arts,
Music Venues
Area: Ostiense
Address: Piazza Bartolomeo Romeno 8
00154 Rome Italy
Phone: +39 06 57067761

#116
Hobo Art Club
Category: Bookstore, Winery
Average Price: Inexpensive
Area: San Giovanni
Address: Via Ascoli Piceno 3
00176 Rome Italy
Phone: +39 06 648019

#117
Li.Boh
Category: Art Gallery, Fashion
Area: San Giovanni
Address: Via Del Pigneto 52
00176 Rome Italy
Phone: +39 06 70304648

#118
**Museo Nazionale Degli
Strumenti Musicali**
Category: Museum
Area: Termini
Address: Piazza Di San Croce IN
Gerusalemme 9A
00185 Rome Italy
Phone: +39 06 7014796

#119
Fatamorgana Ludoteca
Category: Arcade
Area: Termini, San Giovanni
Address: Via Dei Volsci 3
00185 Rome Italy
Phone: +39 06 4468233

#120
Teatro India
Category: Wine Bar,
Performing Arts, Music Venues
Area: Ostiense
Address: Lungotevere Dei Papareschi 1
00146 Rome Italy
Phone: +39 06 684000314

#121
La Riunione Di Condominio
Category: Jazz &Blues, Social Club
Average Price: Inexpensive
Area: Termini
Address: Via Dei Luceri 13
00185 Rome Italy
Phone: +39 06 57301417

#122
Wunderkammern
Category: Art Gallery, Cultural Center
Average Price: Inexpensive
Area: Tuscolano
Address: Via Gabrio Serbelloni 124
00176 Rome Italy
Phone: +39 06 86903806

#123
Villa Ada
Rome Incontra Il Mondo
Category: Music Venues, Festival
Area: Salario
Address: Via Di Ponte Salario
00199 Rome Italy
Phone: +39 06 97602968

#124
Stazione Birra
Category: Pizza, Music Venues, Pub
Average Price: Modest
Area: Phone Number
Address: Via Placanica 172
00118 Rome Italy

#125
Al Vino Al Vino
Category: Winery
Average Price: Modest
Area: Monti
Address: Via Dei Serpenti 19
00184 Rome Italy
Phone: +39 06 485803

#126
Belvedere Cederna
Category: Cinema
Area: Ostia
Address: Clivo Di Acilio
00186 Rome Italy

#127
Cinema Delle Province
Category: Cinema
Area: San Lorenzo
Address: Viale Delle Provincie 41
00162 Rome Italy
Phone: +39 06 44236021

#128
Charity Caf'
Category: Jazz &Blues,
Wine Bar, Cocktail Bar
Average Price: Inexpensive
Area: Monti
Address: Via Panisperna 68
00184 Rome Italy
Phone: +39 06 47825881

#129
Beba Do Samba
Category: Music Venues
Average Price: Inexpensive
Area: San Giovanni
Address: Via De' Messapi 8
00185 Rome Italy
Phone: +39 340 6953499

#130
The Place
Category: Jazz &Blues, Lounge
Average Price: Modest
Area: Prati
Address: Via Alberico II 27
00193 Rome Italy
Phone: +39 06 68307137

#131
Enoteca Vicino
Category: Winery, Italian
Average Price: Inexpensive
Area: San Giovanni
Address: Via Del Pigneto 25
00176 Rome Italy
Phone: +39 06 45441867

#132
Giulio Cesare
Category: Arts/Entertainment
Area: Prati
Address: Viale Giulio Cesare 259
00192 Rome Italy
Phone: +39 06 39720877

#133
Cineclub Alphaville
Category: Cinema
Area: Pigneto
Address: Via Del Pigneto 283
00176 Rome Italy
Phone: +39 339 3618216

#134
Lettere Caff'
Category: Wine Bar, Performing Arts
Average Price: Inexpensive
Area: Trastevere
Address: Via S.Francesco A Ripa 100 /
101, 00153 Rome Italy
Phone: +39 06 97270991

#135
Teatro Sala Umberto
Category: Opera, Ballet, Music Venues
Average Price: Inexpensive
Area: Centro Storico
Address: Via Della Mercede 50
00187 Rome Italy
Phone: +39 06 6794753

#136
Mocobo
Category: Arts/Entertainment
Area: Ostiense
Address: Via Pellegrino Matteucci, 98
00154 Rome Italy
Phone: +39 06 5747503

#137
Enoteca Costantini
Category: Winery
Average Price: Modest
Area: Prati
Address: Piazza Cavour 16
00193 Rome Italy
Phone: +39 06 3203575

#138
Crossover
Category: Music Venues
Area: Termini, San Giovanni
Address: Via Degli Equi 22
00185 Rome Italy
Phone: +39 345 5296500

#139
Eden
Category: Cinema
Area: Prati
Address: Via Cola Di Rienzo 74
00192 Rome Italy
Phone: +39 06 3612449

#140
20 ML
Category: Winery
Average Price:
Area: San Lorenzo
Address: Via Michele Di Lando 20
00162 Rome Italy

#141
I.A.L.S.
Category: Dance Studio,
Arts/Entertainment
Area: Flaminio
Address: Via Cesare Fracassini 60
00196 Rome Italy
Phone: +39 06 3236396

#142
Cinema King
Category: Cinema
Area: Salario
Address: Via Fogliano, 37
00199 Rome Italy
Phone: +39 06 86206732

#143
Arena Del Chiostro Di San Pietro In Vincoli
Category: Stadium/Arena
Area: Monti
Address: Via Eudossiana 18
00184 Rome Italy
Phone: +39 06 9963536

#144
Le Domus Romene
Category: Museum
Area: Centro Storico
Address: Via IV Novembre 119A
00187 Rome Italy
Phone: +39 06 32810

#145
Crypta Balbi
Category: Museum
Area: Centro Storico
Address: Via Delle Botteghe Oscure 31
00186 Rome Italy
Phone: +39 06 39967700

#146
The Aventine Keyhole
Category: Arts/Entertainment
Area: Aventino
Address: Piazza Dei Cavalieri Di Malta
00153 Rome Italy

#147
Grottapinta Lounge
Category: Dance Club, Lounge,
Music Venues
Average Price: Inexpensive
Area: Centro Storico
Address: Via Di Grottapinta 12
00186 Rome Italy

#148
Arcigay Rome
Category: Social Club
Area: Testaccio, Ostiense
Address: Via Nicola Zabaglia 14
00153 Rome Italy
Phone: +39 06 64501102

#149
Spazio IF
Category: Art Gallery, Fashion
Average Price: Modest
Area: Centro Storico
Address: Via Dei Coronari 44A
00186 Rome Italy
Phone: +39 06 64760639

#150
Planetario E Museo Astronomico
Category: Museum
Area: Eur
Address: Piazza Giovanni Agnelli 10
00144 Rome Italy
Phone: +39 06 060608

#151
Ex Elettrofonica
Category: Art Gallery
Area: Borgo
Address: Vicolo Sant'Onofrio 10-11
00165 Rome Italy
Phone: +39 06 64760163

#152
The House Of Love And Dissent
Category: Art Gallery
Area: Monti
Address: Via Leonina, 85
00184 Rome Italy
Phone: +39 06 48903661

#153
Sala Trevi Alberto SordiFilmoteca
Category: Cinema
Area: Centro Storico
Address: Vicolo Del Puttarello, 25
00187 Rome Italy
Phone: +39 06 72294301

#154
Il Tajut
Category: Friulan, Social Club
Area: Esquilino
Address: Via San Giovanni In
Laterano 244, 00184 Rome Italy
Phone: +39 349 6418088

#155
Circuito Cinema
Category: Cinema
Area: Centro Storico
Address: Via Quattro Fontane 23
00184 Rome Italy
Phone: +39 06 4745725

#156
L'image
Category: Art Gallery
Average Price: Inexpensive
Area: Centro Storico
Address: Via Della Scrofa, 67
00186 Rome Italy
Phone: +39 06 6864050

#157
Teatro Due
Category: Opera, Ballet, Music Venues
Average Price: Inexpensive
Area: Centro Storico
Address: Vicolo Due Macelli 37
00187 Rome Italy
Phone: +39 06 6788259

#158
Galleria Monitor
Category: Art Gallery
Area: Centro Storico
Address: Via Sforza Cesarini 43
00186 Rome Italy
Phone: +39 06 39378024

#159
Accademia Filarmonica Romena
Category: Education, Music Venues,
Performing Arts
Area: Flaminio
Address: Via Flaminia, 118
00196 Rome Italy
Phone: +39 06 3201752

#160
Mondopop
Category: Toy Store, Art Gallery,
Bookstore
Average Price: Modest
Area: Flaminio, Centro Storico
Address: Via Dei Greci 30
00187 Rome Italy
Phone: +39 06 36005117

#161
Casa Dei Teatri
Category: Museum, Library
Area: Monteverde
Address: Largo 3 Giugno 1849
00165 Rome Italy
Phone: +39 06 45460691

#162
Istituto Austriaco Di Cultura
Category: Social Club
Area: Parioli
Address: Viale Bruno Buozzi 113
00197 Rome Italy
Phone: +39 06 3608371

#163
Cantine D'Offizi
Category: Winery
Average Price: Inexpensive
Area: San Giovanni
Address: Via Dei Marsi 40
00185 Rome Italy

#164
Ludoteca Casina Di Raffaello
Category: Arts/Entertainment
Area: Pinciano
Address: Viale Della Casina Di Raffaello
00197 Rome Italy
Phone: +39 06 42888888

#165
Fondazione Pastificio Cerere
Category: Art Gallery
Area: San Lorenzo
Address: Via Degli Ausoni, 1
00165 Rome Italy
Phone: +39 06 45422960

#166
Blutopia
Category: Music & Dvds,
Vinyl Records, Jazz &Blues
Area: Pigneto
Address: Via Del Pigneto 116
00176 Rome Italy
Phone: +39 06 69309373

#167
Teatro Allo Scalo
Category: Performing Arts
Area: San Lorenzo, San Giovanni
Address: Via Dei Reti 36
00185 Rome Italy
Phone: +39 340 6485291

#168
Museo Hendrik Christian Andersen
Category: Museum, Bar
Area: Flaminio
Address: Via Pasquale Stanislao Mancini,
20 00196 Rome Italy
Phone: +39 06 3219089

#169
28divino Jazz
Category: Jazz &Blues
Area: San Giovanni
Address: Via Mirandola 21
00182 Rome Italy
Phone: +39 340 8249718

#170
Palalottomatica
Category: Stadium/Arena, Music Venues
Average Price: Modest
Area: Eur
Address: Piazzale Pier Luigi Nervi 1
00144 Rome Italy
Phone: +39 06 540901

#171
Enoteca Bulzoni
Category: Winery
Area: Salario
Address: Viale Parioli, 36
00197 Rome Italy
Phone: +39 06 8070494

#172
Odio l'Estate
Category: Festival
Average Price:
Area: Balduina/Montemario, Aurelia
Address: Piazza Di Villa Carpegna
00165 Rome Italy
Phone: +39 320 3323236

#173
CSA La Torre
Category: Social Club, Italian
Area: Montesacro/Talenti
Address: Via Bertero 13
00156 Rome Italy
Phone: +39 06 822869

#174
Futsal Arena
Category: Stadium/Arena
Area: Corso Francia
Address: Via Del Baiardo
00191 Rome Italy
Phone: +39 06 8606863

#175
Museo Delle Arti E Delle Tradizioni Popolari
Category: Museum
Area: Eur
Address: Piazza G. Marconi 8
00144 Rome Italy
Phone: +39 06 5926148

#176
Atlantico
Category: Music Venues
Average Price: Inexpensive
Area: Eur
Address: Viale Oceano Atlantico 271D
00144 Rome Italy
Phone: +39 06 5915727

#177
Cinema Maestoso
Category: Cinema
Area: San Giovanni
Address: Via Appia Nuova, 416
00179 Rome Italy
Phone: +39 06 45472091

#178
Rome Vintage
Category: Music Venues, Festival
Area: San Giovanni
Address: Via Di Porta San Sebastiano 2
00179 Rome Italy
Phone: +39 06 94800800

#179
Bernabei Liquori
Category: Winery
Area: Trastevere
Address: Via San Francesco A Ripa 48
00153 Rome Italy
Phone: +39 06 5812818

#180
Muzak
Category: Dance Club, Music Venues
Average Price: Inexpensive
Area: Testaccio, Ostiense
Address: Via Di Monte Testaccio 38
00153 Rome Italy
Phone: +39 06 5744712

#181
Arena Villa Mercede
Category: Cinema
Area: Termini, San Lorenzo
Address: Via Tiburtina 113
00185 Rome Italy
Phone: +39 06 9964298

#182
Cinema Mignon
Category: Cinema
Area: Pinciano
Address: Via Viterbo 11
00198 Rome Italy
Phone: +39 06 8559493

#183
Villa Torlonia
Category: Museum, Park
Area: Nomentano
Address: Via Nomentana 70
00161 Rome Italy
Phone: +39 06 0608

#184
Cinema Tiziano
Category: Cinema
Area: Flaminio
Address: Via Guido Reni 2A
00196 Rome Italy
Phone: +39 06 3236588

#185
Cinema Alhambra
Category: Cinema
Area: Balduina/Montemario
Address: Via Pier Delle Vigne 4
00165 Rome Italy
Phone: +39 06 66012154

#186
La Bibliotechina
Category: Dance Club,
Wine Bar, Social Club
Average Price: Inexpensive
Area: Eur
Address: Viale Val Fiorita 10
00144 Rome Italy
Phone: +39 348 3384616

#187
Cinema Antares
Category: Cinema
Area: Nomentano
Address: Viale Adriatico 15
00141 Rome Italy
Phone: +39 06 8186655

#188
Rialto Sant'Ambrogio
Category: Dance Club, Cultural Center
Average Price: Inexpensive
Area: Centro Storico
Address: Via Sant'Ambrogio 4
00186 Rome Italy
Phone: +39 06 68133640

#189
**Libreria Galleria Il Museo
Del Louvre**
Category: Art Gallery, Bookstore
Average Price: Inexpensive
Area: Centro Storico
Address: Via Della Reginella 26-28
00186 Rome Italy
Phone: +39 06 68807725

#190
Teatro Eliseo
Category: Arts/Entertainment
Area: Centro Storico
Address: Via Nazionale 183
00184 Rome Italy
Phone: +39 06 48872222

#191
Pierrot Le Fou
Category: Social Club, Lounge
Area: Monti, Centro Storico
Address: Via Del Boschetto 34
00184 Rome Italy
Phone: +39 339 8839616

#192
Teatro Anfitrione
Category: Opera, Ballet,
Music Venues, Performing Arts
Average Price: Inexpensive
Area: Aventino, Ostiense
Address: Via Di San Saba 24
00153 Rome Italy
Phone: +39 06 5750827

#193
Dorothy Circus Gallery
Category: Art Gallery
Area: Centro Storico
Address: Via Dei Pettinari 76
00186 Rome Italy
Phone: +39 06 68805928

#194
Fondazione Rome Museo
Category: Museum
Area: Centro Storico
Address: Via Del Corso 320
00186 Rome Italy
Phone: +39 06 6786209

#195
Teatro Vittoria
Category: Opera, Ballet, Music Venues
Average Price: Inexpensive
Area: Testaccio, Ostiense
Address: Piazza S. Maria Liberatrice, 11
00153 Rome Italy
Phone: +39 06 5740170

#196
Il Tino Di Vino
Category: Winery
Average Price: Inexpensive
Area: Centro Storico
Address: Via Della Panetteria 42
00107 Rome Italy

#197
Casa Delle Letterature
Category: Arts/Entertainment
Area: Centro Storico
Address: Piazza Dell'orologio 3
00186 Rome Italy
Phone: +39 06 68134697

#198
Fondazione Volume!
Category: Art Gallery
Area: Borgo
Address: Via S. Francesco Di Sales 86/88,
00165 Rome Italy
Phone: +39 06 6892431

#199
Istituto Svizzero Di Rome
Category: Social Club
Area: Centro Storico
Address: Via Ludovisi, 48
00187 Rome Italy
Phone: +39 06 42011271

#200
Lian Club
Category: Music Venues, Food
Area: San Giovanni
Address: Via Flaminia 80
00100 Rome Italy
Phone: +39 347 6507244

#201
Teatro Furio Camilllo
Category: Performing Arts
Area: San Giovanni
Address: Via Camilla 44
00181 Rome Italy
Phone: +39 06 7804476

#202
Acrobax
Area: Magliana
Address: Via Della Vasca Navale 6
00146 Rome Italy
Phone: +39 06 97616630

#203
Teatro Parioli Peppino De Filippo
Category: Opera, Ballet,
Performing Arts
Area: Salario
Address: Via Giosu' Borsi 20
00197 Rome Italy
Phone: +39 06 8073040

#204
Officine Farneto
Category: Music Venues,
Venues &Events
Area: Balduina/Montemario
Address: Via Monti Della Farnesina 77
00135 Rome Italy
Phone: +39 06 83396746

#205
Anzuini
Category: Italian, Grocery, Winery
Average Price: Inexpensive
Area: Eur
Address: Viale Europa 274
00144 Rome Italy
Phone: +39 06 5924583

#206
Defrag
Category: Social Club, Active Life
Area: Salario
Address: Via Delle Isole Curzolane 75
00139 Rome Italy
Phone: +39 320 0486439

#207
Traffic Club
Category: Music Venues
Average Price: Inexpensive
Area: Casilino
Address: Via Prenestina, 738
00176 Rome Italy
Phone: +39 00 393280547412

#208
Voland
Category: Art Gallery,
Colleges &Universities
Average Price: Inexpensive
Area: Monti
Address: Via Del Boschetto, 129
00184 Rome Italy
Phone: +39 06 47823674

#209
Podere Vecciano
Category: Winery
Average Price: Inexpensive
Area: Monti
Address: Via Dei Serpenti 33
00184 Rome Italy
Phone: +39 06 48913812

#210
Unosunove
Category: Art Gallery
Area: Centro Storico
Address: Palazzo Santacroce, Via Degli
Specchi 20, 00186 Rome Italy
Phone: +39 06 97613810

#211
Motelsalieri
Category: Men's Clothing, Art Gallery
Average Price: Modest
Area: Monti
Address: Via Giovanni Lanza, 162
00184 Rome Italy
Phone: +39 06 48989966

#212
Alcazar
Category: Cinema
Area: Trastevere
Address: Via Cardinale Merry Del Val 14
00153 Rome Italy
Phone: +39 06 5880099

#213
Ex Gil
Category: Landmark/Historic, Museum
Area: Trastevere
Address: Largo Ascianghi 5
00153 Rome Italy

#214
Tempio Di Adriano
Category: Museum
Area: Centro Storico
Address: Piazza Di Pietra
00186 Rome Italy
Phone: +39 06 6795937

#215
Terme Di Diocleziano
Category: Museum
Area: Termini
Address: Viale Enrico De Nicola, 79
00185 Rome Italy
Phone: +39 06 39967700

#216
Palazzo Ruspoli Fondazione Memmo
Category: Museum
Area: Centro Storico
Address: Via Del Corso 418
00186 Rome Italy
Phone: +39 06 6874704

#217
Museo Napoleonico
Category: Museum
Area: Centro Storico
Address: Piazza Ponte Umberto I, 1
00186 Rome Italy
Phone: +39 06 6874240

#218
Teatro Lo Spazio
Category: Performing Arts,
Cultural Center
Area: San Giovanni
Address: Via Locri 42
00183 Rome Italy
Phone: +39 06 77076486

#219
Casa Della Memoria E Della Storia
Category: Museum
Area: Borgo
Address: Via San Francesco Di Sales 5
00165 Rome Italy
Phone: +39 06 6876543

#220
Galleria Lorcan O'Neill Rome
Category: Art Gallery
Area: Borgo
Address: Via Orti D'Alibert, 1/E
00165 Rome Italy
Phone: +39 06 68892980

#221
Teatro Vascello
Category: Opera, Ballet, Music Venues
Area: Monteverde
Address: Via Giacinto Carini, 78
00152 Rome Italy
Phone: +39 06 5881021

#222
Warner Village Parco De'medici
Category: Cinema
Area: Eur
Address: Parco De Medici
00148 Rome Italy

#223
Museo Boncompagni Ludovisi Per Le Arti Decorative
Category: Museum
Area: Termini
Address: Via Boncompagni 18
00187 Rome Italy
Phone: +39 06 42013123

#224
Casa Di Goethe
Category: Museum
Area: Flaminio
Address: Via Del Corso 18
00186 Rome Italy
Phone: +39 06 32650412

#225
Teatro Verde
Category: Performing Arts, Education
Area: Trastevere
Address: Circ.Ne Gianicolense, 10
00152 Rome Italy
Phone: +39 06 5882034

#226
Ombralonga Vinerie
Category: Winery
Area: Ostiense
Address: Via Oderisi DA Gubbio, 41
00146 Rome Italy
Phone: +39 06 5594212

#227
Molinari Art Center
Category: Performing Arts
Area: Ostiense
Address: Via Antonino Lo Surdo 51
00146 Rome Italy
Phone: +39 06 5574685

#228
Grauco Cineclub
Category: Cultural Center
Area: San Giovanni
Address: Via Perugia 34
00176 Rome Italy
Phone: +39 06 70300199

#229
Enoteca Di Sero
Category: Winery, Beer,
Wine, Spirits
Area: San Giovanni
Address: Via Macerata 58 B
00176 Rome Italy
Phone: +39 06 70300111

#230
Centrale Preneste
Category: Performing Arts
Area: Pigneto
Address: Via Da Giussano 58
00176 Rome Italy
Phone: +39 06 25393527

#231
Museo Sacrario Delle Bandiere
Category: Museum
Area: Centro Storico
Address: Via Dei Fori Imperiali
00186 Rome Italy
Phone: +39 06 47355002

#232
Galleria Bonomo
Category: Art Gallery
Area: Centro Storico
Address: Via Del Portico D'Ottavia, 13
00186 Rome Italy
Phone: +39 06 683276

#233
Food Tours Of Rome
Category: Tours, Deli
Area: Centro Storico
Address: Piazza Mattei 16
00138 Rome Italy
Phone: +39 328 9473305

#234
**Associazione Italiana
Amici Del Presepio**
Category: Museum
Area: Monti, Centro Storico
Address: Via TOR DE' Conti, 31/A
00184 Rome Italy
Phone: +39 06 6796146

#235
Galleria Edieuropa
Category: Art Gallery
Area: Centro Storico
Address: Piazza Dei Cenci, 56
00186 Rome Italy
Phone: +39 06 68805795

#236
Cinema Reale
Category: Cinema
Area: Trastevere
Address: Piazza Sidney Sonnino 7
00153 Rome Italy
Phone: +39 06 5810234

#237
Vino Rome
Category: Beer, Wine, Spirits
Average Price: Inexpensive
Area: Monti
Address: Via In Selci 84G
00184 Rome Italy
Phone: +39 328 4874497

#238
Stamperia Del Tevere
Category: Art Gallery
Area: Trastevere
Address: Via San Francesco A
Ripa 69, 00153 Rome Italy
Phone: +39 328 2263450

#239
Le Perle
Category: Art Gallery
Area: Centro Storico
Address: Via Dei Chiavari, 56
00186 Rome Italy
Phone: +39 06 6873366

#240
The Deep
Category: Photography Store,
Bookstore, Art Gallery
Area: Trastevere
Address: Via Di San Calisto 9
00153 Rome Italy
Phone: +39 06 45423213

#241
Mostra Dei Bruegel
Category: Art Gallery
Area: Centro Storico
Address: Via Dell'arco Della Pace 5
00186 Rome Italy
Phone: +39 06 68809036

#242
Associazione Culturale Antigone
Category: Performing Arts
Area: Testaccio, Ostiense
Address: Via Amerigo Vespucci, 42
00153 Rome Italy
Phone: +39 06 5755397

#243
Together
Category: Cultural Center
Area: Trastevere
Address: Viale Glorioso 14
00153 Rome Italy

#244
T293
Category: Art Gallery
Area: Centro Storico
Address: Via Dei Leutari 32
00186 Rome Italy
Phone: +39 06 83763242

#245
Vinoteca Novecento
Category: Winery
Average Price: Modest
Area: Centro Storico
Address: Piazza Delle Coppelle, 47
00186 Rome Italy
Phone: +39 06 6833078

#246
Arte In Regola
Category: Art Gallery
Area: Centro Storico
Address: Via Dei Cappellari 92
00186 Rome Italy

#247
Circolo Scandinavo Per Artisti E Scienziati
Area: Borgo
Address: Via Della Lungara, 231
00165 Rome Italy
Phone: +39 06 68131690

#248
Affordable Art Fair
Category: Art Gallery
Area: Testaccio, Ostiense
Address: Piazza Orazio Giustiniani 4
00153 Rome Italy
Phone: +39 390 49657401

#249
Modo
Category: Jazz &Blues
Area: Centro Storico
Address: Vicolo Del Fico 3
00186 Rome Italy
Phone: +39 06 6867452

#250
Mila
Category: Art Gallery
Area: Centro Storico
Address: Via Di Monte Brianzo 49
00186 Rome Italy
Phone: +39 06 68804079

#251
Chiese Parrocchia San Maria Degli Angeli
Category: Museum, Church
Area: Centro Storico
Address: Piazza Della Repubblica
00185 Rome Italy
Phone: +39 06 4880812

#252
Ferrari Store
Category: Toy Store, Art Gallery
Area: Centro Storico
Address: Via Tomacelli 150
00186 Rome Italy

#253
Sala 1
Category: Art Gallery
Area: San Giovanni
Address: Piazza Di Porta San Giovanni 10,
00185 Rome Italy
Phone: +39 06 7008691

#254
Fondazione Giorgio De Chirico
Category: Museum
Area: Centro Storico
Address: Piazza Di Spagna 31
00187 Rome Italy
Phone: +39 06 6796546

#255
Contemporanea
Category: Art Gallery
Area: Centro Storico
Address: Vicolo Sugarelli, 6
00186 Rome Italy
Phone: +39 338 2210224

#256
Enoteca Bruni
Category: Winery
Area: Termini, Centro Storico
Address: Via Ludovisi, 33
00187 Rome Italy
Phone: +39 06 42013326

#257
Alinari
Category: Art Gallery,
Photography Store
Area: Centro Storico
Address: Via Alibert 16
00187 Rome Italy
Phone: +39 06 69941998

#258
Il Burattinaio Del Gianicolo
Category: Performing Arts
Area: Borgo
Address: Viale Del Gianicolo
00165 Rome Italy
Phone: +39 06 5827767

#259
Alif
Category: Art Gallery, Social Club
Area: San Giovanni
Address: Piazza Dei Campani, 9
00185 Rome Italy

#260
LE Rune Magiche Di Moreti David
Category: Performing Arts, Costumes
Area: San Giovanni
Address: Via Casoria, 45
00182 Rome Italy
Phone: +39 06 70614508

#261
Teatro San Carlino
Category: Performing Arts
Area: Pinciano
Address: Viale Dei Bambini Villa Borghese
Pincio 00187 Rome Italy
Phone: +39 06 69922117

#262
Endemica Gallery
Category: Art Gallery
Area: Nomentano
Address: Via Mantova 14
00198 Rome Italy
Phone: +39 06 84240140

#263
Museo Pietro Canonica
Category: Landmark/Historic, Museum
Area: Pinciano
Address: Viale Pietro Canonica 2
00197 Rome Italy
Phone: +39 06 8845702

#264
Instituto Cervantes
Category: Cultural Center,
Language Schools
Area: Nomentano, Pinciano
Address: Via Di Villa Albani 16
00198 Rome Italy

#265
Scuola Romena Di Circo
Category: Sports Club,
Arts/Entertainment
Area: Monteverde
Address: Largo San Vincenzo
De Paoli, 00152 Rome Italy
Phone: +39 338 3552831

#266
Sala Caravaggio
Category: Cinema
Area: Parioli
Address: Via Giovanni Paisiello 24
00198 Rome Italy
Phone: +39 06 8554210

#267
Teatro Mongiovino
Category: Performing Arts,
Opera, Ballet, Music Venues
Area: Ostiense
Address: Via Giovanni Genocchi 15
00145 Rome Italy
Phone: +39 06 5139405

#268
Museo Gregoriano Egizio
Category: Museum
Area: Prati
Address: All'interno Dei Musei Vaticani
00192 Rome Italy

#269
Via Aerea - Vetrina Reale
Dello Shop Virtuale
Category: Street Art
Area: Pigneto, San Giovanni
Address: Circonvallazione Casilina 40
00176 Rome Italy

#270
Cinema Gregory
Category: Cinema
Area: Prati
Address: Via Gregorio VII 180
00165 Rome Italy
Phone: +39 06 6380600

#271
Mago Guarda
Category: Arts/Entertainment
Area: Phone Number
Address: Rome, Rome Italy

#272
Museo Dell'emigrazione Italiana
Category: Museum
Address: P.Zza Dell'ara Coeli,
1 Rome, Rome Italy
Phone: +39 06 69202049

#273
Teatro Villa Torlonia
Category: Performing Arts
Address: Via Nomentana 70
00161 Rome Italy
Phone: +39 06 4404768

#274
Vini Sfusi Vecchia Cantina
Category: Winery
Area: Pigneto
Address: Via Del Pigneto 118
00176 Rome Italy

#275
Teatro Greco
Category: Opera, Ballet
Address: Via Ruggero Leoncavallo 10
00199 Rome Italy
Phone: +39 06 8607513

#276
Mikro
Category: Art Gallery
Area: Nomentano, Salario
Address: Corso Trieste 121
00198 Rome Italy
Phone: +39 06 8417556

#277
Trafalgar Recording Studio
Category: Music Venues
Area: Balduina/Montemario
Address: Via Romeo Romei, 11
00136 Rome Italy
Phone: +39 06 39728201

#278
Wo-Ma'n Home Gallery
Category: Art Gallery
Area: Pigneto
Address: Via Pietro Ruga 24
00176 Rome Italy
Phone: +39 328 9292135

#279
Icon Circolo Arci
Category: Internet Café, Social Club
Average Price: Inexpensive
Area: Tuscolano
Address: Via Sgurgola 7
00179 Rome Italy
Phone: +39 06 95225861

#280
Gotan Club
Category: Sports Wear, Performing Arts
Area: Appia Antica
Address: Via Dei Cessati Spiriti 89
00179 Rome Italy

#281
Bruno Tours
Category: Tours, Museum
Area: Balduina/Montemario
Address: Via Paulo Quinto 29
00167 Rome Italy
Phone: +39 328 9473305

#282
Associazione Musicaealtro
Balduina
Category: Leisure Center,
Cultural Center
Area: Balduina/Montemario
Address: Via Giulio Braida 19
00136 Rome Italy
Phone: +39 06 35496818

#283
Plastic Surgery Tattoo
Category: Shopping
Area: Montesacro/Talenti
Address: Olindo Malagoti 37 Via
00157 Rome Italy

#284
Quadraro Basement
Category: Music Venues
Area: Tuscolano
Address: Via Egerio Levio 25/A
00174 Rome Italy
Phone: +39 06 76965472

#285
Taloni Arte
Category: Flowers, Gifts, Art Gallery
Area: Appia Antica, Eur
Address: Via Alessio Baldovinetti, 114
00142 Rome Italy
Phone: +39 06 5043070

#286
Istinti Musicali
Category: Performing Arts
Area: Casilino
Address: Via Albizzie 22
00172 Rome Italy
Phone: +39 06 24304579

#287
Fantasticland
Category: Arcade
Area: Casilino
Address: Via Dei Platani 180
00172 Rome Italy

#288
Dissonanze
Category: Arts/Entertainment
Area: Pineta Sacchetti
Address: Piazza John F. Kennedy 1
00168 Rome Italy

#289
Leandro Academy
Category: Arts/Entertainment
Area: Tuscolano
Address: Via Quintilio Varo 129
00174 Rome Italy
Phone: +39 348 1482256

#290
Museo Della Mente
Category: Museum
Area: Pineta Sacchetti
Address: Piazza S.Maria Della Piet'5
00135 Rome Italy
Phone: +39 06 68352825

#291
Villaggio Globale
Category: Street Art, Social Club,
Cultural Center
Area: Testaccio, Ostiense
Address: Lungotevere Testaccio, Via Del
Monte Dei Cocci 22
00153 Rome Italy
Phone: +39 347 9074404

#292
Dimmidisi Club
Category: Jazz &Blues, Dance Club
Average Price: Inexpensive
Area: San Lorenzo
Address: Via Dei Volsci 126B
00185 Rome Italy
Phone: +39 06 4461855

#293
Le Cantine Del Re
Category: Winery
Area: Tuscolano
Address: Via Antonio Ciamarra 25
00173 Rome Italy

#294
Walla Walla Live
Category: Music Venues
Area: Ardeatina
Address: Via Tor Pagnotta 371
00143 Rome Italy
Phone: +39 06 5010111

#295
Uci Cinemas
Category: Cinema
Area: Ostiense
Address: Via Enrico Fermi 161
00146 Rome Italy
Phone: +39 06 892960

#296
Antonelli
Category: Winery
Area: Ardeatina
Address: Via Di Tor Pagnotta 364
00143 Rome Italy
Phone: +39 339 3801493

#297
Teatro Dei Satiri
Category: Opera, Ballet, Music Venues
Average Price: Inexpensive
Area: Centro Storico
Address: Via Grotta Pinta, 19
00186 Rome Italy
Phone: +39 06 6871578

#298
Villa Celimontana Circus
Category: Performing Arts,
Music Venues
Area: Esquilino, Aventino
Address: Piazza Ss.Giovanni E Paolo
00184 Rome Italy
Phone: +39 06 583335781

#299
Teatro Ambra Jovinelli
Category: Performing Arts
Area: Termini
Address: Via Guglielmo Pepe, 43
00185 Rome Italy
Phone: +39 06 83082620

#300
CSOA La Strada
Category: Social Club
Area: Ostiense
Address: Via Passino 24
00154 Rome Italy
Phone: +39 06 51436006

#301
Enoteca D'Orio
Category: Specialty Food, Winery
Average Price: Inexpensive
Area: Nomentano
Address: Piazza Regina Margherita 9
00198 Rome Italy
Phone: +39 06 44250905

#302
Teatro Sette
Category: Performing Arts
Area: Nomentano
Address: Via Benevento 23
00161 Rome Italy
Phone: +39 06 44236382

#303
Colonne De Trajan
Category: Arts/Entertainment
Address: 00138 Rome Italy

#304
Circolo Ricreativo Caracciolo
Category: Cultural Center
Area: Prati
Address: Via Francesco Caracciolo 23A
00192 Rome Italy
Phone: +39 06 39733293

#305
26 CC
Category: Art Gallery
Area: Pigneto
Address: Via Castruccio Castracane 26
00176 Rome Italy
Phone: +39 06 98182991

#306
Jolly
Category: Cinema
Area: San Lorenzo
Address: Via Giano Della Bella, 4/6
00162 Rome Italy
Phone: +39 06 44232190

#307
La Vineria
Category: Winery
Area: Pigneto
Address: Via Gentile Da Mogliano 21
00176 Rome Italy
Phone: +39 349 7704311

#308
Politecnico Fandango
Category: Cinema
Area: Flaminio
Address: Via Gianbattista Tiepolo 13A
00196 Rome Italy
Phone: +39 06 36004240

#309
Teatro Olimpico
Category: Opera, Ballet, Music Venues,
Performing Arts
Average Price: Inexpensive
Area: Flaminio
Address: Piazza Gentile Da
Fabriano, 17, 00196 Rome Italy
Phone: +39 06 3265991

#310
Dolce &Salato
Category: Bakery, Winery
Average Price: Inexpensive
Area: Phone Number
Address: Via Dei Sette Metri,
66, 00040 Rome Italy

#311
Escopazzo
Category: Music Venues,
Lounge, Karaoke
Average Price: Inexpensive
Area: Centro Storico
Address: Via d'Aracoeli, 41
00186 Rome Italy
Phone: +39 389 6835618

#312
Teatro Manhattan
Category: Performing Arts
Area: Monti
Address: Via Del Boschetto 58
00184 Rome Italy

#313
Cinema Embassy
Category: Cinema
Area: Salario, Parioli
Address: Via Stoppani, 7
00197 Rome Italy
Phone: +39 06 8070245

#314
Galleria d'Arte De' Serpenti
Category: Social Club
Area: Monti
Address: Via Dei Serpenti 32
00184 Rome Italy
Phone: +39 06 4872212

#315
Profondo Rosso
Category: Museum, Bookstore
Average Price: Modest
Area: Prati
Address: Via Dei Gracchi 260
00192 Rome Italy
Phone: +39 06 3211395

#316
Vini Olii Porchetta
Category: Winery
Average Price: Modest
Area: San Giovanni
Address: Via Del Pigneto 18
00176 Rome Italy
Phone: +39 06 4385445

#317
Museo Di Romeln Trastevere
Category: Museum
Area: Trastevere
Address: Piazza Sant'Egidio 1B
00153 Rome Italy
Phone: +39 06 5816563

#318
Odeon Multiscreen
Category: Arts/Entertainment
Area: Corso Francia
Address: Piazza Jacini, 22
00191 Rome Italy
Phone: +39 06 86391361

#319
Pavart
Category: Art Gallery,
Interior Design, Personal Shopping
Average Price: Inexpensive
Area: Trastevere
Address: Via Dei Genovesi 12A
00153 Rome Italy
Phone: +39 06 5806778

#320
Opera Unica
Category: Art Gallery
Average Price: Inexpensive
Area: Centro Storico
Address: Via Della Reginella 26
00186 Rome Italy
Phone: +39 06 68809645

#321
Teatro Centrale
Category: Opera, Ballet, Music Venues,
Cocktail Bar
Average Price: Inexpensive
Area: Centro Storico
Address: Via Celsa, 6
00186 Rome Italy
Phone: +39 06 6780501

#322
Blurry
Category: Bookstore, Art Gallery
Area: Trastevere
Address: Via Di San Crisogono 33
00153 Rome Italy
Phone: +39 06 96841800

#323
Museo Ebraico Di Rome
Category: Museum
Area: Centro Storico
Address: Lungotevere Cenci
00186 Rome Italy
Phone: +39 06 68400661

#324
Ass. Culturale Cometa
Category: Performing Arts
Area: Testaccio, Ostiense
Address: Via Luca Della Robbia, 47
00153 Rome Italy
Phone: +39 06 57284637

#325
Teatro Belli
Category: Performing Arts
Area: Trastevere
Address: Piazza Sant' Apollonia 11A
00153 Rome Italy
Phone: +39 06 5894875

#326
Atelier Degli Artisti
Category: Art Gallery
Average Price: Inexpensive
Area: Trastevere
Address: Via Dell'arco Di San Calisto 40
00153 Rome Italy
Phone: +39 06 96844351

#327
Tidir'
Category: Active Life
Area: Borgo, Trastevere
Address: Via Del Mattonato 42
00153 Rome Italy
Phone: +39 06 5810626

#328
Versoriente
Category: Shopping
Area: Centro Storico
Address: Vicolo Cellini, 17
00165 Rome Italy
Phone: +39 06 6893506

#329
I Colori Di Dentro
Category: Art Gallery
Area: Centro Storico
Address: Via Dei Banchi Vecchi 28
00186 Rome Italy
Phone: +39 06 6832494

#330
Tricromia
Category: Art Gallery
Area: Centro Storico
Address: Via Di Panico, 35
00186 Rome Italy
Phone: +39 06 6896970

#331
Music Inn
Category: Jazz &Blues
Area: Centro Storico
Address: Largo Dei Fiorentini 3
00186 Rome Italy
Phone: +39 06 68806751

#332
**Museo Nazionale Di
Castel S.Angelo**
Category: Museum
Address: Lungo Tevere Castello 50
Rome, Rome Italy
Phone: +39 06 6819111

#333
**Anfiteatro Della
Quercia Del Tasso**
Category: Performing Arts
Area: Borgo
Address: Passeggiata Del Gianicolo
00165 Rome Italy
Phone: +39 06 5750827

#334
Rock Cycle Store
Category: Art Gallery, Books, Mags
Average Price: Inexpensive
Area: Termini, San Giovanni
Address: Via Dei Volsci 44B
00185 Rome Italy
Phone: +39 06 45473430

#335
Belzebook
Category: Winery
Average Price: Inexpensive
Area: San Giovanni
Address: Via Dei Marsi, 59
00185 Rome Italy

#336
Ippodromo Capannelle
Category: Music Venues
Area: Tuscolano
Address: Via Appia Nuova 1
255, 00040 Rome Italy
Phone: +39 06 716771

#337
Bingo Rouge Et Noire
Category: Casino
Area: Pinciano
Address: Via Salaria 33- 39
00198 Rome Italy

#338
Teatro Delle Muse
Category: Performing Arts
Area: San Lorenzo
Address: Via Forl'43
00161 Rome Italy
Phone: +39 06 44233649

#339
Semidivino Enoteca
Category: Italian, Winery
Area: Nomentano
Address: Via Alessandria 230
00198 Rome Italy
Phone: +39 06 89016293

#340
L'Enoteca Di Monteverde
Category: Winery
Average Price: Inexpensive
Area: Monteverde
Address: Via Federico Ozanam,
40, 00152 Rome Italy
Phone: +39 06 95218694

#341
Teatro Dell'angelo
Category: Performing Arts
Area: Prati
Address: Via Simone De Saint
Bon 19, 00195 Rome Italy
Phone: +39 06 37513571

#342
Cinema Delle Province d'Essai
Category: Cinema
Area: San Lorenzo
Address: Via Delle Provincie 41
00162 Rome Italy
Phone: +39 06 44236021

#343
Fiera Di Rome
Category: Festival
Area: Phone Number
Address: Via Portuense 1645
00148 Rome Italy

#344
Palatiziano
Category: Stadium/Arena
Area: Flaminio
Address: Piazza Apollodoro 10
00196 Rome Italy
Phone: +39 06 36857187

#345
Museo Delle Cere
Category: Museum
Area: Phone Number
Address: Piazza Dei SS.
Apostoli, 68/A, 00187 Rome Italy

#346
Museo Nazionale Preistorico Etnografico
Category: Museum
Area: Eur
Address: Piazza Guglielmo
Marconi 14, 00144 Rome Italy
Phone: +39 06 549521

#347
Sandro Onofri
Category: Cultural Center
Area: Ostia
Address: Via Umberto Lilloni 39/45
00125 Rome Italy

#348
Quarticciolo
Category: Performing Arts, Library
Area: Casilino
Address: Via Ostuni 8
00171 Rome Italy
Phone: +39 06 98951725

#349
Museo Carlo Bilotti
Category: Museum
Area: Centro Storico
Address: Viale Fiorello La Guardia 6
00197 Rome Italy
Phone: +39 06 0608

#350
Casa Dell'architettura
Category: Museum
Area: Termini
Address: Piazza Manfredo Fanti 47
00185 Rome Italy
Phone: +39 06 97604598

#351
Rashomon Club
Category: Music Venues
Average Price: Inexpensive
Address: Via Degli Argonauti 16
00154 Rome Italy

#352
Teatro Italia
Category: Opera, Ballet, Music Venues
Average Price: Inexpensive
Address: Via Bari, 18
00161 Rome Italy
Phone: +39 06 44239286

#353
Giardini Vaticani
Category: Botanical Garden
Average Price:
Area: Citt' Del Vaticano, Prati
Address: Viale Vaticano
00165 Rome Italy
Phone: +39 06 69883145

#354
Clockwork
Category: Social Club
Area: Pigneto
Address: Via Fanfulla DA Lodi, 5/A
00176 Rome Italy
Phone: +39 06 89527498

#355
Cinema Savoy
Category: Cinema
Area: Pinciano
Address: Via Bergamo 25
00198 Rome Italy
Phone: +39 06 85300948

#356
Cinema Admiral
Category: Cinema
Area: Salario
Address: Piazza Verbano 5
00199 Rome Italy
Phone: +39 06 8541195

#357
Strike
Area: Tuscolano
Address: Via U.Partini, 21
00169 Rome Italy
Phone: +39 366 1447867

#358
Teatro Tendastrisce
Category: Music Venues
Area: Casilino
Address: Via Giorgio Perlasca, 69
00155 Rome Italy
Phone: +39 06 25396785

#359
Casa-Museo Di Giacinto Scelsi
Category: Museum
Area: Centro Storico
Address: Via S. Teodoro 8
00186 Rome Italy
Phone: +39 06 69920344

#360
Teatro Colosseo
Category: Performing Arts
Area: Aventino
Address: Via Capo d'Africa 5A
00184 Rome Italy
Phone: +39 06 7004932

#361
Arti E Pensieri
Category: Art Gallery
Area: Esquilino, Aventino
Address: Via Ostilia ,3
00184 Rome Italy

#362
Ermanno Tedeschi Gallery
Category: Art Gallery
Area: Centro Storico
Address: Via Portico D'ottavia, 7
00186 Rome Italy
Phone: +39 06 45551063

#363
Deglizingari Gallery
Category: Art Gallery
Area: Monti
Address: Via Degli Zingari 52
00184 Rome Italy
Phone: +39 06 48907135

#364
White Cube
Category: Art Gallery
Area: Centro Storico
Address: Piazza Mattei 11
00186 Rome Italy
Phone: +39 06 64760164

#365
Mo.C.A.
Category: Art Gallery,
Interior Design
Area: Monti
Address: Piazza Degli Zingari 1
00184 Rome Italy
Phone: +39 06 4742764

#366
Associazione Culturale Teatro
Category: Performing Arts
Area: Trastevere
Address: Via Zanazzo Giggi 1
00153 Rome Italy
Phone: +39 06 5817413

#367
Sales
Category: Art Gallery
Area: Aventino
Address: Via Dei Querceti, 5
00184 Rome Italy
Phone: +39 06 77254794

#368
Teatro Trastevere
Category: Performing Arts
Area: Trastevere
Address: Via Jacopa De' Settesoli, 3
00153 Rome Italy
Phone: +39 06 83664400

#369
Wunderkammer
Category: Art Gallery
Area: Monti
Address: Via Del Boschetto 130
00184 Rome Italy

#370
Niki De Saint Phalle
Category: Arts/Entertainment
Area: Centro Storico
Address: Via Del Corso 320
00186 Rome Italy
Phone: +39 06 62288877

#371
Ass.Culturale Voci Della Terra
Category: Cultural Center
Area: Trastevere
Address: Vicolo Del Bologna 49
00153 Rome Italy
Phone: +39 06 58335689

#372
Museo Della Via Ostiense
Category: Museum
Area: Testaccio, Ostiense
Address: Via Raffaele Persichetti 3
00153 Rome Italy
Phone: +39 06 5651500

#373
Angelini
Category: Winery
Area: Centro Storico
Address: Piazza Del Viminale, 62
00184 Rome Italy
Phone: +39 06 4881028

#374
Galleria Minima
Category: Art Gallery
Area: Centro Storico
Address: Via Del Pellegrino 18
00186 Rome Italy
Phone: +39 06 50915747

#375
Rgb 46 Gallery
Category: Bookstore, Art Gallery
Area: Testaccio, Ostiense
Address: Piazza Santa Maria Liberatrice
46, 00153 Rome Italy
Phone: +39 06 45421608

#376
Dandrieu - Giovagnoni
Category: Art Gallery
Area: Centro Storico
Address: Via Del Collegio Capranica 9
00186 Rome Italy
Phone: +39 06 6990264

#377
Montoro12 Contemporay Art
Category: Art Gallery
Area: Centro Storico
Address: Via Di Montoro12
00186 Rome Italy
Phone: +39 06 68308500

#378
**National Gallery Of Ancient
Art Of Barberini Palace**
Category: Museum
Area: Centro Storico
Address: Via Delle Quattro
Fontane 13, 00184 Rome Italy
Phone: +39 06 32810

#379
Sant'Agnese In Agone
Category: Museum
Area: Centro Storico
Address: Via S. Maria Dell'anima 30/A
00186 Rome Italy
Phone: +39 06 68192134

#380
Galleria Nazionale D'arte Antica
Category: Museum
Area: Borgo
Address: Via Della Lungara 10
00165 Rome Italy
Phone: +39 06 68802323

#381
Teatro Di Documenti
Category: Performing Arts
Area: Testaccio, Ostiense
Address: Via Nicola Zabaglia, 42
00153 Rome Italy
Phone: +39 06 5744034

#382
Teatro Le Maschere
Category: Performing Arts
Area: Trastevere
Address: Via Aurelio Saliceti, 1
00153 Rome Italy
Phone: +39 06 58330817

#383
La Citt' In Tasca
Category: Festival
Area: San Giovanni
Address: Parco Degli Scipioni
Via Di Porta Latina,10
00179 Rome Italy
Phone: +39 06 41733356

#384
Teatro Dei Conciatori
Category: Cinema
Area: Testaccio, Ostiense
Address: Via Dei Conciatori 5A
00154 Rome Italy
Phone: +39 06 45448982

#385
Magazzino d'Arte Moderna
Category: Art Gallery
Area: Centro Storico
Address: Via Dei Prefetti, 17
00186 Rome Italy
Phone: +39 06 6875951

#386
Palazzo Altemps
Category: Museum
Area: Centro Storico
Address: Piazza Di Sant'Apollinare,
46, 00186 Rome Italy
Phone: +39 06 39967700

#387
Sken'
Category: Jazz &Blues, Cabaret
Average Price: Inexpensive
Area: Testaccio, Ostiense
Address: Via Francesco Carletti 5
00154 Rome Italy
Phone: +39 06 5755561

#388
Teatro L'Arciliuto
Category: Performing Arts
Area: Centro Storico
Address: Piazza Montevecchio 5
00186 Rome Italy
Phone: +39 06 6879419

#389
Federica Schiavo Gallery
Category: Art Gallery
Area: Centro Storico
Address: Piazza Montevecchio 16
00186 Rome Italy
Phone: +39 06 45432028

#390
Artsinergy
Category: Art Gallery
Area: Centro Storico
Address: Via Dei Cartari 9
00186 Rome Italy
Phone: +39 06 68892340

#391
Al Ferro Di Cavallo
Category: Bookstore, Art Gallery
Area: Centro Storico
Address: Via Del Governo Vecchio 7
00186 Rome Italy
Phone: +39 06 6893703

#392
Galleria Marie-Laure Fleisch
Category: Art Gallery
Area: Centro Storico
Address: Vicolo Sforza Cesarini 3a
00186 Rome Italy
Phone: +39 06 68891936

#393
Cinema Fiamma
Category: Cinema
Area: Centro Storico
Address: Via Bissolati 45
00187 Rome Italy

#394
American Academy In Rome
Category: Education, Museum
Area: Monteverde
Address: Via Angelo Masina, 5
00153 Rome Italy
Phone: +39 06 5809298

#395
Mosaicari
Category: Art Gallery
Area: Centro Storico
Address: Via Di Panico 75
00186 Rome Italy
Phone: +39 06 6833574

#396
Via Della Comunicazione
Category: Street Art
Area: Testaccio, Ostiense
Address: Via Dei Magazzini Generali 10
00154 Rome Italy

#397
Studio Stefania Miscetti
Category: Art Gallery
Area: Borgo
Address: Via Delle Mantellate 14
00165 Rome Italy
Phone: +39 06 68805880

#398
Fondazione Romeeuropa
Category: Arts/Entertainment
Area: Testaccio, Ostiense
Address: Via Dei Magazzini Generali 20A,
00154 Rome Italy
Phone: +39 06 45553050

#399
Museo Delle Anime Del Purgatorio
Category: Museum
Area: Centro Storico, Prati
Address: Lungotevere Prati 18
00193 Rome Italy
Phone: +39 06 68806517

#400
The Gallery Apart
Category: Art Gallery
Area: Ostiense
Address: Via Francesco Negri 43
00154 Rome Italy
Phone: +39 06 68809863

TOP 500 NIGHTLIFE

Most Recommended by Locals & Trevelers
Ranking (from #1 to #500)

#1
Tazza d'Oro
Average Price: Inexpensive
Category: Bar, Café, Ice Cream
Area: Centro Storico
Address: Via Degli Orfani 84
00186 Rome Italy
Phone: +39 06 6789792

#2
Sant'Eustachio Il Caff'
Average Price: Inexpensive
Category: Bar, Café
Area: Centro Storico
Address: Piazza Sant'Eustachio 81
00186 Rome Italy
Phone: +39 06 68802048

#3
Auditorium Parco Della Musica
Average Price: Modest
Category: Opera, Ballet, Music Venues
Area: Flaminio
Address: Viale Pietro De Coubertin 30
00196 Rome Italy
Phone: +39 06 802411

#4
Antico Caff' Greco
Average Price: Exclusive
Category: Bar, Café
Area: Centro Storico
Address: Via Condotti 86
00187 Rome Italy
Phone: +39 06 6791700

#5
Ai Tre Scalini
Average Price: Modest
Category: Wine Bar, Tapas Bar
Area: Monti
Address: Via Panisperna 251
00184 Rome Italy
Phone: +39 06 48907495

#6
Etabl'
Average Price: Modest
Category: Wine Bar, Café, Mediterranean
Area: Centro Storico
Address: Vicolo Delle Vacche 9
00186 Rome Italy
Phone: +39 06 97616694

#7
Bir &Fud
Average Price: Modest
Category: Pizza, Brewerie, Pub
Area: Trastevere
Address: Via Benedetta 23
00153 Rome Italy
Phone: +39 06 5894016

#8
Hotel De Russie
Average Price: Exclusive
Category: Venues &Events,
Wine Bar, Hotel
Area: Flaminio
Address: Via Del Babuino 9
00187 Rome Italy
Phone: +39 06 328881

#9
Cul De Sac
Average Price: Modest
Category: Italian, Beer,
Wine, Spirits, Wine Bar
Area: Centro Storico
Address: Piazza Pasquino 73
00186 Rome Italy
Phone: +39 06 68801094

#10
Ma Che Siete Venuti A Fa'
Average Price: Modest
Category: Pub, Brewerie
Area: Trastevere
Address: Via Benedetta 25
00153 Rome Italy
Phone: +39 06 97275218

#11
Mizzica
Average Price: Modest
Category: Desserts, Bar
Area: San Lorenzo
Address: Via Catanzaro 30
00161 Rome Italy
Phone: +39 06 44236024

#12
Jerry Thomas Speakeasy
Average Price: Modest
Category: Lounge, Cocktail Bar
Area: Centro Storico
Address: Vicolo Cellini 30
00186 Rome Italy
Phone: +39 06 96845937

#13
Life
Average Price: Modest
Category: Wine Bar, Italian, Pizza
Area: Centro Storico
Address: Via Della Vite 28
00187 Rome Italy
Phone: +39 06 69380948

#14
Gregory's Live Jazz &Dinner Club
Average Price: Modest
Category: Jazz &Blues,
Beer, Wine, Spirits
Area: Centro Storico
Address: Via Gregoriana 54A
00187 Rome Italy
Phone: +39 327 8263770

#15
Grandma Bistrot
Average Price: Modest
Category: Wine Bar,
Breakfast &Brunch, Italian
Area: Tuscolano
Address: Via Dei Corneli 25
00175 Rome Italy
Phone: +39 377 2649540

#16
Cavour 313
Average Price: Expensive
Category: Beer, Wine, Spirits,
Wine Bar
Area: Monti
Address: Via Cavour 313
00184 Rome Italy
Phone: +39 06 6785496

#17
Ferrazza
Average Price: Modest
Category: Wine Bar, Beer
Area: Termini, San Giovanni
Address: Via Dei Volsci 59
00185 Rome Italy
Phone: +39 06 490506

#18
Baccano
Average Price: Expensive
Category: Wine Bar, Italian
Area: Centro Storico
Address: Via Delle Muratte 23
00187 Rome Italy
Phone: +39 06 69941166

#19
La Botticella
Average Price: Modest
Category: Pub, Wine Bar
Area: Centro Storico
Address: Via Tor Millina 32
00186 Rome Italy
Phone: +39 06 6861107

#20
Il Sorchettaro
Average Price: Inexpensive
Category: Desserts, Bar
Area: Termini
Address: Via Cernaia 47A
00185 Rome Italy
Phone: +39 06 83608651

#21
Bar Del Fico
Average Price: Modest
Category: Bar, Café
Area: Centro Storico
Address: Piazza Del Fico 26
00186 Rome Italy
Phone: +39 06 68808413

#22
Centrale Montemartini
Average Price: Inexpensive
Category: Museum, Music Venues
Area: Testaccio, Ostiense
Address: Via Ostiense 106
00154 Rome Italy
Phone: +39 06 0608

#23
Bar San Calisto
Average Price: Inexpensive
Category: Bar
Area: Trastevere
Address: Piazza San Calisto 3
00153 Rome Italy
Phone: +39 06 5895670

#24
Circolo Degli Artisti
Average Price: Modest
Category: Dance Club
Area: San Giovanni
Address: Via Casilina Vecchia 42
00182 Rome Italy
Phone: +39 06 70305684

#25
Caf' Caf'
Average Price: Modest
Category: Mediterranean, Italian, Wine Bar
Area: Aventino
Address: Via De' SS. Quattro 44
00184 Rome Italy
Phone: +39 06 7008743

#26
Antico Arco
Average Price: Exclusive
Category: Wine Bar, Italian
Area: Monteverde
Address: Piazzale Aurelio 7
00152 Rome Italy
Phone: +39 06 5815274

#27
Freni E Frizioni
Average Price: Modest
Category: Wine Bar, Pub
Area: Trastevere
Address: Via Del Politeama 4
00153 Rome Italy
Phone: +39 06 45497499

#28
Moma
Average Price: Expensive
Category: Wine Bar, Italian
Area: Centro Storico
Address: Via San Basilio 42
00187 Rome Italy
Phone: +39 06 42011798

#29
Libreria Del Cinema
Average Price: Modest
Category: Wine Bar, Bookstore
Area: Trastevere
Address: Via Dei Fienaroli 31D
00153 Rome Italy
Phone: +39 06 5817724

#30
Geronimo's
Average Price: Expensive
Category: Pub, Music Venues
Area: Phone Number
Address: Via Appia Nuova 57
00047 Marino Italy
Phone: +39 06 44702320

#31
Zerozero100
Average Price: Modest
Category: Italian, Lounge, Pizza
Area: San Lorenzo, San Giovanni
Address: Via Del Verano 27
00185 Rome Italy
Phone: +39 06 44702346

#32
Hotel Majestic
Average Price: Expensive
Category: Italian, Cocktail Bar
Area: Centro Storico
Address: Via Vittorio Veneto 50
00187 Rome Italy
Phone: +39 06 421441

#33
Momart Caf'
Average Price: Modest
Category: Buffet, Wine Bar
Area: Nomentano
Address: Viale XXI Aprile 19
00162 Rome Italy
Phone: +39 06 86391656

#34
The Fiddler's Elbow
Average Price: Inexpensive
Category: Pub
Address: Via Dell'olmata 43
00184 Rome Italy
Phone: +39 06 4872110

#35
Caff' Della Pace
Average Price: Modest
Category: Café, Bar
Area: Centro Storico
Address: Via Della Pace 3
00186 Rome Italy
Phone: +39 06 6861216

#36
Angelo Mai Altrove
Average Price: Inexpensive
Category: Music Venues,
Dance Club
Area: Aventino, San Giovanni
Address: Via Delle Terme Di
Caracalla 55, 00153 Rome Italy
Phone: +39 06 44702321

#37
Necci 1924
Average Price: Expensive
Category: Wine Bar, Café
Area: Pigneto
Address: Via Fanfulla Da Lodi 68
00176 Rome Italy
Phone: +39 06 97601552

#38
Abbey Theatre Irish Pub
Average Price: Modest
Category: Sports Bar, Pub, Irish
Area: Centro Storico
Address: Via Del Governo Vecchio 51
00186 Rome Italy
Phone: +39 06 6861341

#39
Romoli
Average Price: Modest
Category: Bar, Desserts
Area: Nomentano, Salario
Address: Viale Eritrea 140
00199 Rome Italy
Phone: +39 06 86325077

#40
Enoteca Ferrara
Average Price: Exclusive
Category: Beer, Wine, Spirits
Area: Trastevere
Address: Piazza Trilussa 41
00153 Rome Italy
Phone: +39 06 58333920

#41
Finnegan
Average Price: Modest
Category: Pub
Area: Monti
Address: Via Leonina 66
00184 Rome Italy
Phone: +39 06 4747026

#42
Il Cornettone
Average Price: Inexpensive
Category: Bar, Desserts
Area: Magliana, Ostiense
Address: Via Oderisi Da Gubbio 217
00146 Rome Italy
Phone: +39 06 5587922

#43
Le Mura Live Club
Average Price: Inexpensive
Category: Wine Bar, Music Venues
Area: Termini, San Giovanni
Address: Via Di Porta Labicana, 24
00185 Rome Italy
Phone: +39 06 44702322

#44
Andirivieni
Average Price: Modest
Category: Bar, Italian
Area: Balduina/Montemario, Prati
Address: Via Della Meloria 80
00136 Rome Italy
Phone: +39 06 39735305

#45
Brasserie 4:20
Average Price: Modest
Category: Brasserie, Pub, Wine Bar
Area: Trastevere
Address: Via Portuense 82
00153 Rome Italy
Phone: +39 06 58310737

#46
Pourquoi!
Average Price: Modest
Category: Brasserie, Pub
Area: San Lorenzo, San Giovanni
Address: Via Dei Volsci 82
00185 Rome Italy
Phone: +39 06 44361955

#47
Napoleoni
Average Price: Modest
Category: Bar, Ice Cream
Area: Tuscolano, Appia Antica
Address: Via Appia Nuova 592
00178 Rome Italy
Phone: +39 06 78359574

#48
Ciampini
Average Price: Expensive
Category: Bar, Ice Cream, Café
Area: Centro Storico
Address: Piazza S. Lorenzo In Lucina 29,
00186 Rome Italy
Phone: +39 06 6876606

#49
Scholars Lounge Pub
Average Price: Modest
Category: Pub, American
Area: Centro Storico
Address: Via Del Plebiscito 101B
00186 Rome Italy
Phone: +39 06 69202208

#50
Forte Fanfulla
Average Price: Modest
Category: Music Venues
Area: Pigneto
Address: Via Fanfulla Da Lodi 5
00176 Rome Italy
Phone: +39 06 44702323

#51
Romena Mente
Average Price: Modest
Category: Bar, Café
Area: Ostiense
Address: Circonvallazione
Ostiense 136, 00154 Rome Italy
Phone: +39 06 51605131

#52
Maranega
Average Price: Modest
Category: Bar, Café
Area: Centro Storico
Address: Piazza Campo De' Fiori 48
00186 Rome Italy
Phone: +39 06 68300331

#53
Baccanale Trastevere
Average Price: Modest
Category: Pub, Italian
Area: Trastevere
Address: Via Della Lungaretta 81
00153 Rome Italy
Phone: +39 06 45448268

#54
Officine Beat
Average Price: Expensive
Category: Wine Bar, Pub, Italian
Area: Termini, San Giovanni
Address: Via Degli Equi 29
00185 Rome Italy
Phone: +39 06 95218779

#55
Ombre Rosse
Average Price: Modest
Category: Jazz &Blues, Bar
Area: Trastevere
Address: Piazza Sant'Egidio 12-13
00153 Rome Italy
Phone: +39 06 5884155

#56
Salotto 42
Average Price: Expensive
Category: Cocktail Bar
Area: Centro Storico
Address: Piazza Di Pietra 42
00186 Rome Italy
Phone: +39 06 6785804

#57
Magick Bar
Average Price: Inexpensive
Category: Lounge, Wine Bar
Area: Flaminio, Prati
Address: Lungotevere Oberdan 2
00196 Rome Italy
Phone: +39 06 5748277

#58
Conte Staccio
Average Price: Modest
Category: Music Venues,
Lounge, Italian
Area: Testaccio, Ostiense
Address: Via Di Monte Testaccio 65B
00153 Rome Italy
Phone: +39 06 57289712

#59
Caff' Letterario
Average Price: Expensive
Category: Bar, Books, Mags,
Music &Video
Area: Testaccio, Ostiense
Address: Via Ostiense 95
00154 Rome Italy
Phone: +39 06 57302842

#60
Jailbreak
Average Price: Expensive
Category: Music Venues, Pub
Area: Tiburtino
Address: Via Tiburtina 870
00155 Rome Italy
Phone: +39 00 39064063155

#61
Rosticcer'
Average Price: Exclusive
Category: Bar
Area: Centro Storico
Address: Corso Rinascimento 83
00186 Rome Italy
Phone: +39 06 68808345

#62
Bar Hungaria
Average Price: Expensive
Category: Bar, Burgers, Café
Area: Salario
Address: Piazza Ungheria 7
00198 Rome Italy
Phone: +39 06 8551432

#63
Casa Del Jazz
Average Price: Modest
Category: Jazz &Blues
Area: Ostiense
Address: Viale Di Porta Ardeatina 55
00154 Rome Italy
Phone: +39 06 704731

#64
Hotel Locarno
Average Price: Expensive
Category: Lounge, Hotel, Cocktail Bar
Area: Flaminio
Address: Via Della Penna 22
00186 Rome Italy
Phone: +39 06 3610841

#65
Er Caffettiere
Average Price: Modest
Category: Café, Bar
Area: Monti
Address: Via Urbana 72
00184 Rome Italy
Phone: +39 320 4168532

#66
Lo Zodiaco
Average Price: Expensive
Category: Bar, Italian
Area: Balduina/Montemario
Address: Viale Del Parco Mellini 88
00136 Rome Italy
Phone: +39 06 35496744

#67
Bar Lillo
Average Price: Inexpensive
Category: Café, Bar
Area: Trastevere
Address: Via Dei Genovesi 39
00153 Rome Italy
Phone: +39 06 5817142

#68
Henry Cow
Average Price: Modest
Category: Bar
Area: Termini
Address: Via Flavia 61
00187 Rome Italy
Phone: +39 06 484823

#69
Lanificio 159
Average Price: Modest
Category: Music Venues
Area: Montesacro/Talenti
Address: Via Di Pietralata 159
00157 Rome Italy
Phone: +39 06 41780081

#70
Duke's
Average Price: Exclusive
Category: Bar, American
Area: Salario
Address: Viale Parioli 200
00197 Rome Italy
Phone: +39 06 80662455

#71
Fluid
Average Price: Expensive
Category: Lounge
Area: Centro Storico
Address: Via Del Governo Vecchio 46
00186 Rome Italy
Phone: +39 06 6832361

#72
Caff' Boh'mien
Average Price: Modest
Category: Café, Wine Bar
Area: Monti
Address: Via Degli Zingari 36
00184 Rome Italy
Phone: +39 339 7224622

#73
Bar Celestino
Average Price: Inexpensive
Category: Café, Pub
Area: San Giovanni
Address: Via Degli Ausoni 62
00185 Rome Italy
Phone: +39 06 490517

#74
Big Mama
Average Price: Expensive
Category: Jazz &Blues,
Music Venues
Area: Trastevere
Address: Vicolo Di San Francesco A Ripa
18, 00153 Rome Italy
Phone: +39 06 5812551

#75
Civetta Sul Com'
Average Price: Inexpensive
Category: Pub,
Recreation Center
Area: San Giovanni
Address: Via Cereate 8
00183 Rome Italy
Phone: +39 06 7003752

#76
Piper Club
Average Price: Exclusive
Category: Dance Club
Area: Salario
Address: Via Tagliamento 9
00198 Rome Italy
Phone: +39 06 8555398

#77
Meeting Place
Average Price: Modest
Category: Bar, Café,
Coffee &Tea
Area: San Lorenzo
Address: Piazza Bologna 1A
00162 Rome Italy
Phone: +39 06 44237704

#78
La Fontana
Average Price: Modest
Category: Wine Bar, Italian
Area: Centro Storico
Address: Vicolo De' Modelli 56
00187 Rome Italy
Phone: +39 390 669924087

#79
Marinari Caff'
Average Price: Modest
Category: Internet Café, Bar
Area: Salario
Address: Viale Libia 10
00199 Rome Italy
Phone: +39 06 44702324

#80
L'Emporio Alla Pace
Average Price: Inexpensive
Category: Café, Bar
Area: Centro Storico
Address: Via Della Pace 28
00186 Rome Italy
Phone: +39 06 68802938

#81
Dulcamara
Average Price: Expensive
Category: Italian, Wine Bar
Area: Corso Francia
Address: Via Flaminia 449
00191 Rome Italy
Phone: +39 06 3332108

#82
Bali
Average Price: Modest
Category: Indonesian, Lounge
Area: Trastevere
Address: Via Del Mattonato 29
00153 Rome Italy
Phone: +39 06 5896089

#83
Alexanderplatz Jazz Club
Average Price: Expensive
Category: Jazz &Blues
Area: Prati
Address: Via Ostia 9
00192 Rome Italy
Phone: +39 06 39742171

#84
Goa Club
Average Price: Expensive
Category: Dance Club, Bar
Area: Ostiense
Address: Via Giuseppe Libetta 13
00154 Rome Italy
Phone: +39 06 95558820

#85
Osteria Dell'ingegno
Average Price: Expensive
Category: Italian, Wine Bar
Area: Centro Storico
Address: Piazza Di Pietra 45
00186 Rome Italy
Phone: +39 06 6780662

#86
Palombini
Average Price: Expensive
Category: Bar, Café
Area: Eur
Address: Piazzale Konrad Adenauer 12
00144 Rome Italy
Phone: +39 06 5911700

#87
00 - Doppio Zero
Average Price: Modest
Category: Bar, Food, Pizza
Area: Testaccio, Ostiense
Address: Via Ostiense 68
00154 Rome Italy
Phone: +39 06 44702325

#88
Settembrini
Average Price: Expensive
Category: Wine Bar, Italian
Area: Prati
Address: Via Luigi Settembrini 25
00195 Rome Italy
Phone: +39 06 3232617

#89
Coso Wine
Average Price: Modest
Category: Italian, Wine Bar
Area: Centro Storico
Address: Via In Lucina 16L
00186 Rome Italy
Phone: +39 06 68210420

#90
Coming Out
Average Price: Modest
Category: Gay Bar
Area: Esquilino, Aventino
Address: Via Di San Giovanni In
Laterano 8 00184 Rome Italy
Phone: +39 06 7009871

#91
Mokarabia
Average Price: Modest
Category: Bar, Café
Area: Pinciano
Address: Piazza Fiume 77
00198 Rome Italy
Phone: +39 06 84241134

#92
Otium Club
Average Price: Modest
Category: Wine Bar, Pub
Area: Ostiense
Address: Via Roberto De Nobili 3B
00154 Rome Italy
Phone: +39 333 3643072

#93
Akbar
Average Price: Modest
Category: Cocktail Bar, Jazz &Blues
Area: Trastevere
Address: Piazza In Piscinula 51
00153 Rome Italy
Phone: +39 06 5800681

#94
Arte5
Average Price: Expensive
Category: Art Gallery, Jazz &Blues
Area: Centro Storico
Address: Corso Vittorio Emanuele II 5
00186 Rome Italy
Phone: +39 06 69921298

#95
Bar Del Cappuccino
Average Price: Inexpensive
Category: Bar, Café
Area: Centro Storico
Address: Via Arenula 50
00186 Rome Italy
Phone: +39 06 68806042

#96
Casina Valadier
Average Price: Exclusive
Category: Italian, Lounge
Area: Pinciano, Flaminio
Address: Piazza Bucarest
00187 Rome Italy
Phone: +39 06 69922090

#97
Four Green Fields
Average Price: Modest
Category: Pub, Brewerie
Area: Prati
Address: Via Costantino Morin 38
00195 Rome Italy
Phone: +39 06 3725091

#98
Tortuga
Average Price: Modest
Category: Bar, Café
Area: Nomentano, Salario
Address: Piazza Trasimeno 4
00198 Rome Italy
Phone: +39 06 8558289

#99
Fandango Incontro
Average Price: Inexpensive
Category: Wine Bar, Museum
Area: Centro Storico
Address: Via Dei Prefetti 22
00186 Rome Italy
Phone: +39 06 97601104

#100
Shari Vari
Average Price: Expensive
Category: Dance Club, Cocktail Bar
Area: Centro Storico
Address: Via Di Torre Argentina 78
00186 Rome Italy
Phone: +39 06 68806936

#101
Mim' E Coc'
Average Price: Modest
Category: Italian, Coffee &Tea, Wine Bar
Area: Centro Storico
Address: Via Del Governo Vecchio 72
00186 Rome Italy
Phone: +39 06 68301850

#102
Antonini
Average Price: Expensive
Category: Desserts, Ice Cream, Bar
Area: Prati
Address: Via Sabotino 19
00195 Rome Italy
Phone: +39 06 3725052

#103
Bar Viminale
Average Price: Modest
Category: Bar, Café
Area: Centro Storico
Address: Via Del Viminale 47
00184 Rome Italy
Phone: +39 06 486941

#104
Bar Brunori
Average Price: Modest
Category: Café, Bar
Area: Aventino, Ostiense
Address: Largo Giovanni Chiarini 2
00154 Rome Italy
Phone: +39 06 5746418

#105
Tavola Calda
Average Price: Modest
Category: Bar
Area: Borgo
Address: Via Della Cava Aurelia 64
00165 Rome Italy
Phone: +39 06 630852

#106
Habana
Average Price: Modest
Category: Pub, Karaoke
Area: Centro Storico
Address: Via Dei Pastini 120
00186 Rome Italy
Phone: +39 06 6781983

#107
Baylon Caf'
Average Price: Modest
Category: Cocktail Bar
Area: Trastevere
Address: Via Di San Francesco A
Ripa 151, 00153 Rome Italy
Phone: +39 06 5814275

#108
8Millimetri
Average Price: Inexpensive
Category: Cocktail Bar
Area: Trastevere
Address: Via Del Moro 8
00153 Rome Italy
Phone: +39 06 64562508

#109
Lancelot
Average Price: Inexpensive
Category: Pub, Italian
Area: Termini, San Giovanni
Address: Via Dei Volsci 77
00185 Rome Italy
Phone: +39 06 4454675

#110
Sciascia Caff'
Average Price: Modest
Category: Café, Lounge
Area: Prati
Address: Via Fabio Massimo 80A
00192 Rome Italy
Phone: +39 06 3211580

#111
Chakra Caf'
Average Price: Modest
Category: Pub, Wine Bar
Area: Trastevere
Address: Piazza Di San Rufina 13
00153 Rome Italy
Phone: +39 338 2917593

#112
The Old Cottage
Average Price: Modest
Category: Pub
Area: Borgo
Address: Piazza Santa Maria Alle Fornaci
2, 00191 Rome Italy
Phone: +39 06 6382774

#113
Bar Panth'on
Average Price: Modest
Category: Bar
Area: Centro Storico
Address: Via Degli Orfani
00186 Rome Italy
Phone: +39 06 44702326

#114
Streat
Average Price: Modest
Category: Bar, Italian
Area: San Giovanni
Address: Piazza Dei Campani 6
00185 Rome Italy
Phone: +39 06 44702327

#115
Stazione Birra
Average Price: Expensive
Category: Music Venues, Pub
Area: Phone Number
Address: Via Placanica 172
00118 Rome Italy
Phone: +39 06 44702328

#116
Harry's Bar
Average Price: Expensive
Category: Bar
Area: Termini
Address: Via Veneto 150
00187 Rome Italy
Phone: +39 06 484643

#117
Carrot's
Average Price: Modest
Category: Italian, Sports Bar
Area: Parioli
Address: Piazza Euclide 1
00197 Rome Italy
Phone: +39 06 8074594

#118
Big Hilda Caff'
Average Price: Modest
Category: Pub, Wine Bar
Area: Trastevere
Address: Vicolo Del Cinque 33
00100 Rome Italy
Phone: +39 06 5803303

#119
Hopside
Average Price: Expensive
Category: Pub, Burgers, Gluten-Free
Area: Ostiense
Address: Via Francesco Negri 39
00154 Rome Italy
Phone: +39 06 69313081

#120
Caff' San Lorenzo
Average Price: Modest
Category: Pub
Area: Termini, San Giovanni
Address: Via Dei Sabelli 50
00185 Rome Italy
Phone: +39 06 4454880

#121
Be Bop
Average Price: Modest
Category: Jazz &Blues
Area: Testaccio, Ostiense
Address: Via Giuseppe Giulietti 14
00154 Rome Italy
Phone: +39 06 5755582

#122
Gotha
Average Price: Expensive
Category: Wine Bar
Area: Salario
Address: Viale Parioli 144
00197 Rome Italy
Phone: +39 06 8080325

#123
Pasticceria Siciliana Svizzera
Average Price: Expensive
Category: Bar, Desserts
Area: Balduina/Montemario, Aurelia
Address: Piazza Pio XI 10
00165 Rome Italy
Phone: +39 06 6374974

#124
Caf' Friends
Average Price: Modest
Category: Lounge
Area: Trastevere
Address: Piazza Trilussa 34
00153 Rome Italy
Phone: +39 06 5816111

#125
Latte+
Average Price: Expensive
Category: Cocktail Bar
Area: San Giovanni
Address: Via Albalonga 31
00183 Rome Italy
Phone: +39 06 770091

#126
Gelateria Tony
Average Price: Modest
Category: Bar, Ice Cream,
Frozen Yogurt
Area: Ostiense
Address: Largo Alberto Missiroli 13
00151 Rome Italy
Phone: +39 06 58201002

#127
Sciam
Average Price: Expensive
Category: Hookah Bar, Middle Eastern
Area: Centro Storico
Address: Via Del Pellegrino 56
00186 Rome Italy
Phone: +39 06 68308957

#128
George Byron Caf'
Average Price: Modest
Area: Centro Storico
Address: Via Nazionale 250
00184 Rome Italy
Phone: +39 06 47825579

#129
Casina Appia
Average Price: Inexpensive
Category: Lounge
Area: Appia Antica
Address: Via Appia Nuova 620
00179 Rome Italy
Phone: +39 347 9531368

#130
Bibenda Wine Concept
Average Price: Expensive
Category: Wine Bar, Winery
Area: Aventino
Address: Via Capo d'Africa 21
00184 Rome Italy
Phone: +39 06 77206673

#131
Il Pasticciaccio
Average Price: Modest
Category: Lounge, Café
Area: Esquilino
Address: Via Merulana 34
00185 Rome Italy
Phone: +39 06 4826928

#132
Il Maritozzaro
Average Price: Modest
Category: Bar, Café
Area: Trastevere
Address: Via Ettore Rolli 50
00153 Rome Italy
Phone: +39 06 5810781

#133
Enoteca Trimani
Average Price: Exclusive
Category: Wine Bar, Winery, Beer, Wine
Area: Termini
Address: Via Goito 20
00185 Rome Italy
Phone: +39 06 4469661

#134
La Maison
Average Price: Exclusive
Category: Dance Club
Area: Centro Storico
Address: Vicolo Dei Granari 3
00186 Rome Italy
Phone: +39 06 6833312

#135
0,75 - Zerosettantacinque
Average Price: Modest
Category: Wine Bar, Pub, Cocktail Bar
Area: Aventino
Address: Via Dei Cerchi 65
00186 Rome Italy
Phone: +39 06 6875706

#136
Obik' Mozzarella Bar
Average Price: Modest
Category: Italian, Pizza, Lounge
Area: Centro Storico
Address: Piazza Campo Dei Fiori 16
00186 Rome Italy
Phone: +39 06 68802366

#137
Trinity College Pub
Average Price: Modest
Category: Sports Bar
Area: Centro Storico
Address: Via Del Collegio Romeno 6
00186 Rome Italy
Phone: +39 06 6786472

#138
Teatro Salone Margherita
Average Price: Expensive
Category: Opera, Ballet, Music Venues
Area: Centro Storico
Address: Via Due Macelli 75
00187 Rome Italy
Phone: +39 06 6798269

#139
Brunello
Average Price: Exclusive
Category: Wine Bar, Italian
Area: Termini, Centro Storico
Address: Via Vittorio Veneto 70A
00187 Rome Italy
Phone: +39 06 48902867

#140
Pumma Re'
Average Price: Expensive
Category: Lounge, Cucina Campana
Area: Prati
Address: Via Andrea Doria 41M
00192 Rome Italy
Phone: +39 06 39727392

#141
Vineria Reggio
Average Price: Expensive
Category: Wine Bar
Area: Centro Storico
Address: Piazza Campo De' Fiori 15
00186 Rome Italy
Phone: +39 06 68219526

#142
Supper Club
Average Price: Expensive
Category: Bar
Area: Centro Storico
Address: Via De Nari 14
00186 Rome Italy
Phone: +39 06 68807207

#143
Black Out Rock Club
Average Price: Modest
Category: Dance Club, Music Venues
Area: Casilino
Address: Via Casilina 713
00177 Rome Italy
Phone: +39 06 2415047

#144
Ducati Caff'
Average Price: Modest
Category: Lounge, Café, Italian
Area: Centro Storico
Address: Via Delle Botteghe Oscure 35
00186 Rome Italy
Phone: +39 06 68891718

#145
Giggetto Al Portico d'Ottavia
Average Price: Expensive
Category: Romen, Pub
Area: Centro Storico
Address: Via Del Portico d'Ottavia 21A
00186 Rome Italy
Phone: +39 06 6861105

#146
Ar Galletto
Average Price: Exclusive
Category: Italian, Pub
Area: Centro Storico
Address: Piazza Farnese 104
00186 Rome Italy
Phone: +39 06 6861714

#147
Giulio Passami L'Olio
Average Price: Expensive
Category: Italian, Pub, Wine Bar
Area: Centro Storico
Address: Via Di Monte Giordano 28
00186 Rome Italy
Phone: +39 06 68803288

#148
Qube
Average Price: Modest
Category: Dance Club, Music Venues
Area: Pigneto
Address: Via Di Portonaccio 212
00159 Rome Italy
Phone: +39 06 4385445

#149
L'euclide
Average Price: Modest
Category: Desserts, Bar, Ice Cream
Area: Parioli
Address: Piazza Euclide 45
00197 Rome Italy
Phone: +39 06 80687522

#150
Alpheus
Average Price: Modest
Category: Dance Club
Area: Testaccio, Ostiense
Address: Via Del Commercio 36
00154 Rome Italy
Phone: +39 06 5747826

#151
Druid's Rock
Average Price: Modest
Category: Pub
Area: Termini
Address: Piazza Dell'esquilino 1
00184 Rome Italy
Phone: +39 06 4741329

#152
Bar Pappagallo
Average Price: Expensive
Category: Pub
Area: Balduina/Montemario
Address: Via Anastasio II 45
00165 Rome Italy
Phone: +39 06 6380406

#153
Sotto Casa Di Andrea
Average Price: Inexpensive
Category: Pub
Area: San Lorenzo, San Giovanni
Address: Via Dei Reti 25
00185 Rome Italy
Phone: +39 347 8146544

#154
INIT Club
Average Price: Modest
Category: Bar, Dance Club,
Music Venues
Area: San Giovanni
Address: Via Della Stazione
Tuscolana 133, 00182 Rome Italy
Phone: +39 06 97277724

#155
Birrifugio
Average Price: Modest
Category: Pub, Romen
Address: Via Federico Rosazza 6
00153 Rome Italy
Phone: +39 06 58303189

#156
Teatro Ghione
Average Price: Inexpensive
Category: Opera, Ballet, Music Venues
Area: Borgo
Address: Via Delle Fornaci 37
00165 Rome Italy
Phone: +39 06 6372294

#157
Rising Love
Average Price: Modest
Category: Music Venues
Area: Testaccio, Ostiense
Address: Via Delle Conce 14
00154 Rome Italy
Phone: +39 06 89520643

#158
Room 26
Average Price: Expensive
Category: Dance Club
Area: Eur
Address: Piazza Marconi 31
00144 Rome Italy
Phone: +39 06 5976540

#159
Villa Celimontana
Average Price: Inexpensive
Category: Opera, Ballet,
Music Venues, Park
Area: Aventino
Address: Via Della Navicella 12
00184 Rome Italy
Phone: +39 06 5897807

#160
Il Fiammifero Strano
Average Price: Inexpensive
Category: Food, Bar
Area: Termini, Centro Storico
Address: Via Lombardia 32
00187 Rome Italy
Phone: +39 06 4880072

#161
Un Angolo Divino
Average Price: Modest
Category: Beer, Wine, Spirits,
Wine Bar
Area: San Giovanni
Address: Via Tuscolana 225
00181 Rome Italy
Phone: +39 06 89684891

#162
Vicious Club
Average Price: Modest
Category: Dance Club
Area: Esquilino, San Giovanni
Address: Via Achille Grandi 7A
00185 Rome Italy
Phone: +39 06 70614349

#163
Dolce Vita
Average Price: Modest
Category: Bar, Italian
Area: Centro Storico
Address: Piazza Navona 70
00186 Rome Italy
Phone: +39 06 68806221

#164
Beerland
Average Price: Modest
Category: Brewerie, Bar
Area: Trastevere
Address: Via Di Ponte Sisto 76
00153 Rome Italy
Phone: +39 06 58200700

#165
La Pinta
Average Price: Modest
Category: Pub
Area: Termini, San Giovanni
Address: Via Degli Equi 39
00185 Rome Italy
Phone: +39 06 44703982

#166
Il Baretto
Average Price: Modest
Category: Coffee &Tea, Café, Bar
Area: Monteverde
Address: Via Garibaldi 28
00153 Rome Italy
Phone: +39 06 58205716

#167
Seamus Heaney
Average Price: Modest
Category: Pub
Area: San Lorenzo
Address: Viale Delle Provincie 154
00162 Rome Italy
Phone: +39 06 44236805

#168
La Riunione Di Condominio
Average Price: Modest
Category: Jazz &Blues, Social Club
Area: Termini
Address: Via Dei Luceri 13
00185 Rome Italy
Phone: +39 06 57301417

#169
Caff' Dell'orologio
Average Price: Modest
Category: Bar
Area: Flaminio
Address: Piazzale Flaminio 34
00196 Rome Italy
Phone: +39 06 3610956

#170
29 Metri Quadri
Average Price: Inexpensive
Category: Lounge, Wine Bar, Pub,
Brewerie, Tapas Bar
Area: Corso Francia
Address: Piazzale Di Ponte Milvio 31
00191 Rome Italy
Phone: +39 06 33219542

#171
Art Caf'
Average Price: Expensive
Category: Dance Club, Café,
Coffee &Tea
Area: Pinciano
Address: Viale Galoppatoio 33
00198 Rome Italy
Phone: +39 06 44702329

#172
Big Star
Average Price: Modest
Category: Pub
Area: Trastevere
Address: Via Mameli 25
00153 Rome Italy
Phone: +39 339 7644575

#173
Il Pentagrappolo
Average Price: Modest
Category: Nightlife
Area: Aventino
Address: Via Celimontana, 21/B
00184 Rome Italy
Phone: +39 06 7096301

#174
Tbar
Average Price: Modest
Category: Lounge, Wine Bar,
Italian, Brewerie
Area: Ostiense
Address: Viale Ostiense 182A
00154 Rome Italy
Phone: +39 06 5740009

#175
Cargo
Average Price: Modest
Category: Pub
Area: San Giovanni
Address: Via Del Pigneto 20
00176 Rome Italy
Phone: +39 06 97617820

#176
Haus Garten Bagel Bar
Average Price: Modest
Category: Bar, Bagels, American
Area: Prati
Address: Piazza Monte Grappa 1
00195 Rome Italy
Phone: +39 06 32120073

#177
Lowenhaus - Birreria Bavarese
Average Price: Modest
Category: Pub, Brewerie, German
Area: Flaminio
Address: Via Della Fontanella 16
00187 Rome Italy
Phone: +39 06 3230410

#178
Aristocampo
Average Price: Modest
Category: Food, Bar, Italian
Area: Corso Francia
Address: Piazzale Di Ponte Milvio, 38
00191 Rome Italy
Phone: +39 06 44702330

#179
Avalon
Average Price: Modest
Category: Pub, Italian
Area: San Giovanni
Address: Via Terni 21
00182 Rome Italy
Phone: +39 06 7015755

#180
The Drunken Ship
Average Price: Modest
Category: Pub, Sports Bar
Area: Centro Storico
Address: Piazza Campo De' Fiori 20
00186 Rome Italy
Phone: +39 06 68300535

#181
White
Average Price: Modest
Category: Bar, Dance Club, Italian
Area: Centro Storico
Address: Via Degli Avignonesi 73
00187 Rome Italy
Phone: +39 06 97278949

#182
Malavite
Average Price: Inexpensive
Category: Pub
Area: San Giovanni
Address: Via Del Pigneto 36
00176 Rome Italy
Phone: +39 06 77200016

#183
Ris Caf'
Average Price: Modest
Category: Pub, Italian, Breakfast &Brunch
Area: Prati
Address: Piazza Risorgimento 16
00192 Rome Italy
Phone: +39 06 39754330

#184
Hera Hora
Average Price: Inexpensive
Category: Bar
Area: San Giovanni
Address: Via Degli Aurunci 30
00185 Rome Italy
Phone: +39 340 9235142

#185
Magnolia Lounge Bar
Average Price: Modest
Category: Bar, Café
Area: Centro Storico
Address: Piazza Campo De' Fiori 4
00186 Rome Italy
Phone: +39 06 68309367

#186
Rosati
Average Price: Expensive
Category: Bar
Area: Flaminio
Address: Piazza Del Popolo 4
00187 Rome Italy
Phone: +39 06 97749804

#187
Lo Yeti
Average Price: Modest
Category: Café, Bar
Area: San Giovanni
Address: Via Perugia 4
00176 Rome Italy
Phone: +39 06 7025633

#188
Bar Dei Belli
Average Price: Modest
Category: Bar
Area: Termini
Address: Via Tiburtina 76
00185 Rome Italy
Phone: +39 06 4453840

#189
Crossing's
Average Price: Expensive
Category: Pub
Area: San Giovanni
Address: Viale Furio Camillo 111
00181 Rome Italy
Phone: +39 06 78359124

#190
Gelateria Tony
Average Price: Modest
Category: Ice Cream, Bar
Area: Monteverde
Address: Piazza San Giovanni Di Dio 1
00152 Rome Italy
Phone: +39 06 535007

#191
Beba Do Samba
Average Price: Modest
Category: Music Venues
Area: San Giovanni
Address: Via De' Messapi 8
00185 Rome Italy
Phone: +39 340 6953499

#192
The Place
Average Price: Expensive
Category: Jazz &Blues, Lounge
Area: Prati
Address: Via Alberico II 27
00193 Rome Italy
Phone: +39 06 68307137

#193
Jamboree
Average Price: Expensive
Category: Pub, Sports Bar
Area: Salario
Address: Via Tagliamento 77
00198 Rome Italy
Phone: +39 06 45493387

#194
Le Coppelle 52
Average Price: Modest
Category: Lounge, Wine Bar
Area: Centro Storico
Address: Piazza Delle Coppelle 52
00186 Rome Italy
Phone: +39 349 7404620

#195
Charity Caf'
Average Price: Inexpensive
Category: Wine Bar, Cocktail Bar
Area: Monti
Address: Via Panisperna 68
00184 Rome Italy
Phone: +39 06 47825881

#196
Coming Out Shop
Average Price: Modest
Category: Adult Entertainment
Area: Esquilino, Aventino
Address: Via Di San Giovanni In Laterano
26 00184 Rome Italy
Phone: +39 06 44702331

#197
Albrecht
Average Price: Expensive
Category: German, Pub, Gluten-Free
Area: Centro Storico
Address: Via Rasella 52
00187 Rome Italy
Phone: +39 06 4880457

#198
Lettere Caff'
Average Price: Modest
Category: Wine Bar, Performing Arts
Area: Trastevere
Address: Via S.Francesco A Ripa 100 /
101, 00153 Rome Italy
Phone: +39 06 97270991

#199
45 Giri
Average Price: Exclusive
Category: Dance Club, Italian
Area: Ostiense
Address: Via Giuseppe Libetta 19
00154 Rome Italy
Phone: +39 06 57288666

#200
Foffo Bar
Average Price: Inexpensive
Category: Bar
Area: San Lorenzo
Address: Piazzale Delle Provincie 1
00162 Rome Italy
Phone: +39 06 44236379

#201
La Taverna Del Grano
Average Price: Modest
Category: Italian, Pub
Area: Tuscolano
Address: Piazza Tribuni 31
00175 Rome Italy
Phone: +39 06 45425262

#202
La Barcaccia
Average Price: Exclusive
Category: Bar, Café
Area: Centro Storico
Address: Piazza Di Spagna 71
00187 Rome Italy
Phone: +39 06 6797497

#203
Palalottomatica
Average Price: Expensive
Category: Stadium/Arena, Music Venues
Area: Eur
Address: Piazzale Pier Luigi Nervi 1
00144 Rome Italy
Phone: +39 06 540901

#204
Caff' Ponte Milvio
Average Price: Modest
Category: Wine Bar, Café
Area: Corso Francia
Address: Piazzale Ponte Milvio 44
00191 Rome Italy
Phone: +39 06 3333461

#205
Saxophone
Average Price: Modest
Category: Pub
Area: Prati
Address: Via Germanico, 26
00192 Rome Italy
Phone: +39 06 39723039

#206
Antico Caff' Dell'isola
Average Price: Inexpensive
Category: Pub
Area: Trastevere, Centro Storico
Address: Via Di Ponte Quattro Capi 18
00186 Rome Italy
Phone: +39 06 6877662

#207
Caruso
Average Price: Modest
Category: Dance Club
Area: Testaccio, Ostiense
Address: Via Monte Testaccio 36
00153 Rome Italy
Phone: +39 06 5745019

#208
Beige
Average Price: Modest
Category: Cocktail Bar
Area: Trastevere
Address: Via Del Politeama 13
00153 Rome Italy
Phone: +39 347 1284186

#209
Mario Tornatora
Average Price: Expensive
Category: Chocolatier, Venues &Events
Area: Ostiense
Address: Via Oderisi Da Gubbio 27
00146 Rome Italy
Phone: +39 06 5593658

#210
Cantina Castrocielo
Average Price: Modest
Category: Beer, Wine, Wine Bar, Italian
Area: Eur
Address: Viale Degli Astri 35
00144 Rome Italy
Phone: +39 06 5204979

#211
Teatro Sala Umberto
Average Price: Modest
Category: Opera, Ballet, Music Venues
Area: Centro Storico
Address: Via Della Mercede 50
00187 Rome Italy
Phone: +39 06 6794753

#212
Bibelot Dolci
Average Price: Modest
Category: Lounge, Desserts
Area: Tuscolano
Address: Via Delle Cave 42A
00181 Rome Italy
Phone: +39 06 7803913

#213
Tree Bar
Average Price: Modest
Category: Bar, Romen
Area: Flaminio, Parioli
Address: Via Flaminia 226
00196 Rome Italy
Phone: +39 06 32652754

#214
Grottapinta Lounge
Average Price: Modest
Category: Dance Club, Music Venues
Area: Centro Storico
Address: Via Di Grottapinta 12
00186 Rome Italy
Phone: +39 06 44702332

#215
Antico Caff' Santamaria
Average Price: Expensive
Category: Bar
Area: Termini
Address: Via Carlo Alberto 1
00185 Rome Italy
Phone: +39 06 4465863

#216
Terra Satis
Average Price: Inexpensive
Category: Wine Bar
Area: Trastevere
Address: Piazza Dei Ponziani 1a
00153 Rome Italy
Phone: +39 06 97603734

#217
Fior Di Luna
Average Price: Modest
Category: Ice Cream, Bar
Area: Monteverde
Address: Via Paola Falconieri 117
00152 Rome Italy
Phone: +39 06 536084

#218
King Arthur
Average Price: Modest
Category: Pub
Address: Via Carlo Pirzio Biroli 176d
00043 Ciampino Italy
Phone: +39 06 44702333

#219
Bar Tritone
Average Price: Modest
Category: Bar
Area: Centro Storico
Address: Via Del Tritone 144
00187 Rome Italy
Phone: +39 06 44702334

#220
Gustosito
Average Price: Inexpensive
Category: Bar, Café
Area: Ostiense
Address: Via Libetta 25
00154 Rome Italy
Phone: +39 06 5781367

#221
Bar Del Ponticello
Average Price: Modest
Category: Bar, Café
Area: Ostiense
Address: Via Ostiense 421
00142 Rome Italy
Phone: +39 06 5410109

#222
Mad For Beer
Average Price: Inexpensive
Category: Pub
Area: Monteverde
Address: Via Federico Ozanam 62
00152 Rome Italy
Phone: +39 340 5709150

#223
Rer'
Average Price: Expensive
Category: Nightlife
Area: Corso Francia
Address: Flaminia Vecchia 475 Via
00191 Rome Italy
Phone: +39 06 3340483

#224
Caff' Stella Ruschena
Average Price: Modest
Category: Bar
Area: Flaminio, Parioli
Address: Via Flaminia
00196 Rome Italy
Phone: +39 06 44702335

#225
The Dog And Duck
Average Price: Expensive
Category: Pub, Wine Bar
Area: Trastevere
Address: Via Della Luce 70
00153 Rome Italy
Phone: +39 06 45474798

#226
Da &Da
Average Price: Modest
Category: Bar
Area: San Lorenzo
Address: P.Le Del Verano 90/91
00185 Rome Italy
Phone: +39 06 4462617

#227
Shamrock Irish Pub
Average Price: Modest
Category: Pub
Area: Monti, Centro Storico
Address: Via Del Colosseo 1 C
00184 Rome Italy
Phone: +39 06 6791729

#228
Teatro Due
Average Price: Modest
Category: Opera, Ballet, Music Venues
Area: Centro Storico
Address: Vicolo Due Macelli 37
00187 Rome Italy
Phone: +39 06 6788259

#229
L'Albero Cocciuto
Average Price: Modest
Category: Pizza, Pub, Italian
Area: Tuscolano
Address: Viale Appio Claudio 221
00174 Rome Italy
Phone: +39 06 64780600

#230
Banana Republic
Average Price: Modest
Category: Bar
Area: Prati
Address: Via Giovanni Bettolo 3A
00195 Rome Italy
Phone: +39 06 3723291

#231
Luppolo 12
Average Price: Inexpensive
Category: Beer Garden, Beer
Area: Termini, San Lorenzo
Address: Via Dei Marrucini 12
00185 Rome Italy
Phone: +39 333 6750672

#232
C'era Una Volta... Il Caff'
Average Price: Modest
Category: Bar, Café
Area: Montesacro/Talenti, Tiburtino
Address: Via Tiburtina 441
00159 Rome Italy
Phone: +39 06 43533502

#233
Birreria Trilussa
Average Price: Modest
Category: Pub
Area: Trastevere
Address: Via Benedetta 18
00153 Rome Italy
Phone: +39 06 5819067

#234
Casina Dei Pini
Average Price: Expensive
Category: Italian, Café, Bar
Area: Nomentano
Address: Viale Di Villa Massimo 8A
00161 Rome Italy
Phone: +39 06 44244707

#235
Il Melograno Caf'
Average Price: Inexpensive
Category: Lounge
Area: Tuscolano
Address: Viale Giulio Agricola 41
00174 Rome Italy
Phone: +39 06 71546716

#236
Faenas
Average Price: Modest
Category: Nightlife
Area: Trastevere
Address: Via Portuense, 47
00153 Rome Italy
Phone: +39 06 64562336

#237
Ice Club
Average Price: Modest
Category: Pub
Area: Monti
Address: Via Della Madonna Dei
Monti 18, 00184 Rome Italy
Phone: +39 06 97845581

#238
Mr. Brown
Average Price: Inexpensive
Category: Pub
Area: Trastevere
Address: Vicolo Del Cinque 29
00153 Rome Italy
Phone: +39 06 58122913

#239
Rhome
Average Price: Expensive
Category: Dance Club, Italian
Area: Centro Storico
Address: Piazza Augusto Imperatore 42
00186 Rome Italy
Phone: +39 06 68301430

#240
Elle Restaurant
Average Price: Expensive
Category: Dance Club, Piano Bar
Area: Centro Storico
Address: Via Veneto 81
00187 Rome Italy
Phone: +39 06 42010164

#241
Gilda
Average Price: Expensive
Category: Dance Club
Area: Centro Storico
Address: Via Mario De' Fiori 97
00187 Rome Italy
Phone: +39 06 6784838

#242
Atlantico
Average Price: Modest
Category: Music Venues
Area: Eur
Address: Viale Oceano Atlantico 271D
00144 Rome Italy
Phone: +39 06 5915727

#243
Vida Do Brasil
Average Price: Inexpensive
Category: Bar
Area: San Giovanni
Address: Via Del Pigneto 22
00176 Rome Italy
Phone: +39 06 70614518

#244
Merulana Caf'
Average Price: Modest
Category: Pub
Area: Esquilino, San Giovanni
Address: Via Merulana 138,138a-138b
00185 Rome Italy
Phone: +39 06 7004221

#245
Bar Settimiano
Average Price: Inexpensive
Category: Bar, Café, Coffee &Tea
Area: Borgo, Trastevere
Address: Via Porta Settimiana 1
00153 Rome Italy
Phone: +39 06 5810468

#246
Os Club
Average Price: Expensive
Category: Lounge
Area: Esquilino
Address: Via Delle Terme Di Traiano 4A
00184 Rome Italy
Phone: +39 06 48930379

#247
Rome Beer Company
Average Price: Modest
Category: Burgers, Beer Garden
Area: Corso Francia
Address: Piazzale Ponte Milvio 40
00191 Rome Italy
Phone: +39 06 3337048

#248
Senza Fondo
Average Price: Modest
Category: Pub
Area: Prati
Address: Via Germanico 168C
00192 Rome Italy
Phone: +39 06 3211415

#249
Bar Per'
Average Price: Inexpensive
Category: Bar
Area: Centro Storico
Address: Via Di Monserrato 46
00186 Rome Italy
Phone: +39 06 6879548

#250
Barnum Caf'
Average Price: Modest
Category: Wine Bar, Juice Bar
Area: Centro Storico
Address: Via Del Pellegrino 87
00186 Rome Italy
Phone: +39 06 64760483

#251
The Random
Average Price: Expensive
Category: Dance Club, Karaoke
Area: San Lorenzo, San Giovanni
Address: Viale Dello Scalo San
Lorenzo 99, 00185 Rome Italy
Phone: +39 06 44360773

#252
La Cabala
Average Price: Expensive
Category: Dance Club
Area: Centro Storico
Address: Via Dei Soldati 25B
00186 Rome Italy
Phone: +39 06 68309415

#253
Flann O' Brien
Average Price: Inexpensive
Category: Irish, Pub
Area: Centro Storico
Address: Via Nazionale 17
00184 Rome Italy
Phone: +39 00 39064880418

#254
692
Average Price: Modest
Category: Lounge, Italian, Cocktail Bar
Area: Tuscolano
Address: Via Tuscolana 692
00181 Rome Italy
Phone: +39 06 76968667

#255
Pepy's Bar
Average Price: Modest
Category: Pub
Area: Centro Storico
Address: Piazza Barberini 56
00187 Rome Italy
Phone: +39 06 4874491

#256
Muzak
Average Price: Inexpensive
Category: Dance Club, Music Venues
Area: Testaccio, Ostiense
Address: Via Di Monte Testaccio 38
00153 Rome Italy
Phone: +39 06 5744712

#257
Caf' 500
Average Price: Modest
Category: Bar, Italian
Area: Balduina/Montemario
Address: Via Taddeo Da Sessa 18
00165 Rome Italy
Phone: +39 06 6626139

#258
Ciampini 2
Average Price: Expensive
Category: Bar, Italian
Area: Centro Storico
Address: Via Della Fontanella Di
Borghese 59 00186 Rome Italy
Phone: +39 06 68135108

#259
Mate Bar
Average Price: Modest
Category: Pub
Area: Trastevere
Address: Via Benedetta 17
00153 Rome Italy
Phone: +39 06 58331645

#260
Il Serpente
Average Price: Modest
Category: Pub
Area: San Giovanni
Address: Via Dei Marsi 21
00185 Rome Italy
Phone: +39 00 3906490946

#261
Blind Pig
Average Price: Modest
Category: Pub, Brewerie
Area: San Giovanni
Address: Via Gino Capponi 45
00141 Rome Italy
Phone: +39 06 78345642

#262
Shamrock Irish Pub Celio
Average Price: Modest
Category: Pub, Italian
Area: Aventino
Address: Via Capo d'Africa 26D
00184 Rome Italy
Phone: +39 06 7002583

#263
Mr. Pucci
Average Price: Modest
Category: Pub
Area: Trastevere
Address: Piazza Mastai 18
00153 Rome Italy
Phone: +39 06 58334333

#264
L'Alibi
Average Price: Modest
Category: Dance Club, Gay Bar
Area: Testaccio, Ostiense
Address: Via Di Monte Testaccio 44
00153 Rome Italy
Phone: +39 06 5743448

#265
Ketumbar
Average Price: Expensive
Category: Dance Club, Italian
Area: Testaccio, Ostiense
Address: Via Galvani 24
00153 Rome Italy
Phone: +39 00 390657305338

#266
Sloppy
Average Price: Modest
Category: American, Bar
Area: Centro Storico
Address: Piazza Campo De' Fiori 6
00186 Rome Italy
Phone: +39 06 68802637

#267
La Bibliotechina
Average Price: Modest
Category: Dance Club, Wine Bar
Area: Eur
Address: Viale Val Fiorita 10
00144 Rome Italy
Phone: +39 348 3384616

#268
Cantina Paradiso
Average Price: Modest
Category: Wine Bar, Café
Area: Trastevere
Address: Via San Francesco A Ripa 73
00153 Rome Italy
Phone: +39 06 5899799

#269
Oppio Caff'
Average Price: Modest
Category: Dance Club, Mexican, Wine Bar
Area: Esquilino, Aventino
Address: Via Delle Terme Di Tito, 72
00184 Rome Italy
Phone: +39 06 4745262

#270
Trimani
Average Price: Expensive
Category: Wine Bar, Beer, Wine, Spirits
Area: Termini
Address: Via Cernaia 37
00185 Rome Italy
Phone: +39 06 4468351

#271
Vinallegro
Average Price: Inexpensive
Category: Wine Bar
Area: Trastevere
Address: Piazza Giuditta Tavani
Arquati 114, 00153 Rome Italy
Phone: +39 06 44702336

#272
Il Tartarughino
Average Price: Expensive
Category: Italian, Piano Bar
Area: Centro Storico
Address: Via Della Scrofa 1
00186 Rome Italy
Phone: +39 06 6864131

#273
Bar Dell'orologio
Average Price: Modest
Category: Coffee &Tea, Bar
Area: Flaminio
Address: Piazzale Flaminio 34
00196 Rome Italy
Phone: +39 06 3610956

#274
Teatro Vittoria
Average Price: Modest
Category: Opera, Ballet,
Music Venues
Area: Testaccio, Ostiense
Address: Piazza S. Maria Liberatrice,
11, 00153 Rome Italy
Phone: +39 06 5740170

#275
Teatro Anfitrione
Average Price: Modest
Category: Opera, Ballet, Music Venues,
Performing Arts
Area: Aventino, Ostiense
Address: Via Di San Saba 24
00153 Rome Italy
Phone: +39 06 5750827

#276
Enoteca Spiriti
Average Price: Modest
Category: Wine Bar
Area: Centro Storico
Address: Via Di S. Eustachio 5
00186 Rome Italy
Phone: +39 06 68892199

#277
Primo Caf'
Average Price: Modest
Category: Wine Bar
Area: Centro Storico
Address: Piazza Campo De' Fiori 6
00186 Rome Italy
Phone: +39 06 64760179

#278
Old Trafford
Average Price: Modest
Category: Brewerie, Pub
Area: Prati
Address: Via Angelo Emo 61
00136 Rome Italy
Phone: +39 06 39735450

#279
Equarantadue
Average Price: Modest
Category: Lounge, Café
Area: Eur
Address: Via Laurentina 599
00143 Rome Italy
Phone: +39 06 54221740

#280
Caff' Arabo
Average Price: Inexpensive
Category: Bar
Area: Trastevere
Address: Via Ippolito Nievo, 20
00153 Rome Italy
Phone: +39 06 44702337

#281
Living Room Caf'
Average Price: Modest
Category: Coffee &Tea, Lounge
Area: Termini
Address: Via Solferino 9
00185 Rome Italy
Phone: +39 06 44703976

#282
Rialto Sant'Ambrogio
Average Price: Inexpensive
Category: Dance Club, Cultural Center
Area: Centro Storico
Address: Via Sant'Ambrogio 4
00186 Rome Italy
Phone: +39 06 68133640

#283
Il Tavolinetto
Average Price: Modest
Category: Bar, Italian
Area: Termini
Address: Via Massimo d'Azeglio 46
00184 Rome Italy
Phone: +39 06 4823913

#284
La Taverna Di Tom Bombadil
Average Price: Modest
Category: Pub
Area: Salario
Address: Via Casperia 33
00199 Rome Italy
Phone: +39 06 86201417

#285
Traffic Club
Average Price: Inexpensive
Category: Music Venues
Area: Casilino
Address: Via Prenestina, 738
00176 Rome Italy
Phone: +39 00 393280547412

#286
Highlander Pub
Average Price: Modest
Category: Brewerie, Italian, Pub
Area: Casilino
Address: Viale Della Primavera 213
00172 Rome Italy
Phone: +39 06 44702338

#287
Tam O'Shanter Scottish Pub
Average Price: Modest
Category: Pub
Area: Prati
Address: Via Crescenzio 2
00193 Rome Italy
Phone: +39 06 68134866

#288
Antica Biblioteca Valle
Average Price: Modest
Category: Wine Bar, Italian, Buffet
Area: Centro Storico
Address: Largo Del Teatro Valle 7
00186 Rome Italy
Phone: +39 06 6896005

#289
Bulldog Inn
Average Price: Modest
Category: Pub
Area: Centro Storico
Address: Corso Vittorio Emanuele II, 107,
00186 Rome Italy
Phone: +39 06 6871537

#290
Red
Average Price: Modest
Category: Italian, Wine Bar, Lounge
Area: Flaminio
Address: Viale Pietro De Coubertin 12
00196 Rome Italy
Phone: +39 06 80691630

#291
The Donegal
Average Price: Modest
Category: Pub
Area: Ostiense
Address: Viale Marco Polo 47B
00154 Rome Italy
Phone: +39 06 57284499

#292
Bleid
Average Price: Modest
Category: Pub
Area: Ostiense
Address: Viale Giustiano, 17
00145 Rome Italy
Phone: +39 06 45494681

#293
Caf' Friends
Average Price: Expensive
Category: Bar, Café
Area: Centro Storico
Address: Via Della Scrofa 60
00186 Rome Italy
Phone: +39 06 6861416

#294
Bar Durante
Average Price: Inexpensive
Category: Bar
Area: Flaminio, Centro Storico
Address: Via Della Frezza 55
00186 Rome Italy
Phone: +39 06 3227189

#295
Mc Queen
Average Price: Modest
Category: Pub
Area: Prati
Address: Via Aurelia 77
00165 Rome Italy
Phone: +39 06 631872

#296
La Cannoleria Siciliana
Average Price: Inexpensive
Category: Desserts, Cafeteria, Cocktail Bar
Area: San Giovanni
Address: Piazza Dei Re Di Rome10
00183 Rome Italy
Phone: +39 06 70497456

#297
Buskers Pub
Average Price: Modest
Category: Pub
Area: Ostiense
Address: Viale Leonardo Da Vinci 287
00145 Rome Italy
Phone: +39 06 92599275

#298
Level Club
Average Price: Modest
Category: Lounge, Dance Club
Area: Centro Storico
Address: Vicolo Del Fico 3
00186 Rome Italy
Phone: +39 06 68808866

#299
Hostaria Dell'Orso
Average Price: Modest
Category: Italian, Dance Club
Area: Centro Storico
Address: Via Dei Soldati 25C
00186 Rome Italy
Phone: +39 06 68301192

#300
Lapsutinna
Average Price: Modest
Category: Pub, Brewerie
Area: Prati
Address: Via Giordano Bruno 25
00195 Rome Italy
Phone: +39 347 7844622

#301
Razmataz Al Pigneto
Average Price: Inexpensive
Category: Wine Bar
Area: San Giovanni
Address: Via Macerata 58A
00176 Rome Italy
Phone: +39 06 99925688

#302
Disco Pub 3 Jol'
Average Price: Modest
Category: Gay Bar, Karaoke
Area: Termini, San Lorenzo
Address: Via Tiburtina 812
00185 Rome Italy
Phone: +39 06 44702339

#303
Bar Campidoglio
Average Price: Modest
Category: Bar
Area: Centro Storico
Address: Piazza Aracoeli 11
00186 Rome Italy
Phone: +39 06 6785593

#304
**Tempio BAR Gestione Di
Schiafone Mario**
Average Price: Modest
Category: Bar
Area: Centro Storico
Address: Piazza Della Rotonda, 16
00186 Rome Italy
Phone: +39 06 6861007

#305
Bum Bum Di Mel
Average Price: Inexpensive
Category: Pub
Area: Trastevere
Address: Via Del Moro 17
00153 Rome Italy
Phone: +39 06 97616676

#306
**Lo Spuntino - Gastronomia
Luncheonette**
Average Price: Inexpensive
Category: Bar, Italian, Sandwiches
Area: Cassia
Address: Via Cassia 927 G
00189 Rome Italy
Phone: +39 06 30362143

#307
Panamino
Average Price: Inexpensive
Category: Café, Bar
Area: Salario
Address: Via Panama12
00198 Rome Italy
Phone: +39 06 8415561

#308
RDC
Average Price: Inexpensive
Category: Nightlife
Area: Termini
Address: Via Dei Luceri 13
00185 Rome Italy
Phone: +39 06 44702340

#309
Mondi Caff'
Average Price: Expensive
Category: Bar, Coffee &Tea
Area: Casilino
Address: Viale Della Serenissima 12
00177 Rome Italy
Phone: +39 06 2593194

#310
Jackie'o
Average Price: Expensive
Category: Nightlife
Area: Termini
Address: Via Boncompagni,11
00187 Rome Italy
Phone: +39 06 42885457

#311
Bril'
Average Price: Modest
Category: Wine Bar
Area: Tuscolano
Address: Via Genzano 77
00179 Rome Italy
Phone: +39 06 7800156

#312
28Basement
Average Price: Inexpensive
Category: Pub
Area: Salario
Address: Via Lucrino 28B
00199 Rome Italy
Phone: +39 347 0706044

#313
Supperclub
Average Price: Exclusive
Category: Nightlife
Area: Centro Storico
Address: Via De'nari Pantheon 14
Rome, Rome Italy
Phone: +39 06 68807207

#314
Dad' Chalet
Average Price: Modest
Category: Bar
Area: Monteverde
Address: Via Sabiniano 30
00165 Rome Italy
Phone: +39 339 4441090

#315
Gay Street
Average Price: Modest
Category: Gay Bar
Area: Esquilino, Aventino
Address: Via San Giovanni In Laterano
00184 Rome Italy
Phone: +39 06 44702341

#316
Co.So Cocktail&Social
Average Price: Modest
Category: Cocktail Bar
Area: Pigneto
Address: Via Braccio Da Montone 80
00176 Rome Italy
Phone: +39 06 44702342

#317
Orvm Bar
Average Price: Expensive
Category: Cocktail Bar
Area: Termini
Address: Via Vittoria Veneto 125
00197 Rome Italy
Phone: +39 06 44702343

#318
Open Gate
Average Price: Expensive
Category: Nightlife
Area: Centro Storico
Address: Via San Nicola Da Tolentino 4
00187 Rome Italy
Phone: +39 06 42011931

#319
Cacio E Pepe
Average Price: Modest
Category: Nightlife, Pizza
Area: Trastevere
Address: Vicolo Del Cinque 15
00153 Rome Italy
Phone: +39 06 89572853

#320
Ni.Bi.Ru Spacebar
Average Price: Inexpensive
Category: Lounge
Area: Testaccio, Ostiense
Address: Via Del Gazometro 14
00154 Rome Italy
Phone: +39 338 3688400

#321
Olfattorio
Average Price: Exclusive
Category: Bar, Shopping
Area: Flaminio
Address: Via Di Ripetta, 34
00186 Rome Italy
Phone: +39 06 3612325

#322
Debo's La Birraia
Average Price: Modest
Category: Pub
Area: Monteverde
Address: Via Antonio Toscani 70
00152 Rome Italy
Phone: +39 06 88542311

#323
La Parolaccia &Sons
Average Price: Inexpensive
Category: Pub
Area: Trastevere
Address: Vicolo Del Cinque, 2
00153 Rome Italy
Phone: +39 06 44702344

#324
The Druid's Den
Average Price: Modest
Category: Sports Bar, Pub
Area: Monti
Address: Via Di San Martino Ai Monti 28
00184 Rome Italy
Phone: +39 06 48904781

#325
Pinci Bar
Average Price: Inexpensive
Category: Bar, Street Vendors
Area: Centro Storico
Address: Via San Bernadette 1/7 Rome,
Rome Italy
Phone: +39 06 6623000

#326
Bar Berti Dal 1951
Average Price: Inexpensive
Category: Bar, Beer, Wine, Spirits
Area: Trastevere
Address: Via Natale Del Grande 46
00153 Rome Italy
Phone: +39 06 5817552

#327
Zanussi
Average Price: Modest
Category: Dance Club
Area: San Giovanni
Address: Piazza Tarquinia 5E
00183 Rome Italy
Phone: +39 06 70493859

#328
**Caffetteria Spinelli
Di Spinelli Giovanni**
Average Price: Modest
Category: Bar
Area: Centro Storico
Address: Piazza Del Viminale, 18
00184 Rome Italy
Phone: +39 06 4817117

#329
Oasies Bar
Average Price: Modest
Category: Bar
Area: Termini
Address: Via Villafranca
00185 Rome Italy
Phone: +39 06 44702345

#330
Ar Gabbio
Average Price: Modest
Category: Wine Bar
Area: Termini
Address: Via Dei Ramni 28
00185 Rome Italy
Phone: +39 347 7734206

#331
La Mescita
Average Price: Modest
Category: Bar
Area: San Lorenzo
Address: Viale Ippocrate, 174
00161 Rome Italy
Phone: +39 06 4454383

#332
Moriondo E Gariglio
Average Price: Exclusive
Category: Bar, Desserts
Area: Centro Storico
Address: Via Pie' Di Marmo 21
00186 Rome Italy
Phone: +39 06 45437170

#333
Jessly Birreria
Average Price: Modest
Category: Pub, Cocktail Bar
Area: Salario
Address: Via Amatrice 32
00199 Rome Italy
Phone: +39 06 86328027

#334
Marr'
Average Price: Inexpensive
Category: Pub
Area: Termini, San Lorenzo
Address: Via Dei Marrucini 12
00185 Rome Italy
Phone: +39 349 2502570

#335
Aristocampo
Average Price: Inexpensive
Category: Dive Bar
Area: Trastevere
Address: Vicolo Del Bologna 36
00153 Rome Italy
Phone: +39 06 44702346

#336
Il Re Della Notte
Average Price: Modest
Category: Beer, Wine, Spirits, Bar
Area: Magliana
Address: Via Oderisi Da Gubbio, 141
00146 Rome Italy
Phone: +39 06 22184715

#337
Essence
Average Price: Modest
Category: Wine Bar, Italian
Area: Casilino
Address: Via Dei Platani 4
00172 Rome Italy
Phone: +39 06 24400442

#338
Bar Primavera
Average Price: Modest
Category: Bar
Area: Casilino
Address: Via Delle Albizzie 54
00172 Rome Italy
Phone: +39 06 24402696

#339
Valori Caff'
Average Price: Modest
Category: Bar, Café
Area: Pigneto
Address: Piazza Dei Condottieri 44
00176 Rome Italy
Phone: +39 06 27800369

#340
Caff' Castello
Average Price: Modest
Category: Bar, Café
Area: Prati
Address: Via Di Porta Castello 9
00193 Rome Italy
Phone: +39 06 302330

#341
Il Cocomerino
Average Price: Expensive
Category: Bar, Italian, Pizza
Area: Pineta Sacchetti
Address: Viale Cortina D'ampezzo 377
00135 Rome Italy
Phone: +39 06 3055948

#342
Tutti A Prua
Average Price: Modest
Category: Pub
Area: Prati
Address: Piazza Cavour 17B
00193 Rome Italy
Phone: +39 06 3212498

#343
Teatro Manzoni
Average Price: Modest
Category: Opera, Ballet, Music Venues,
Performing Arts
Area: Prati
Address: Via Monte Zebio, 14
00195 Rome Italy
Phone: +39 06 3223634

#344
Del Frate Wine Bar
Average Price: Modest
Category: Wine Bar
Area: Prati
Address: Via Degli Scipioni 118
00192 Rome Italy
Phone: +39 06 3236437

#345
Teatro Olimpico
Average Price: Modest
Category: Opera, Ballet, Music Venues,
Performing Arts
Area: Flaminio
Address: Piazza Gentile Da Fabriano, 17,
00196 Rome Italy
Phone: +39 06 3265991

#346
Panificio Nazzareno
Average Price: Modest
Category: Baguettes, Cocktail Bar
Area: Corso Francia
Address: Piazzale Di Ponte Milvio 35
00135 Rome Italy
Phone: +39 06 33220720

#347
Studio 7
Average Price: Modest
Category: Dance Club
Area: Cassia
Address: Via Grottarossa 175
00189 Rome Italy
Phone: +39 06 33263215

#348
Tennent's Pub
Average Price: Inexpensive
Category: Pub
Area: Cassia
Address: Via Mariano Vibio 43
00189 Rome Italy
Phone: +39 06 33264609

#349
Euclide
Average Price: Expensive
Category: Bar, Café
Area: Corso Francia
Address: Via Flaminia Nuova Km. 8.200
00191 Rome Italy
Phone: +39 06 3333225

#350
Sha Bar
Average Price: Modest
Category: Pub
Area: Prati
Address: Via Pietro Borsieri 7
00195 Rome Italy
Phone: +39 06 37514981

#351
Elliot Pub
Average Price: Modest
Category: Pub
Area: Balduina/Montemario
Address: Via Delle Medaglie d'Oro 115
00136 Rome Italy
Phone: +39 06 39736212

#352
Pandora
Average Price: Inexpensive
Category: Café, Bar
Area: Balduina/Montemario
Address: Via Trionfale 75D
00136 Rome Italy
Phone: +39 06 39754613

#353
3Jol'
Average Price: Modest
Category: Bar
Area: Tiburtino
Address: Via Tiburtina 812
00159 Rome Italy
Phone: +39 06 4063928

#354
Caf' De Paris
Average Price: Expensive
Category: Bar, Italian
Area: Centro Storico
Address: Via Vittorio Veneto 91
00187 Rome Italy
Phone: +39 06 42011090

#355
Friends
Average Price: Modest
Category: Bar
Area: Termini, Pinciano
Address: Via Piave 71
00187 Rome Italy
Phone: +39 06 42014285

#356
Elegance Caf'
Average Price: Expensive
Category: Bar
Area: Centro Storico
Address: Via Vittorio Veneto 91
00187 Rome Italy
Phone: +39 06 42016700

#357
Il Pettirosso Due
Average Price: Modest
Category: Bar, Café
Area: San Lorenzo
Address: Via Tiburtina 328
00159 Rome Italy
Phone: +39 06 43253216

#358
Nuovo Onda Caf'
Average Price: Inexpensive
Category: Sports Bar
Area: San Lorenzo
Address: Via Tiburtina 451
00159 Rome Italy
Phone: +39 06 4395035

#359
Industrial Eat
Average Price: Modest
Category: Pizza, Buffet, Bar, Italian
Area: Nomentano
Address: Piazza Alessandria 11
00198 Rome Italy
Phone: +39 06 44231862

#360
Teatro Italia
Average Price: Modest
Category: Opera, Ballet, Music Venues
Area: San Lorenzo
Address: Via Bari, 18
00161 Rome Italy
Phone: +39 06 44239286

#361
Radio Caf'
Average Price: Modest
Category: Bar
Area: Esquilino, Termini
Address: Via Principe Umberto 67
00185 Rome Italy
Phone: +39 06 44361110

#362
Giuliani Caff'
Average Price: Modest
Category: Desserts, Bar, Café
Area: Termini
Address: Via Volturno 60
00185 Rome Italy
Phone: +39 06 4455443

#363
Dimmidisi Club
Average Price: Modest
Category: Jazz &Blues, Dance Club
Area: San Lorenzo
Address: Via Dei Volsci 126B
00185 Rome Italy
Phone: +39 06 4461855

#364
Legend American Pub
Average Price: Expensive
Category: Pub, Burgers
Area: Termini, San Giovanni
Address: Via Dei Latini 25
00185 Rome Italy
Phone: +39 06 4463881

#365
Cocorico
Average Price: Modest
Category: Pub, Italian
Area: San Giovanni
Address: Via Dei Latini 74
00185 Rome Italy
Phone: +39 06 4465460

#366
Dietro Le Quinte
Average Price: Modest
Category: Café, Sandwiches, Bar
Area: Salario
Address: Via Tirso 85
00198 Rome Italy
Phone: +39 06 45421672

#367
Trevi Club By Micca Club
Average Price: Modest
Category: Dance Club
Area: Centro Storico
Address: Via Degli Avignonesi 73
00187 Rome Italy
Phone: +39 06 45443003

#368
Barley Wine
Average Price: Modest
Category: Pub, Wine Bar
Area: Tuscolano
Address: Via Dei Consoli 115
00175 Rome Italy
Phone: +39 06 45687489

#369
Er Baretto L'Arte Del Caff'
Average Price: Expensive
Category: Bar, Café
Area: Monti
Address: Via Del Boschetto 132
00184 Rome Italy
Phone: +39 06 4820444

#370
Gino Bar
Average Price: Inexpensive
Category: Café, Bar
Area: Centro Storico
Address: Via Di San Basilio 52
00187 Rome Italy
Phone: +39 06 483671

#371
Rio Bar
Average Price: Inexpensive
Category: Bar
Area: Termini
Address: Via Curtatone
00185 Rome Italy
Phone: +39 06 4940630

#372
Caff' Trombetta
Average Price: Inexpensive
Category: Coffee &Tea, Bar, Café
Area: Termini
Address: Via Marsala 44
00185 Rome Italy
Phone: +39 06 4941193

#373
Tre Castelli
Average Price: Modest
Category: Bar, Café, Coffee &Tea
Area: Appia Antica
Address: Via Andrea Mantegna 55
00147 Rome Italy
Phone: +39 06 5128825

#374
Bar 3 G
Average Price: Modest
Category: Café, Bar
Area: Appia Antica
Address: Via Giuseppe Cerbara 96
00147 Rome Italy
Phone: +39 06 51607867

#375
Dea Di Rome
Average Price: Modest
Category: Bar, Beauty &Spas
Area: Ardeatina
Address: Via Andrea Millevoi 49
00134 Rome Italy
Phone: +39 06 51962780

#376
On The Rox
Average Price: Modest
Category: Pub
Area: Testaccio, Ostiense
Address: Via Galvani 54
00153 Rome Italy
Phone: +39 06 57284415

#377
Papageno Caff'
Average Price: Modest
Category: Wine Bar, Coffee &Tea
Area: Aventino
Address: Viale Aventino 123
00153 Rome Italy
Phone: +39 06 5742149

#378
BAR Il Seme E La Foglia 2
Average Price: Inexpensive
Category: Bar
Area: Testaccio, Ostiense
Address: Via Galvani, 18
00153 Rome Italy
Phone: +39 06 5743008

#379
Taste Of Heaven
Average Price: Modest
Category: Dance Club, Italian
Area: Ostiense
Address: Viale Di Porta Ardeatina 119
00154 Rome Italy
Phone: +39 06 5743772

#380
Nuova Caff' Testaccio
Average Price: Expensive
Category: Bar
Area: Testaccio, Ostiense
Address: Via Giovanni Branca 62
00153 Rome Italy
Phone: +39 06 5746919

#381
Mastro Titta
Average Price: Modest
Category: Pub
Area: Testaccio, Ostiense
Address: Via Del Porto Fluviale 5C
00154 Rome Italy
Phone: +39 06 5747420

#382
Tr3ntatr3
Average Price: Modest
Category: Italian, Lounge
Area: Testaccio, Ostiense
Address: Via Di Monte Testaccio 33
00153 Rome Italy
Phone: +39 06 5755142

#383
Sken'
Average Price: Modest
Category: Jazz &Blues, Cabaret
Area: Testaccio, Ostiense
Address: Via Francesco Carletti 5
00154 Rome Italy
Phone: +39 06 5755561

#384
Gran Caff' Imperiale
Average Price: Inexpensive
Category: Bar
Area: Testaccio, Ostiense
Address: Via Del Gazometro, 20/24
00154 Rome Italy
Phone: +39 06 5757357

#385
Bar Gli Archi
Average Price: Inexpensive
Category: Bar
Area: Monteverde
Address: Via Fratelli Bonnet 4
00152 Rome Italy
Phone: +39 06 5803891

#386
Associazione Garbo
Average Price: Expensive
Category: Dance Club, Gay Bar
Area: Trastevere
Address: Vicolo Di Santa Margherita 1
00153 Rome Italy
Phone: +39 06 5812766

#387
Bar Pasticceria Fiorini
Average Price: Modest
Category: Bar
Area: Monteverde
Address: Viale Di Villa Pamphili 31A
00152 Rome Italy
Phone: +39 06 5814508

#388
Kebab In Trastevere
Average Price: Inexpensive
Category: Bar, Kebab
Area: Trastevere
Address: Via Natale Del Grande 17
00153 Rome Italy
Phone: +39 06 5819863

#389
The Club 98
Average Price: Modest
Category: Wine Bar, Lounge
Area: Ostiense
Address: Via Di Monteverde 98
00151 Rome Italy
Phone: +39 06 58203969

#390
Old Moon
Average Price: Modest
Category: Bar
Area: Monteverde, Ostiense
Address: Circonvallazione Gianicolense
232, 00152 Rome Italy
Phone: +39 06 58233702

#391
Kilo Brasil
Average Price: Expensive
Category: Brazilian, Dance Club
Area: Trastevere
Address: Via Portuense 74
00153 Rome Italy
Phone: +39 06 58340151

#392
Lochness Pub
Average Price: Modest
Category: Pub
Area: Trastevere
Address: Viale Portuense 94
00153 Rome Italy
Phone: +39 06 5895979

#393
Gran Caff' Eur
Average Price: Modest
Category: Bar, Café
Area: Eur
Address: Viale Dell'aeronautica 25
00144 Rome Italy
Phone: +39 06 5916796

#394
Parco Rosati
Average Price: Modest
Category: Bar, Italian
Area: Eur
Address: Via Delle Tre Fontane 24
00144 Rome Italy
Phone: +39 06 5916849

#395
Casina Dei Tre Laghi
Average Price: Modest
Category: Bar, Ice Cream
Area: Eur
Address: Viale Oceania 90
00144 Rome Italy
Phone: +39 06 5924507

#396
Orange Caff'
Average Price: Modest
Category: Coffee &Tea,
Juice Bar, Bar
Area: Eur
Address: Viale Europa 3B
00144 Rome Italy
Phone: +39 06 5925079

#397
Domino Bar
Average Price: Inexpensive
Category: Coffee &Tea, Bar
Area: Eur
Address: Viale Europa 13
00144 Rome Italy
Phone: +39 06 5926066

#398
Chattanooga Saloon
Average Price: Exclusive
Category: Pub, Mexican
Area: Appia Antica
Address: Via Benedetto Croce 61
00142 Rome Italy
Phone: +39 06 59604290

#399
Rosy O'Grady
Average Price: Modest
Category: Brewerie, Pub
Area: Monteverde, Borgo
Address: Via Della Cava Aurelia 155B
00165 Rome Italy
Phone: +39 06 632714

#400
Casina Donati
Average Price: Inexpensive
Category: Tobacco Shop, Bar, Café
Area: San Giovanni
Address: Piazzale Appio 9
00183 Rome Italy
Phone: +39 06 677254847

#401
Teatro Centrale
Average Price: Modest
Category: Opera, Ballet, Music Venues,
Cocktail Bar
Area: Centro Storico
Address: Via Celsa, 6
00186 Rome Italy
Phone: +39 06 6780501

#402
Giamaica Caffe'
Average Price: Expensive
Category: Bar
Area: Centro Storico
Address: Via Del Tritone, 54
00187 Rome Italy
Phone: +39 06 6780807

#403
Bar Gambero Due
Average Price: Modest
Category: Café, Bar
Area: Centro Storico
Address: Via Della Croce 40
00187 Rome Italy
Phone: +39 06 6782696

#404
D'Angelo
Average Price: Expensive
Category: Desserts, Bar
Area: Centro Storico
Address: Via Della Croce 30
00187 Rome Italy
Phone: +39 06 6783924

#405
The Nag's Head
Average Price: Modest
Category: Dance Club
Area: Centro Storico
Address: Via IV Novembre 138B
00187 Rome Italy
Phone: +39 06 6794620

#406
BAR Gelateria Fontana Di Trevi
Average Price: Inexpensive
Category: Bar
Area: Centro Storico
Address: PZA Trevi, 90
00100 Rome Italy
Phone: +39 06 6797764

#407
Mad Jack's
Average Price: Modest
Category: Pub
Area: Centro Storico
Address: Via Arenula, 20
00186 Rome Italy
Phone: +39 06 68301060

#408
Soci't' Lut'ce
Average Price: Modest
Category: Cocktail Bar
Area: Centro Storico
Address: Piazza Montevecchio 17
00186 Rome Italy
Phone: +39 06 68301472

#409
Cantina Del Vecchio
Average Price: Modest
Category: Wine Bar, Beer, Wine, Spirits, Party &Event Planning
Area: Centro Storico
Address: Via Dei Coronari 30
00186 Rome Italy
Phone: +39 06 6832407

#410
Bar Mariscoli
Average Price: Inexpensive
Category: Bar
Area: Centro Storico
Address: Via Giulia 84
00186 Rome Italy
Phone: +39 06 6861310

#411
Camilloni A Sant'Eustachio
Average Price: Modest
Category: Coffee &Tea, Bar, Café
Area: Centro Storico
Address: Piazza Sant'Eustachio 54
00186 Rome Italy
Phone: +39 06 6864995

#412
Baccanale
Average Price: Modest
Category: Pub, Italian
Area: Centro Storico
Address: Piazza Campo De' Fiori 32
00186 Rome Italy
Phone: +39 06 6865163

#413
Teatro Dei Satiri
Average Price: Inexpensive
Category: Opera, Ballet, Music Venues
Area: Centro Storico
Address: Via Grotta Pinta, 19
00186 Rome Italy
Phone: +39 06 6871578

#414
ZTL Ristoclub
Average Price: Modest
Category: Italian, Lounge
Area: Centro Storico
Address: Via Di Santa Eufemia 8
00187 Rome Italy
Phone: +39 06 69942041

#415
Moroni Bar Cioccolateria
Average Price: Expensive
Category: Desserts, Bar
Address: Via Gallia 169
00183 Rome Italy
Phone: +39 06 7003421

#416
My Bar
Average Price: Modest
Category: Gay Bar
Area: Esquilino, Aventino
Address: Via Di San Giovanni In Laterano 12 00184 Rome Italy
Phone: +39 06 7004425

#417
La Pace Del Cervello
Average Price: Modest
Category: Pub, Italian, Pizza
Area: Esquilino, Aventino
Address: Via Dei Strada Statale Quattro 63, 00100 Rome Italy
Phone: +39 06 7005173

#418
Antica Caffetteria
Average Price: Modest
Category: Wine Bar
Area: San Giovanni
Address: Via Pinerolo 27
00182 Rome Italy
Phone: +39 06 7022563

#419
Bar La Dolce Vita
Average Price: Modest
Category: Bar
Area: Tuscolano
Address: Viale Giulio Agricola 142
00174 Rome Italy
Phone: +39 06 71072493

#420
Killjoy
Average Price: Modest
Category: Pub
Area: San Giovanni
Address: Via Appia Nuova, 1228
00183 Rome Italy
Phone: +39 06 7183984

#421
Pasticceria Casoria
Average Price: Inexpensive
Category: Desserts, Bar, Café
Area: Tuscolano
Address: Viale Antonio Ciamarra 59
00173 Rome Italy
Phone: +39 06 72901088

#422
Rebacco
Average Price: Modest
Category: Wine Bar
Area: San Giovanni
Address: Via Pomezia 12
00183 Rome Italy
Phone: +39 06 77590412

#423
Caff' Elite
Average Price: Modest
Category: Coffee &Tea, Bar
Area: San Giovanni
Address: Via Appia Nuova 486
00179 Rome Italy
Phone: +39 06 78349221

#424
Remigio Champagne E Vino
Average Price: Modest
Category: Champagne Bar
Area: Tuscolano
Address: Via Santa Maria Ausiliatrice 23
00181 Rome Italy
Phone: +39 06 78392311

#425
Orologio Club
Average Price: Inexpensive
Category: Pub
Area: Tuscolano
Address: Via Numitore 17
00181 Rome Italy
Phone: +39 06 7840892

#426
MBM Biliardi
Average Price: Modest
Category: Amateur Sports Teams, Hobby
Shop, Pool Halls
Area: Esquilino
Address: Via Bixio 89
00185 Rome Italy
Phone: +39 06 7880113

#427
Toma's
Average Price: Modest
Category: Bar, Café
Address: Piazza Euclide 26
00197 Rome Italy
Phone: +39 06 8075659

#428
Bambu's
Average Price: Modest
Category: Coffee &Tea, Bar
Area: Salario, Parioli
Address: Viale Parioli, 79i
00197 Rome Italy
Phone: +39 06 8084885

#429
Dervock
Average Price: Modest
Category: Pub
Area: Nomentano
Address: Via Valsolda 37 -39
00141 Rome Italy
Phone: +39 06 8173667

#430
Monte Gennaro Caff'
Average Price: Inexpensive
Category: Wine Bar, Café
Area: Bufalotta
Address: Piazza Monte Gennaro 30
00139 Rome Italy
Phone: +39 06 8184385

#431
Devil's Chair
Average Price: Modest
Category: Pub
Area: Nomentano
Address: Via Tripolitania 190
00199 Rome Italy
Phone: +39 06 83607737

#432
Inofficina
Average Price: Modest
Category: Nightlife, Italian
Area: Montesacro/Talenti
Address: Via Mesula 12
00158 Rome Italy
Phone: +39 06 83707012

#433
Il Grifone
Average Price: Modest
Category: Bar
Area: Pinciano
Address: Via Isonzo 3
00198 Rome Italy
Phone: +39 06 8416656

#434
Primbar
Average Price: Modest
Category: Bar
Area: Pinciano
Address: Via Salaria 77
00198 Rome Italy
Phone: +39 06 8553849

#435
Zeus Pub
Average Price: Inexpensive
Category: Beer, Brewerie, Pub
Area: Nomentano
Address: Piazza Armellini 7
00162 Rome Italy
Phone: +39 06 86321748

#436
Il Siciliano
Average Price: Inexpensive
Category: Bar, Tobacco Shop
Area: Salario
Address: Piazza Acilia 15
00199 Rome Italy
Phone: +39 06 86322191

#437
Sofa Wine Bar
Average Price: Modest
Category: Wine Bar
Area: Nomentano
Address: Via Cimone 181
00141 Rome Italy
Phone: +39 06 86897655

#438
Caff'Italy
Average Price: Inexpensive
Category: Bar, Café, Sandwiches
Area: Bufalotta
Address: Via Adolfo Celi 33
00139 RM Italy
Phone: +39 06 87071451

#439
Caff' Fiorenza
Average Price: Modest
Category: Bar, Café
Area: Bufalotta
Address: Via Carlo Ludovico
Bragaglia 68, 00139 RM Italy
Phone: +39 06 87071515

#440
Caff' Rosati
Average Price: Inexpensive
Category: Desserts, Bar, Caterer
Area: Nomentano
Address: Piazzale Adriatico 6
00141 Rome Italy
Phone: +39 06 87183777

#441
Bar Ginky
Average Price: Modest
Area: Nomentano, Salario
Address: Piazza Istria 10
00198 Rome Italy
Phone: +39 06 8841685

#442
H2o
Average Price: Modest
Category: Wine Bar
Area: Testaccio, Ostiense
Address: Via Del Gazometro 18
00154 Rome Italy
Phone: +39 06 89531856

#443
**Festa Dell'unit' Rome
Terme Di Caracalla**
Average Price: Modest
Category: Dance Club
Area: Aventino
Address: Via Del Circo Massimo
00153 Rome Italy
Phone: +39 06 90206052

#444
Anima Mundi
Average Price: Modest
Category: Lounge
Area: Aventino, Centro Storico
Address: Via Del Velabro 1
00186 Rome Italy
Phone: +39 06 96030061

#445
Cheese And Cheers
Average Price: Modest
Category: Pub
Area: Monteverde
Address: Via Paola Falconieri, 47b
00152 Rome Italy
Phone: +39 06 96039525

#446
Bros
Average Price: Modest
Category: Bar, Brazilian
Area: Trastevere
Address: Via Goffredo Mameli 45
00153 Rome Italy
Phone: +39 06 97270660

#447
Stairs
Average Price: Modest
Category: Bar
Area: Trastevere
Address: Via Della Scala 43
00153 Rome Italy
Phone: +39 06 97277421

#448
Caff' Cant'
Average Price: Modest
Category: Coffee &Tea, Gay Bar
Area: Tuscolano, Appia Antica
Address: Piazza Cesare Cant' 11
00179 Rome Italy
Phone: +39 06 97618350

#449
Barrique
Average Price: Modest
Category: Bar
Area: Appia Antica
Address: Via Amedeo Crivellucci 8
00179 Rome Italy
Phone: +39 06 97658297

#450
Magazzino 33
Average Price: Modest
Category: Dance Club
Area: Trastevere
Address: Via Portuense 88
00153 Rome Italy
Phone: +39 320 0511179

#451
Caff' Degli Orti
Average Price: Modest
Category: Beer Garden, Lounge
Area: Corso Francia
Address: Viale Di Tor Di Quinto
00191 Rome Italy
Phone: +39 328 6116483

#452
Re Noir
Average Price: Expensive
Category: Lounge
Area: Salario
Address: Piazza Belotti 25
00139 Rome Italy
Phone: +39 338 1885993

#453
Jarro
Average Price: Inexpensive
Category: Lounge, Wine Bar
Area: Corso Francia
Address: Piazzale Di Ponte Milvio 32
00191 Rome Italy
Phone: +39 338 7079573

#454
La Palma Club
Average Price: Modest
Category: Art Gallery,
Jazz &Blues, Italian
Area: San Lorenzo
Address: Via Giuseppe Mirri 35
00159 Rome Italy
Phone: +39 339 5275019

#455
Derry Rock Pub
Average Price: Inexpensive
Category: Pub
Area: Prati
Address: Via Degli Scipioni 96
00192 Rome Italy
Phone: +39 339 7097098

#456
Gay Village
Average Price: Modest
Area: Eur
Address: Via Delle Tre Fontane
00144 Rome Italy
Phone: +39 340 7538396

#457
Fantasie Di Sicilia
Average Price: Inexpensive
Category: Bar, Desserts, Sicilian
Area: San Lorenzo
Address: Via Dei Monti Di Pietralata 27
00157 Rome Italy
Phone: +39 342 8233224

#458
Oracolo Pellerossa
Average Price: Inexpensive
Category: Dance Club
Area: San Lorenzo, San Giovanni
Address: Via Scalo San Lorenzo 36A
00185 Rome Italy
Phone: +39 345 3558058

#459
Rummeria QS
Average Price: Modest
Category: Pub
Area: Trastevere
Address: Via Moroni 53
00153 Rome Italy
Phone: +39 347 5055355

#460
B-Cool
Average Price: Modest
Category: Pub, Italian
Area: Nomentano
Address: Via Val Chisone 3
00141 Rome Italy
Phone: +39 347 5831407

#461
Elen Bar Centrifugheria
Average Price: Modest
Category: Juice Bar
Area: Centro Storico
Address: Via Capo Le Case 27
00187 Rome Italy
Phone: +39 347 9224699

#462
Sard Wonder
Average Price: Inexpensive
Category: Pub
Area: Termini
Address: Via Dei Volsci 5
00185 Rome Italy
Phone: +39 349 0566538

#463
Docks
Average Price: Modest
Category: Dance Club
Area: Testaccio, Ostiense
Address: Riva Ostiense
00154 Rome Italy
Phone: +39 349 3584582

#464
Sott'An Treno
Average Price: Expensive
Category: Nightlife, Italian
Area: Monteverde
Address: Piazzale Enrico Dunant 67
00143 Rome Italy
Phone: +39 349 4227912

#465
In Vino Veritas
Average Price: Modest
Category: Beer Garden
Area: Borgo, Trastevere
Address: Via Garibaldi 2A
00153 Rome Italy
Phone: +39 349 8154801

#466
Escopazzo
Average Price: Modest
Category: Music Venues, Lounge, Karaoke
Area: Centro Storico
Address: Via d'Aracoeli, 41
00186 Rome Italy
Phone: +39 389 6835618

#467
Mama Tequila
Average Price: Modest
Category: Beer, Wine, Spirits, Pub
Area: Balduina/Montemario
Address: Largo Millesimo 1
00168 Rome Italy
Phone: +39 390 635508800

#468
Mapi Caf'
Average Price: Modest
Category: Tea Room, Piano Bar
Area: Nomentano
Address: Piazza Regina Margherita 10
00198 Rome Italy
Phone: +39 392 0792617

#469
New Age Caf'
Average Price: Modest
Category: Wine Bar, Pub, Cocktail Bar
Area: Pinciano
Address: Via Nizza 23
00198 Rome Italy
Phone: +39 392 5937952

#470
Ugo Jey
Average Price: Modest
Category: Lounge, Italian
Area: Eur
Address: Via Laurentina 74
00144 Rome Italy
Phone: +39 392 9411359

#471
Help
Average Price: Modest
Category: Pub, Brewerie, Pizza
Area: Salario
Address: Via Giovanni Animuccia 24
00199 Rome Italy
Phone: +39 393 0854667

#472
Pub 800
Average Price: Modest
Category: Pub
Area: San Lorenzo
Address: Piazza Pontida 4
00162 Rome Italy
Phone: +39 393 9040317

#473
The Odd Room
Average Price: Inexpensive
Category: Pub
Area: Termini, San Giovanni
Address: Via Dei Sabelli 47
00185 Rome Italy
Phone: +39 06 44702347

#474
Bar Britannia
Average Price: Inexpensive
Category: Sports Bar
Area: San Giovanni
Address: Via Britannia, 12/14/16
00183 Rome Italy
Phone: +39 06 44702348

#475
Caffe Life
Average Price: Inexpensive
Category: Bar, Cafetería, Tobacco Shop
Area: Casilino
Address: Viale Della Primavera 135
00172 Rome Italy
Phone: +39 06 44702349

#476
Locanda Blues
Average Price: Inexpensive
Category: Jazz &Blues, European
Area: Phone Number
Address: Via Cassia 1284
00189 Rome Italy
Phone: +39 06 44702350

#477
Bar San Paolo
Average Price: Inexpensive
Category: Bar, Café
Area: Ostiense
Address: Via Gaspare Gozzi 15
00145 Rome Italy
Phone: +39 06 44702351

#478
Il Localino
Average Price: Inexpensive
Category: Bar
Area: Termini
Address: Via Dei Luceri, 13
00185 Rome Italy
Phone: +39 06 44702352

#479
Zoobar
Average Price: Inexpensive
Category: Dance Club
Area: Phone Number
Address: Via Bencivenga 1
00141 Rome Italy
Phone: +39 06 44702353

#480
Bar Tabacchi Mo.Di.
Average Price: Inexpensive
Category: Tobacco Shop, Dive Bar
Area: Phone Number
Address: Via Cassia 1142
00189 Rome Italy
Phone: +39 06 44702354

#481
Coffee Pot Park
Average Price: Inexpensive
Category: Bar
Area: San Lorenzo, San Giovanni
Address: Largo Settimio Passamonti
00185 Rome Italy
Phone: +39 06 44702355

#482
Max's Bar
Average Price: Modest
Category: Bar
Area: Pinciano
Address: Via Po 1
00198 Rome Italy
Phone: +39 06 44702356

#483
Caff' Del Parco
Average Price: Modest
Category: Bar
Area: Montesacro/Talenti
Address: Via Tino Buazzelli 9
00137 Rome Italy
Phone: +39 06 44702357

#484
Birreria Marconi
Average Price: Modest
Category: Pub
Area: Monti
Address: Via Santa Prassede 9
00184 Rome Italy
Phone: +39 06 44702358

#485
Casa Clementina
Average Price: Modest
Category: Wine Bar, Dance Club
Area: Monti
Address: Via Clementina 9
00184 Rome Italy
Phone: +39 06 44702359

#486
Caffetteria Mazzini
Average Price: Modest
Category: Bar, Café
Area: Prati
Address: Viale Mazzini 75
00195 Rome Italy
Phone: +39 06 44702360

#487
Rashomon Club
Average Price: Modest
Category: Music Venues
Area: Ostiense
Address: Via Degli Argonauti 16
00154 Rome Italy
Phone: +39 06 44702361

#488
Estate Romena Lungotevere
Average Price: Modest
Category: Nightlife
Area: Testaccio, Ostiense
Address: Trilussa Lungotevere Piazza
00153 Rome Italy
Phone: +39 06 44702362

#489
Baruffa Caf'
Average Price: Modest
Category: Bar, Café
Area: Phone Number
Address: Piazza Della Libert' 27,
00040 Castel Gandolfo Italy
Phone: +39 06 44702363

#490
Magnebevo E Sto Ar Pigneto
Average Price: Modest
Category: Pub
Area: San Giovanni
Address: Via Macerata 3
00176 Rome Italy
Phone: +39 06 44702364

#491
Brancaleone
Average Price: Modest
Category: Dance Club
Area: Phone Number
Address: Rome, Rome Italy
Phone: +39 06 44702365

#492
Without Music Club
Average Price: Modest
Category: Bar
Area: Testaccio, Ostiense
Address: Via Dei Magazzini
Generali, 4/D, 00154 Rome Italy
Phone: +39 06 44702366

#493
Bar Dell'universit'
Average Price: Modest
Category: Café, Bar
Area: Phone Number
Address: Via Orazio Raimondo 15
00173 Rome Italy
Phone: +39 06 44702367

#494
Cuv'e
Average Price: Modest
Category: Lounge, Karaoke, Bar
Area: Nomentano, Salario
Address: Via Topino 23
00199 Rome Italy
Phone: +39 06 44702368

#495
Animal Social Club
Average Price: Modest
Category: Dance Club
Area: San Lorenzo
Address: Via Di Portonaccio 22
00159 Rome Italy
Phone: +39 06 44702369

#496
La Quintessa
Average Price: Modest
Category: Lounge, Italian
Area: Phone Number
Address: Via Spiaggia Del Lago 20 00040
Castel Gandolfo Italy
Phone: +39 06 44702370

#497
Ny.Lon
Average Price: Expensive
Category: Bar
Area: Trastevere
Address: Via Del Politeama 12
00153 Rome Italy
Phone: +39 06 44702371

#498
Antico Caff' Del Teatro
Average Price: Expensive
Category: Café, Bar
Area: Centro Storico
Address: Via Del Teatro Di Marcello 42
00186 Rome Italy
Phone: +39 06 44702372

#499
Bar Villa Balestra
Average Price: Expensive
Category: Bar
Area: Parioli
Address: Via Bartolomeo Ammannati
00198 Rome Italy
Phone: +39 06 44702373

#500
Iceclub Pub
Average Price: Exclusive
Category: Pub
Area: Esquilino, Aventino
Address: Madonna Dei Monti 18 Via
00184 Rome Italy
Phone: +39 06 44702374

Printed in Great Britain
by Amazon

72742416R00098